3500

ERZSÉBET HEGYI

SOLFEGE
ACCORDING
TO THE
KODÁLY-CONCEPT

ERZSÉBET HEGYI

SOLFEGE ACCORDING TO THE KODÁLY-CONCEPT

CHAPTERS I TO V

TRANSLATED BY FRED MACNICOL

ZOLTÁN KODÁLY PEDAGOGICAL INSTITUTE OF MUSIC
KECSKEMÉT 1975

The music examples in this book are quoted by permission of **Edwin Ashdown Ltd., London;**
Boosey & Hawkes Ltd., London; J. & W. Chester Ltd., London; Durand & Cie, Paris;
Editio Musica, Budapest; Oxford University Press, London; Ricordi & Co., Milano;
Edition Salabert, Paris; Universal Edition A. G., Wien.

ISBN 963 01 0118 1
Printed in Hungary

CONTENTS

CHAPTER II
(The staff notation material uses C, C sharp and C flat as "d")

CHAPTER III
(The staff notation material uses F and F sharp as "d")

CHAPTER IV
(The staff notation material uses B and B flat as "d")

11

CHAPTER V

SUPPLEMENT
Music material for ear training exercises

INTRODUCTION

Here comes a bluebird through the window, Hey, diddle-dum a day day day.

If we place the notes used by this melody in order we will find there are no more than five in it:

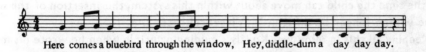

If we continue to write these notes in both directions we will see that the five different notes come in such positions within the octave that major seconds and minor thirds follow each other in a certain definite order: the two minor thirds which occur are connected by either one or two major seconds:

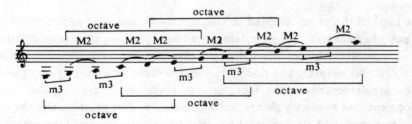

A five-note system which is positioned in this way within the octave is called anhemitonic pentatony.

Anhemitonic pentatony is to be found not only in the folksongs of the most diverse nations but also in gregorian melodic culture:

Al - le - lu - ja,   al - le - lu - ja,   al - le - lu - ja.

17

The melodic patterns of this pentatonic system are extremely clear, even their great variety does not preclude simplicity, for their intervals do not include any diminished or augmented interval or the upward or downward minor second. For precisely these reasons varied vocal practice in pentatony can lay the foundations of secure intonation, on which it will later become possible for seven-degree diatony to build without difficulty, and to this latter an extended range of notes, supplemented by the altered notes, can then be added. In 1943, Kodály wrote: "One of the chief causes of the failure in our school singing teaching so far is an accumulation of difficulties. The complications of rhythm and pitch suddenly confuse the unprepared child completely, and there are few who can cope with them... The greatest problem in intonation is the semitone... the pentatonic melodies are interesting and show variety ... and can be sung with perfect clarity. By the time the child can move about within this system, the insertion of the semitone will no longer be difficult." **(Visszatekintés I,** p. 133.)

Keeping all this in mind was Kodály's guiding principle when he wrote his music education works. Among these volumes it is the 333 Elementary Exercises which provide the best material for use at the beginning, because the systematic development of typical pentatonic phrases which this volume employs encourages secure innervation of them.

Thus the vocal material of the first chapter in this solfege book also covers essentially the melodies of the 333 Elementary Exercises, supplemented in the sight-singing vocal material (p. 66) by melodic quotations taken from musical literature using a pentatonic range of notes. But besides unison vocal material, certain two-part exercises (Kodály: Let Us Sing Correctly), various sections to develop the ear and musical memory, and theoretical information and conscious development of it are also included, none of which are to be omitted from solfege studies.

The logic of the order adopted in chapters II—IV and — if necessary — in the later published chapters VI—IX is determined by the system of relative solmization. The inner construction of the individual chapters, however, remains similar to that of the first chapter: the Kodály material is taken as a starting point and this is then supplemented by the most diverse kinds of ear training and memory development, the necessary theoretical information and its practice, and the unison or two-five-part sight-singing vocal material taken from musical literature.

The essence of the relative solmization mentioned above is that as all major keys are exactly alike in the order of whole tones and semitones, the keynote of any major key may be called "do" (further on "d"). As a result of this movable "d" the different degrees of the major scale may also be given constant names: "r" is always the second degree, "m" the third, and so on. Therefore the intervals between the different solfa names are also constant. For example, d—m is always a major third, etc.

18

The relative minor of a major key starts three notes down so the keynote of a minor key is always "l".

Although according to the key signatures we can have fifteen different major and minor keys, according to the notes themselves "d" can be placed in one of only seven positions:

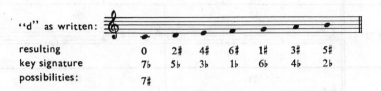

"d" as written:							
resulting key signature possibilities:	0 7#	2# 5♭	4# 3♭	6# 1♭	1# 6♭	3# 4♭	5# 2♭

The interrelationships between the keys belonging to the individual "d" positions are most clearly shown by representation on the fifth-pillar:

key signature	major key	minor key	1st "d"	2nd "d"	3rd "d"	4th "d"	5th "d"	6th "d"	7th "d"
7#	C#	A#	→						
6#	F#	D#							→
5#	B	G#						→	
4#	E	C#					→		
3#	A	F#				→			
2#	D	B			→				
1#	G	E		→					
0	C	A	→						
1♭	F	D							→
2♭	B♭	G						→	
3♭	E♭	C					→		
4♭	A♭	F				→			
5♭	D♭	B♭			→				
6♭	G♭	E♭		→					
7♭	C♭	A♭	→						

19

The same expressed in staff notation:

	0	7♯	7♭
1st "d"	d l,	d l,	d l,

	1♯	6♭
2nd "d"	d l,	d l,

	2♯	5♭
3rd "d"	d l,	d l,

	3♯	4♭
4th "d"	d l,	d l,

	4♯	3♭
5th "d"	d l,	d l,

	5♯	2♭
6th "d"	d l,	d l,

	6♯	1♭
7th "d"	d l,	d l,

Each of chapters II—IV and VI—IX in the solfege book is based on one single "d" position: II — C, C flat, C sharp "d"; III — F, F sharp "d"; IV — B flat, B "d"; VI — E flat, E "d"; VII — A flat, A "d"; VIII — D flat, D "d"; IX — G flat, G "d". This means that the staff notation material of each individual chapter (Kodály exercises, sight-singing, melody dictation and memorizing) is related to the given "d", or may be combined with a "d" position already learned.

That the "d" positions in the book succeed one another by progressing in the direction of the flat keys is explained by the fact that in the baroque and Viennese classical styles the great majority of modulations lead to the dominant, and so the dominant key of the latest "d" which has been reached by moving downwards on the fifth-pillar always represents a "d" position which has been dealt with in detail in the preceding chapter. For example, if the melodies containing F as "d"

20

in the third chapter modulate to the dominant key and thus arrive in C, the "d" position of this dominant key will already be perfectly familiar from the second chapter.

With the exeption of the chord studies from Chapter III onwards, the material in Chapters II—IV and VI—IX also takes pentatony as a starting point but this is later extended to seven-degree diatony, and then completed by alteration. The chordal analyses and singings and the related ear training exercises, however, remain within the framework of diatony till the end of Chapter VII so as to provide a firm foundation for the study of altered chords which will follow afterwards.

Chapter V contains detailed musical — melodic, rhythmic, formal — analyses of American folksongs of which some are already being used in many places by American singing teachers in school singing teaching.

The musical material in the book includes, alongside the Kodály exercises (the "Kodály Choral Method"), unison and two-five-part extracts from the renaissance, baroque and Viennese classical periods, and also — quite independently of musicological style periods — musical quotations using a pentatonic range.

In each individual chapter each of the different kinds of study material — the development of the Kodály exercises, technical exercises, the ear training material, the parts for memory development, harmonic analysis, sight-singing material — forms a separate unit so that the interrelationships between the stages of development between the areas of study may become clearer. In the teaching process, however, the various sections belonging to one chapter should not be separated from one another, but must form a permanent and organic unit in the progress in each chapter. The detailed Planning Suggestions are designed to encourage this co-ordination.

To work through each chapter at least fifteen(-twenty) lessons and intensive home study to complement them are necessary if the students have not previously had systematic experience of this way of working. As this volume contains chapters I—V, it represents a whole school year study material.

CHAPTER I

ORIENTATION IN PENTATONY

The folksong in the Introduction used an anhemitonic pentatonic range of notes where the individual notes come at a distance of a major second or a minor third from each other:

In this pentatonic system there is also, apart from the two minor thirds, one major third, which always comes as a result of the two adjacent major seconds:

This major third can be sung most naturally by using the d—m solfa names. In this way the solfa names of the anhemitonic pentatonic system are:

m, s, l, d r m s l d' r' m' s' l'

In this order the major second adjacent notes receive the names d—r , r—m and s—l , while the minor third pentatonically adjacent notes become l,—d and m—s.

KODÁLY MATERIAL

Unison Pentatonic Melodies

333 ELEMENTARY EXERCISES

Section I (1—19): d—r range
(major second)

Some of the exercises — 7, 8, 14, 15 and 19 — require more practice because of rhythmic difficulties. For this reason it is best to leave these till the end by which time the students will have had some vocal practice.

Among the singing forms there are some which are easier and some which are more difficult. Which way and how many ways the individual exercises are to be sung is something to be determined by the degree of difficulty of the given melody and the musical knowledge of the students. In any event until a certain degree of vocal ability evolves in them it is best to spend more time using development of 1—1 melody.

Thus in the first singing through of the material the above mentioned exercises 7, 8, 14, 15 and 19 should be omitted. The others can be sung in the following ways, both individually and in groups:

1. Accompanied by beating the metrical units (see p. 64).

2. Beating time: $\frac{2}{4}$ ⇂↑ $\frac{3}{4}$ △ (See p. 64.)

3. With one-bar ostinato accompaniment formed from the rhythmic elements of the exercises. (For example: $\frac{2}{4}$ ♫ ♩ ; $\frac{2}{4}$ ♩ ♫ ; $\frac{3}{4}$ ♩ ♫ ♩ ; $\frac{3}{4}$ ♩ ♩ ♫).

4. Accompanied by rhythm canon: in the second bar of singing, begin tapping (or clapping) the rhythm of the first bar and let this difference of one bar remain between the singing and the rhythm tapping throughout.

Stages recommended in singing accompanied by ostinato or rhythm canon:

a) The students sing the melody while the teacher taps (claps) the rhythm accompaniment.

b) Students and teacher exchange roles.

c) One group of students sings, another group makes the rhythm.

d) The two groups exchange roles.

e) The same performed by two students; let them exchange roles, too.

f) One individual carries out the two-part task on his own.

5. In an answering form: two groups — or individuals — take part in the singing by alternating with each other motif by motif. This task has a double purpose:

a) The development of inner hearing, since the student who takes over the singing from another can only come in at exactly the right time if he himself follows and hears his colleague's singing.

b) To evolve a feeling for form, for in the exercises not only two-bar motifs appear: there are also three-bar motifs. (To begin with it is as well to discuss together the formal construction and the way the motifs follow each other.)

Answering singing should be accompanied by beating time, beating the metric units, or an easy ostinato, so that the metrical pulse remains the same in spite of the alternation in the singing.

The five exercises which have so far been omitted from the series of melodies present rhythm difficulties which are really grouped round three rhythm patterns:

Sixteenth movement (♫♪);

Syncopation (♪♩♪);

A rest smaller than the beat unit, coming in a stressed — or relatively stressed — place (𝄾♪).

The practice of these melodies requires special care.

♫♪ = 7

a) One group provides a slow metric unit beat (palm or fingertips), the other group sings the melody with a $\frac{2}{4}$ ♩ ♫ ostinato (tapping or clapping) — after two introductory bars of rhythm:

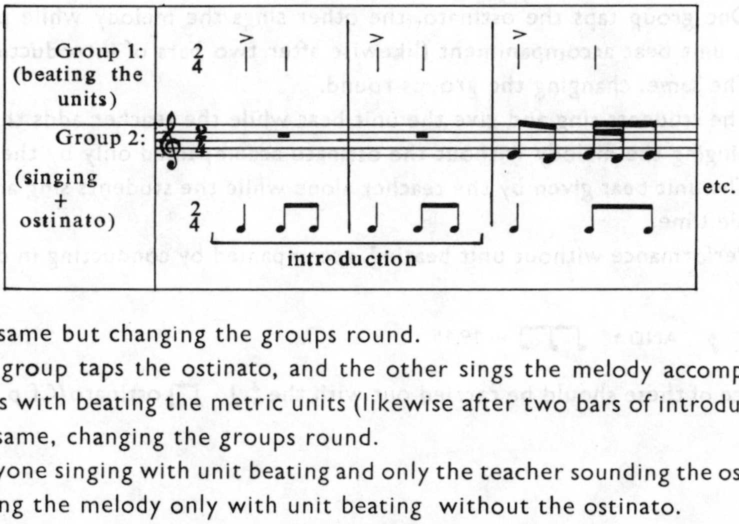

b) The same but changing the groups round.

c) One group taps the ostinato, and the other sings the melody accompanying themselves with beating the metric units (likewise after two bars of introduction).

d) The same, changing the groups round.

e) Everyone singing with unit beating and only the teacher sounding the ostinato.

f) Singing the melody only with unit beating without the ostinato.

g) The metric unit beating provided only by the teacher, while the students sing and conduct in duple time.

h) Individual performance accompanied by beating time (without unit beating).

♪ ♩ ♪ = 8

This should be practised in ways similar to those given for No. 7.

Once a successful performance has been achieved, accompaniment using the
$\frac{2}{4}$ ♩ ♫ | ♫ ♩ two-bar ostinato can also be tried, remembering the necessary stages.

, ♫♩ = 14

a) One group provides a metrical unit beat (fingertips or palm) while the other sings the melody to a $\frac{2}{4}$ ♫ ♩ ostinato (tapping or clapping) — after two introductory bars.

b) The same, the groups exchanging roles.

c) One group taps the ostinato, the other sings the melody while providing a metric unit beat accompaniment (likewise after two bars of introduction).

d) The same, changing the groups round.

e) The students sing and give the unit beat while the teacher adds the ostinato.

f) Singing the melody without the ostinato accompanied only by the unit beat.

g) The unit beat given by the teacher alone while the students sing and conduct in duple time.

h) Performance without unit beating, accompanied by conducting in duple time.

♫ , ♪ AND , ♫♩ = 19,15

Practice of these should be carried out with the $\frac{2}{4}$ ♩ ♫ ostinato (Cf. p. 27, No. 7).

28

Section II (20—29): d—l, —s, range
(min. 3rd
↘maj. 2nd)

(The sign to the right down of the solfa name indicates that the notes concerned are below "d".)

Before beginning to sing the melodies:

a) Practise the pentatonic trichord d—l,—s, beginning on notes of different pitch so that the sound of the descending minor third + major second after each other will develop in the students as soon as possible. For example:

(Trichord is the name for three adjacent notes in a given tonal system — in this case, pentatony.)

b) Sing this same trichord in an upward direction as well in a similar way. For example:

c) Write the trichord on the blackboard with the staff notation existing in the exercises (▤) and, pointing to the notes, have the students sing them, varying the order as much as possible, using solmization but at the absolute pitch prescribed by the staff notation. (This pointing can produce, for example, the following melody: d—l,—d—l,—s,—l,—d—s,—l,—s,—d—l,—d—s,—l, etc.)

Work on the exercises should follow the pattern set in Section I, employing logical steps and variety (see pp. 26—27, points 1—5). When ostinato accompaniment is used, we should try to use all the rhythmic patterns which have so far been met -— with the exception of ♫♩ — not only for the sake of variety but also to develop rhythmic sense.

Section IV (31—47): r—d—l, range

(maj. 2nd
⟶ min. 3rd)

Stages in preparation:

a) Singing the melody of the pentatonic trichord r—d—l, in a downward and upward direction as well at different pitch levels:

b) Note-finding practice from staff notation (see p. 29, point c)) with the notes of the trichord written on the blackboard (⎯⎯).

In the exercises of Section IV there are two metrical novelties: bars of $\frac{4}{4}$ and $\frac{1}{4}$.

$\frac{4}{4} = 30$ (See p. 64.)

Since the rhythm of the melody moves in even quarters, it is excellently suitable for practising the beating of $\frac{4}{4}$ time (♩). It should be sung in groups and then individually but always accompanied by beating time.

ALTERNATION OF $\frac{2}{4}$ AND $\frac{1}{4} = 37$

The melody should be practised in the following ways:

a) With a rhythm accompaniment which divides the eighth movement between the two hands:

b) Accompanying by beating the metrical units with alternating left and right hand (in the $\frac{1}{4}$ bar only the stressed left to beat):

(In practice forms a) and b) it is useful to perform the melody with repeat.)

   c) With a differentiated rhythm ostinato: $\frac{2}{4}$ ♪♩ ♪ and $\frac{1}{4}$ ♫

   d) Conducting in time: $\frac{2}{4}$ ↕ and $\frac{1}{4}$ ↻

All these stages can be used for both groups and individuals.

   Singing of the other exercises of Section IV should be carried out in as varied a way as possible and similarly to those in Section I and II.

Section V (48—55): m—r—d range
(maj. 2nd
maj. 2nd)

Before singing the melodies it is very important to practise the major second + major second melodic pattern thoroughly as in each of the trichords so far there has been a minor third and so melodic memories and innervations are bound up with minor third phrases. We should therefore use both stages of the preparatory practice:

   a) Sing the trichord in descending and ascending directions, starting from different pitch levels.

   b) Sing the notes from staff notation ( ). The exercises should be worked on as with the previous ones.

Section VI (56—139): r—d—l,—s, range
(maj. 2nd
min. 3rd
maj. 2nd)

It is no accident that there are 83 melodies in this group. For the phrases of the pentatonic tetrachord r—d—l,—s, require a great deal of practice. (Tetrachord: four adjacent notes in a given tonal system — in the present case, pentatony.) Continuous singing of these notes in one direction — whether upwards or down-

31

wards — is made difficult by the minor third between the two major seconds, while different variations in the order of the notes demand attention because of the fourth-fifth alternations (d—s,; r—l,; r—s,). It is therefore advisable to spend more time on these melodies so that the new interval relationships will become reinforced by as much repetition as possible.

Both kinds of preparatory practice (singing the tetrachords in descending and ascending order, and note-finding practice from staff notation) should be carried out on each occasion and as intensively as possible.

Apart from the new melodic phrases there are four points in the exercises which need special care:

The $\frac{4}{4}$ metre;

The new rhythm pattern ♪ ♩. ;

Change of metre between $\frac{3}{4}$ and $\frac{2}{4}$;

The rhythm pattern ♫♩ which has occurred earlier but which once more requires special practice.

$\frac{4}{4}$ = 56, 57

The two melodies should primarily be practised while conducting in $\frac{4}{4}$ for so far there has been little opportunity for this (Section IV 33). The even pulse of the rhythm is a great help in this.

After beating time is innervated the exercises should be sung with an ostinato. The $\frac{4}{4}$ ostinato is the same in extent as a two-bar ostinato accompanying a $\frac{2}{4}$ melody, but within one bar it seems a more compact and more easily perceptible unit. $\frac{4}{4}$ ostinatos: either ♫ ♩ ♩ ♫ or ♩ ♫ ♫ ♩ etc.

♪ ♩. = 61

The melody can be sung with several different rhythm accompaniments, for example the $\frac{4}{4}$ ♩ ♫ ♫ ♩ ostinato (so that the ♪ will not become shorter than it ought to be):

a) One group beats the metric units with the palm, and another group sings the melody with ostinato accompaniment (after two introductory bars of rhythm):

b) The same but changing the groups round.

c) The group giving the unit beat sings the melody while the other group only taps the ostinato.

d) The same but changing the groups round.

e) Everyone sings the melody with continuous metrical unit beating and the ostinato is given by the teacher alone. (Take care that the ♪ should have its proper length.)

f) Volunteers perform the three-part exercise individually:

This last task is excellently suitable for the development of concentration ability. Those to become teachers have indeed a great need for simultaneously carried out three-part activities. They can only carry out control work in several directions securely and with facility if they have already acquired a certain degree of practice in this kind of concentration through their own activity.

ALTERNATION OF $\frac{3}{4}$ AND $\frac{2}{4}$ = 120

The exercise can also be sung in several ways:

a) Accompanied by beating the metric units with alternate hands:

b) Alternating conducting in time ($\frac{3}{4}$ and $\frac{2}{4}$).

c) With a combination of a $\frac{3}{4}$ and a $\frac{2}{4}$ ostinato. For example:

$\frac{3}{4}$ ♩ ♫ ♩ and $\frac{2}{4}$ ♩ ♫

or: $\frac{3}{4}$ ♩ ♩ ♫ and $\frac{2}{4}$ ♪ ♩ ♪

♫♩ = 80, 87, 122, 123

The exercises containing the rhythm pattern ♫♩ should be taken separately

33

from the others and practised as a separate group and very thoroughly so that the sixteenth movement can become accepted among the rhythmic experiences, which so far have mostly contained ♩ and ♪ values.

This sixteenth pattern has already occurred in the seventh melody of Section I but in the present case it is associated with a more difficult melody. For this reason it is advisable to go through certain practice stages. For example:

№ 80: $\frac{2}{4}$ ♩ ♫ or $\frac{2}{4}$ ♪ ♩ ♪ ostinato

№ 87: $\frac{2}{4}$ ♫♫ | ♪ ♩ ♪ ‖ or $\frac{2}{4}$ ♫ ♫ | ♪ ♩ ♪ ‖ two-bar ostinato, etc.

Section III (30): r—d—s, range
(maj. 2nd
↘ perf. 4th)

This three-note melodic phrase uses notes which are not immediately adjacent in pentatony: actually it extracts one of the perfect fourths of pentatony (d—s,) and adds to it its upper major second changing note (d—r—d). To sing the ↘ maj.2nd perf.4th or ↗ maj.2nd perf.4th patterns quickly is no easy task. For this reason it is necessary to devote special care to the vocal practice of this set of notes in both directions. In this case this part of the preparatory practice is considerably more important than singing from staff notation since the students have acquired great practice in this latter during the singing of the melodies in Section VI.

Section VII (140—171): m—r—d—l, range
(maj. 2nd
↘ maj. 2nd
↘ min. 3rd)

The tetrachord containing the d—m major third comes in two different written forms: with the G—B major third, the note G is "d", while in the exercises containing the F—A major third the note F is "d". It is advisable to keep the exercises belonging to these two different staff notation positions separate so that the "d" positions will become fixed better.

34

THE MELODIES TO BE SUNG WITH G "d" ARE:
140, 141, 143, 145, 146, 150, 151, 152—156, 159, 161—163, 166—171.

To prepare them:

a) Solfa singing of the m—r—d—l₁ tetrachord upwards and downwards at various pitches;

b) Note-finding practice of the tetrachord connected with G "d" in staff notation:

In the melodies written with "d" on G there is no new musical element whatsoever. It is nevertheless advisable to practise three of the melodies specially:

№ 163, in which $\frac{2}{4}$ and $\frac{1}{4}$ metres alternate as in № 37, which has already been learned (see p. 30).

№ 151, in which a syncopated rhythm pattern (♪ ♩ ♪) occurs very frequently.

№ 159, in which the rhythm patterns ♫ ♩ and ♩ ♫ come one after the other.

THE MELODIES WRITTEN WITH "d" ON F ARE:
142, 144, 147—149, 157, 158, 160, 164. 165,

These should be prepared in the same way as the melodies sung earlier with "d" on G:

a) Solfa singing of the m—r—d—l₁ tetrachord (as revision).

b) Note-finding practice with the staff notation of the tetrachord written with F as "d":
The ways of singing the exercises should be similar to the above.

Section IX (215—238): s—m—r—d range
(min. 3rd
 ↘ maj. 2nd
    ↘ maj. 2nd)

No special problem is caused by singing the notes of the tetrachord successively in one direction (either upwards or downwards). Among the patterns it presents, note-placing problems are frequently posed by s—r and r—s. For this reason great attention must be paid to these in the course of phrase singing from staff notation. (For example: d—r—m—s—m—r—s—r—m—s—d—s—r—m—r—s—d etc.)

Apart from the s—r and r—s patterns there are no melodic or rhythmic difficulties to be found in the exercises. Thus the more difficult forms of practice should be used in singing them:

1. Add the most recently practised ♪ ♩. , ♫ ♩ and ♫ ♩ rhythm patterns to the ostinato accompaniments.

2. Select two-bar or three-bar ostinatos as well, depending on the extent of the motifs. For example,

for 217: $\frac{2}{4}$ ♪ ♩ ♪ | ♪ ♩ ♪ | , ♪ ♩ ‖

for 223: $\frac{2}{4}$, ♪ ♩ | , ♪ , ♪ ‖

for 215: $\frac{4}{4}$ ♩ ♫ ♪ ♩. | ♩ , ♪ ♩ ‖ etc.

3. Sing certain bars — accompanied by continuous metric unit beating — with no more than "inner" singing: the first or second bar of two-bar motifs, or the middle bar of three-bar motifs.

The following stages are possible:

a) Answering singing (performed by two groups or individuals). For example, № 224:

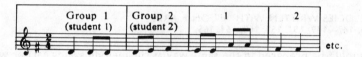

b) Alternating voice and piano (individual performance):

c) Alternating inner singing and singing aloud (individual performance):

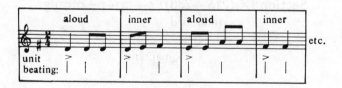

This kind of practising way should also sometimes be started with inner singing.

Section VIII (172—193, 195, 197, 198, 200—214):
m—r—d—l,—s, range
(A complete pentatonic set of notes.)

In these melodies it is possible to speak of pentatonic tonality. It is, of course, true that the melodies do not go beyond the range of the sixth but within this range all the notes of pentatony appear. The tonality can thus be determined depending on the final note of the exercises: if the final note is "l", the mode is "l" pentatonic; if the final note is "s", the mode is "s", pentatonic, etc. The majority of the melodies are in "l" pentatonic (172—179, 181, 182, 184, 188, 189, 192, 202—205, 207, 209, 210, 212) but there are also several "s" pentatonic exercises (180, 190, 193, 195, 198, 201, 211), "d" pentatonic (185—187, 191, 200, 208 214) and even "r" pentatonic (183, 197, 206, 213).

With the extension of the set of notes to five degrees, we encounter an important new interval — the major sixth s, —m. It is therefore necessary to concentrate principally on this pattern in the note-finding practice from staff notation.

Apart from one exception there is a G—B major third in all the melodies. Only exercise 178 contains an F—A major third. It is nevertheless useful to sing on the basis of both "d" positions in the note-finding exercises:

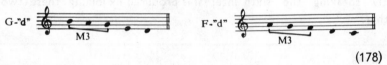

(178)

New musical elements in Section VIII:

The major sixth interval;

The ♩. ♪ rhythm pattern;

The ¢ metre.

s,—m MAJOR SIXTH = 175, 193, 200, 204, 205, 213, 214

The order of difficulties presented by the major sixth patterns in the exercises:

a) № 200: Upward major sixth with melodic preparation of the highest note "m", heard twice. The note "m" of the sixth leap "recalls" the already sung highest note.

b) № 205: Major sixth occurring in ascending melodic sequence.

c) № 214: The highest note "m" of the upward major sixth is prepared only by the very exposed main note "d" which determines the tonality.

d) № 175, 193: In these melodies it is necessary to hear and intonate the s,—m major sixth as an independent interval since it occurs as the opening phrase of the melody.

37

e) № 204: The downward major sixth is securely prepared by the melodic phrases preceding it:

The high note "m" is an organic part of the upward moving d—r—m melodic line, while the lowest note "s", is merely a return to the last low note before the ascent in the melody.

f) № 213: A downward sixth without any preparation. In the two-bar motif, however, it is not the sixth interval but the well known s,—d phrase which dominates. Thus once again sure hearing of the principal note "d", makes perfect intonation of this major sixth possible:

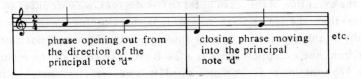

Strictly speaking the sixth interval is produced by joining these two details together.

♩. ♪ = 188

The melody should be sung with a) a ♩ ♫ ostinato, b) a rhythm canon entering in the second bar, c) with beating the metrical units and d) a ♪ ♩ ♪ ostinato.

¢ = 202 (See p. 64.)

a) The students should sing this melody in quick tempo with ♩ ♫ ♩ ♫ ostinato accompaniment, and meanwhile the teacher should add a two-part rhythm accompaniment. The singing should begin in the third bar — that is, after two bars of introduction:

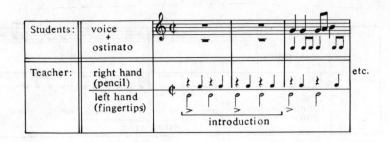

Students:	voice + ostinato	(music notation)
Teacher:	right hand (pencil) left hand (fingertips)	(music notation) etc. introduction

. b) This same way of performing the melody should be supplemented by the teacher counting the ♩ metric units aloud:

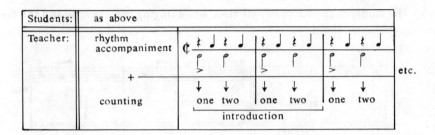

Students:	as above	
Teacher:	rhythm accompaniment + counting	(music notation) etc. one two one two one two introduction

c) One group of students taps the ♩ ♫ ♩ ♫ ostinato and counts the ♩ metric units aloud while the other group, after two bars of introduction, only sings the melody:

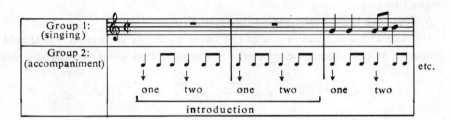

Group 1: (singing)	(music notation)
Group 2: (accompaniment)	(music notation) etc. one two one two one two introduction

d) The same, the groups exchanging roles.

e) Using this same way of performing, the singing group also beats the ♩ units:

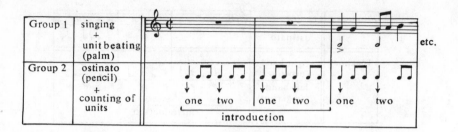

Group 1	singing + unit beating (palm)			
Group 2	ostinato (pencil) + counting of units	one two	one two	one two

introduction

f) The same, the groups exchanging roles.

g) Everyone sings the melody accompanied by beating the ♩ metric units and the teacher counts the units aloud.

h) The students conduct in duple time while singing the exercise and the teacher counts the units aloud:

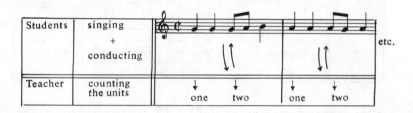

Students	singing + conducting		
Teacher	counting the units	one two	one two

i) Omitting the counting aloud, a volunteer performs the melody accompanied by duple-time conducting. The others also conduct and listen closely to their colleague's singing.

j) Everyone sings, accompanied by beating time.

The ostinato accompaniments of the other melodies in Section VIII should be formed so as to include as many of the rhythm patterns so far learned as possible:

For example, a three-bar ostinato for Ex. 175:

three-bar motif

ostinato:

or

Section X (239—270) and Section VIII (194, 196, 199):
l—s—m—r—d range

These exercises, similarly to those in the preceding Section VIII, embrace the entire pentatonic range. But here all the melodies, with the single exception of № 248, all have "d", as the final note, and are thus in the "d" pentatonic mode.

In the l—s—m—r—d set of notes it is the other major sixth of pentatony — d—l — that stands out as a new interval. In the present case the importance of this is not merely that the students are again practising a major sixth but that after much practice in using lower "l", they are now gaining experience in interval relations connected to upper "l". Thus in note-finding exercises using staff notation this "l" is necessary so that it has to assume its principal role, and at the same time all intervals which, through being connected to this upper "l", produce novel melodic patterns. To gain practice in these many melodic lines such as the following should be sung from staff notation using D as "d" (♮𝄞) l—s—l—m—r— s—l—r—m—d—l—r—l—s—d etc.

Musical elements requiring special practice in the exercises in the group:

The ♪𝅘𝅥𝅭. rhythm pattern;

The d—l major sixth;

The ‚ 𝅘𝅥𝅮𝅘𝅥 ‚ staff notation.

♪ 𝅘𝅥. = 268

This rhythm pattern has already appeared in Ex. 61 of Section VI (see p. 32). Here, however, it occurs in a more difficult environment: it is at the beginning of the melody, without any preparation. Precisely because of this the suggested forms of practice below are preceded by a two-bar introduction which uses only beating the metric units.

a) One group should provide a continuous unit beat while the other sings the melody with an ostinato:

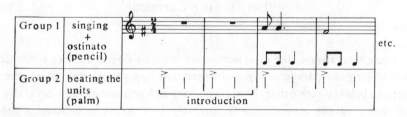

b) The same, the groups exchanging roles.
c) The melody is sung with a two-bar 𝅘𝅥 𝅘𝅥𝅮𝅘𝅥 | 𝅘𝅥𝅘𝅥 ♪ | ostinato:

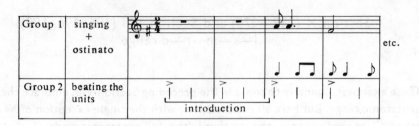

Group 1	singing + ostinato						etc.
Group 2	beating the units			introduction			

d) The same, the groups exchanging roles.

e) The melody to be practised accompanied only by beating the metric units.

f) Try the forms given in a) and c) with individuals performing the three parts (singing — ostinato [right hand] — unit beating [left hand]).

d—l MAJOR SIXTH = 256, 267, 194

The easiest of the three occurrences of the d—l major sixth — considering the environment — seems to be that in which the major sixth appears in both directions successively (256), and the most difficult that in which it comes as the opening phrase of the melody (194).

γ $\sqrt{}$ γ $= 270$

The staff notation of γ $\sqrt{}$ γ seems new but it belongs essentially among the problem area of rests coming in a stressed part of the bar, and the students have already met this in singing the melodies in Section I (exercises 14 and 19, see p. 28).

Two-Part Material

"Let Us Sing Correctly"

". . . those who always sing in unison never learn to sing in correct pitch. Correct unison singing can, paradoxically, be learned only by singing in two parts: the voices adjust and balance each other. Those who have a clear aural conception of the sound C—G will sing the interval C—G correctly." "Correct intonation is the main purpose of the present exercises; rhythmic difficulties are therefore avoided." (Foreword)

These indispensable two-part exercises for secure and pure intonation, with the exception of the last two, likewise move within the pentatonic system. "The scale will sound correct only when its pillars are established in advance, and these pillars are the notes of the pentatonic scale: C—D—E—G—A, or in solmisation d—r—m—s—l." (Foreword)

Of the exercises in the volume the first to be sung should be

   a) those in which only one part moves

   b) those which contain the notes d—m—s + l,—d—m

   c) those in which the intervals which sound simultaneously are not larger than an octave.

Taking these points into consideration 34 two-part exercises can be listed in this chapter. The singing of the exercises seems most useful in the following groupings which have been divided into lessons:

Lesson	Notes used	C—"d"	F—"d"	Lesson	Notes used	C—"d"	F—"d"
1st	d-d'	1, 2.		7th	l,-d-m		18, 19, 20.
	d-s	3.		8th	l,-d-m		21.
2nd	d-s-d'	4, 5.			m,-l,-d-m		22, 23.
	d-m-s	6.		9th	d-m-s		26, 27.
3rd	d-m	7.			d-m-s-l		28.
	d-m-d'	8, 9.		10th	d-m-s-d'	30.	
4th	d-m-d'	10, 11.			d-m-s-l-d'	29.	
	d-m-s	12, 24.		11th	d-m-s-l	31.	
5th	s,-d-s		13, 14.		d-m-s-l-d'	32.	
	s,-d-m-s		15.	12th	d-m-s-l-d'	33, 34.	
6th	d-m-s		16, 25.				
	s,-d-m-s		17.				

Kodály writes as follows in the foreword to the volume (1941): "In order to achieve satisfactory results care must be taken

1. that at each lesson no more than one or two new exercises should be learned." (It is concerning first of all the teaching of little children.) "The old ones should always be repeated.

2. . . . no instrument is used. The pitch should be given orally.

3. . . . at first the exercises should be practised at a slow pace, breath being taken after every note; even later the speed should never be too fast, so as to allow for proper control of every note.

4. Every exercise should be repeated at once with exchanged parts, at the same pitch if the range permits, otherwise at a different pitch, higher or lower.

5. As preparation for the exercises let us practise the major and minor triads (d—m—s and l,—d—m) in various positions (m—s—d'; s,—d—m; d—m—l; m—l—d'); . . . For every exercise in which the melodic line rises two should be practised in which it falls."

The distribution into lessons given in the table above (p. 43) is a suggestion for the teacher, prepared by taking the range ot fhe notes and pitch into consideration. Stages to be used in singing:

1. Slow note-finding practice to hand-signs, using the set of notes and intervals in the exercises to be sung, and at the absolute pitch.

2. Grouping of students and establishment of the order of singing the exercises selected.

3. Two-part singing of the exercises.

a) The teacher should accompany the singing by beating the half notes so that the newly produced intervals will sound together in group singing as well.

b) Every exercise should be sung immediately with the groups exchanging parts so that each part may have a chance to observe the moving intervals.

c) After singing through each exercise there should be a rest of two half notes so that it will be possible to sing the planned exercises without any stopping or interruption.

For example, the singing of the three exercises planned for the first lesson will sound as follows:

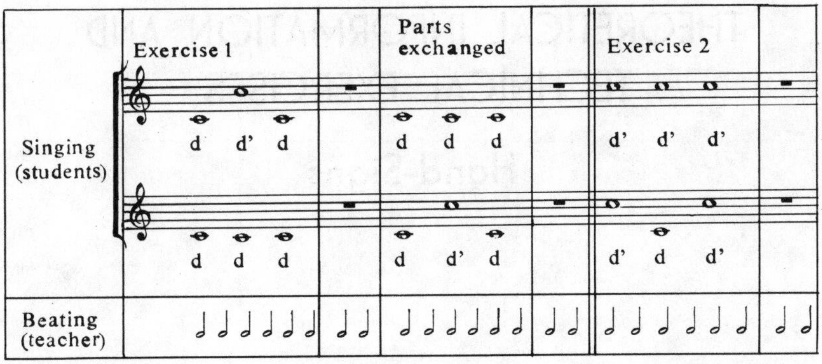
Exercise 1
Parts exchanged
Exercise 2
Singing (students)
d d' d
d d d
d' d' d'
d d d
d d' d
d' d d'
Beating (teacher)

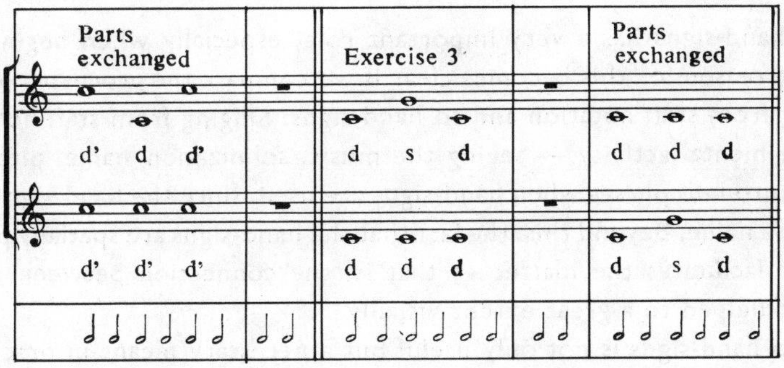
Parts exchanged
Exercise 3
Parts exchanged
d' d d'
d s d
d d d
d' d' d'
d d d
d s d

THEORETICAL INFORMATION AND TECHNICAL EXERCISES

Hand-Signs

Singing to hand-signs has a very important role, especially when beginning such studies. The reason for this becomes clear if we compare the processes of solmization singing from staff notation and to hand-signs. Singing from staff notation is a three-phase mental activity — seeing the music, solmization name, pitch. This is condensed into two phases when hand-signs are used, since the hand-sign coincides with the solfa name. Beyond this, the fact that the hand-signs are spatially positioned also further facilitates the matter — that is, the connection between name and pitch is also helped to a great extent visually.

Singing to hand-signs is not only useful but a necessary means in practising the interval relationships until the association between printed music and name becomes sufficiently automatic. For this reason it is necessary at the beginning to devote some minutes to practice of this in every lesson.

Hand-signs for the pentatonic notes:

| d | r | m | s | l |

Solfa singing to hand-signs has a double purpose in the early stages:

a) Preparation of the melodic patterns and intervals due to appear in the musical material for the lessons.

b) Developing the sound of the pentatonic tonal system as securely as possible in the students by intensive practice of various pentatonic phrases.

Within the framework of this second aim belongs the gradual extension of the set of notes used at the moment, in preparation for the melodic world of the following chapter (II). Since there are melodies which go beyond the octave range in the Kodály exercises and sight-singing material in Chapter II, hand-signs practising has to evolve in the students sensitivity towards this kind of melodic movement.

When it is a case of adult students, the hand-signs for all five pentatonic notes can be used from the very first lesson, but the principle of progressivity should not be forgotten in the order of the melodic patterns. For example:

Daily aim	The hand-sign melody of the realization (for example):
Developing the pentatonic set of notes with "d" as principal note (usuallay with adjacent note phrases)	d-r-m-r-d-r-m-d-r-m-d-r-m-r-d — m-s-m-s-m-r-d-m-s-m- d-r-m + s -d-r-m-d — m-s-l-s-m-r-d-m-s-l-s-l-m-s-r-m-s-d + l
Downward extention of the pentatonic notes	d-r-m-d-m-s-m-r-d-m-s-l-s-l-s-m-l-s-m-r-s-m-d-r-d — repetition + -l,-s,-l,-d-m-r-d-m-s-l-m-r-s-m-d-m-r-d-s,-l,-s,-d l,-s,
Upward extention of the pentatonic notes	d-l,-d-r-m-d-l,-s,-d-m-s-m-s-l-s-m-r-s-m-r-d — repetition + m-s-l-d'-l-s-d'-l-s-m-r-d-m-l-d'-s-d'-l-s-m-d-r-d-l,-s,-d d'

In what follows some new pentatonic interval pattern should be added on each occasion to the melodic movement already practised (mainly on the basis of the musical material to be sung from the music), or the already familiar interval relationships should be sung but grouped around a different principal note.

Practice in Pentatony

The note-groups of pentatony

We can see in the 333 Elementary Exercises how careful Kodály was to have the students become thoroughly orientated in certain pentatonic groups of two, three, or four notes before carrying out intensive practising of complete pentatony.

Over however great a range we write the notes of anhemitonic pentatony, we will still find only two kinds of adjacent notes: the major second and the minor third.

Thus it is a combination of these two intervals that produces the pentatonic note-groups which consist of adjacent notes. These note-groups are:

TWO-NOTE GROUP (= bichord: two notes adjacent to one another in the given system — in this case, pentatony):

	structure	solmization possibilities
a)	major second	d-r r-m s-l
b)	minor third	m-s l-d'

THREE-NOTE GROUP (= trichord: three adjacent notes in the given system — in this case, pentatony):

	structure	solmization possibilities
a)	maj. 2nd ↘ min. 3rd	r-d-l, l-s-m
b)	min. 3rd ↘ maj. 2nd	s-m-r d-l,-s,
c)	maj. 2nd ↘ maj. 2nd	m-r-d

FOUR-NOTE GROUP (= tetrachord: four notes adjacent to one another in the given system — in this case, pentatony):

	structure	solmization possibilities
a)	min. 3rd \\ maj. 2nd \\ maj. 2nd	s-m-r-d (pentatonic tetrachord of major character)
b)	maj. 2nd \\ maj. 2nd \\ min. 3rd	m-r-d-l, (pentatonic tetrachord of minor character)
c)	maj. 2nd \\ min. 3rd \\ maj. 2nd	r-d-l,-s, l-s-m-r
d)	min. 3rd \\ maj. 2nd \\ min. 3rd	d'-l-s-m (this does not appear in the melodies of the 333 Elementary Exercises)

The intervals of the pentatonic note-groups

Since there is a distance of either a major second or a minor third between notes which are adjacent in pentatony, the distances between notes which are not adjacent are also produced by the different variations in combining these two intervals with one another.

1. The distances between every third notes (the intervals between the outer notes of pentatonic trichords):

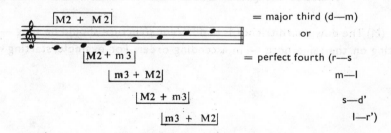

In trichords consisting only of major seconds, the distance between the two outer notes is a major third, but in those consisting of a major second and a minor third the perfect fourth is the largest interval.

2. The distance between every fourth note (the intervals between the outer notes of pentatonic tetrachords):

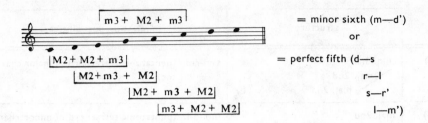

⌐ m3 + M2 + m3 ⌐	= minor sixth (m—d')
	or
⌐M2 + M2 + m3⌐	= perfect fifth (d—s
⌐M2 + m3 + M2⌐	r—l
⌐M2 + m3 + M2⌐	s—r'
⌐m3 + M2 + M2⌐	l—m')

Where there are two major seconds among the three components the perfect fifth comes as the largest interval, and where there are two minor thirds the outer notes are separated by a minor sixth.

Practising the pentatonic note-groups

1. (M)* Pentatonic trichords of different structure should be sung in a descending line, from the same pitch (e. g. from A), using all the solmization possibilities:

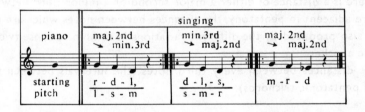

piano	singing		
	maj. 2nd → min. 3rd	min.3rd → maj.2nd	maj. 2nd → maj.2nd
starting pitch	r - d - l, l - s - m	d - l, - s, s - m - r	m - r - d

2. (M) The downward trichords of different structure should be sung — likewise starting on the same note — in ascending order. For example, starting with "d":

* The letter M before an exercise indicates that the students should know the exercise from memory.

50

piano	d	r	m	s	l
starting pitch	d - l, - s,	r - d - l,	m - r - d	s - m - r	l - s - m
	m3 ↘ M2	M2 ↘ m3	M2 ↘ M2	m3 ↘ M2	M2 ↘ m3

The series should also be started with "r", "m", "s" and "l".

3. (M) The same should be practised in a descending order. For example, beginning with "s":

piano	s	m	r	d	l,
starting pitch	s - m - r	m - r - d	r - d - l,	d - l, - s,	l, - s, -m,

The series should also be begun with the other solfa names as starting notes.

4. (M) The first way of practising should be used with ascending trichords:

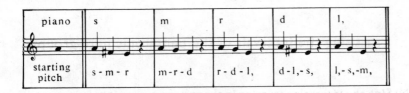

piano	M2 ↗ m3	m3 ↗ M2	M2 ↗ M2
starting pitch	l, - d - r / m - s - l	s, - l, - d / r - m - s	d - r - m

5. (M) Practise upward trichords in an ascending order, beginning, for example, with "r":

piano	r	m	s	l	d'
starting pitch	r - m - s	m - s - l	s - l - d'	l - d'- r'	d'- r'- m'
	m3 / M2 ↗	M2 / m3 ↗	m3 / M2 ↗	M2 / m3 ↗	M2 / M2 ↗

Begin the series with the other solmization names, too.

6. (M) Do the same in descending order, beginning, for example, with "l":

To be sung with the other starting notes as well.

7. (M) The exercises described under 1—6 should also be practised with groups of four notes (tetrachords), but only once quick and secure intonation of the various trichords causes no trouble.

Practising the intervals of the pentatonic note-groups

1. (M) Sing the intervals occurring in three-note groups in a downward direction, beginning with the smallest:

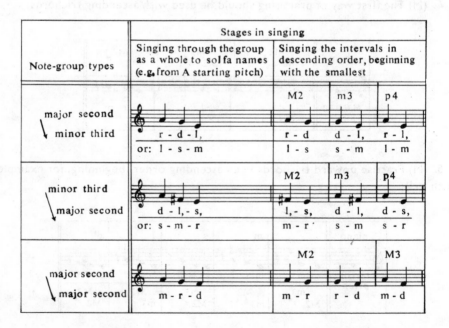

2. (M) Practise the intervals of the note-groups in the same way but starting with the largest:

52

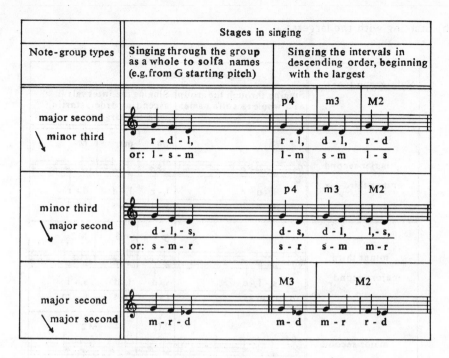

Stages in singing

Note-group types	Singing through the group as a whole to solfa names (e.g. from G starting pitch)	Singing the intervals in descending order, beginning with the largest		
		p4	m3	M2
major second ↓ minor third	r - d - l, or: l - s - m	r - l, / l - m	d - l, / s - m	r - d / l - s
		p4	m3	M2
minor third ↓ major second	d - l, - s, or: s - m - r	d - s, / s - r	d - l, / s - m	l, - s, / m - r
		M3		M2
major second ↓ major second	m - r - d	m - d	m - r	r - d

3. (M) Sing the intervals of the three-note groups upwards.

a) Starting with the smallest:

Stages in singing

Note-group types	Singing through the group as a whole to solfa names (e.g. from D starting pitch)	Singing the intervals in ascending order, starting with the smallest		
		M2	m3	p4
↗ major second minor third	l, - d - r or: m - s - l	d - r / s - l	l, - d / m - s	l, - r / m - l
		M2	m3	p4
↗ minor third major second	s, - l, - d or: r - m - s	s, - l, / r - m	l, - d / m - s	s, - d / r - s
			M2	M3
↗ major second major second	d - r - m		d - r / r - m	d - m

b) Starting with the largest:

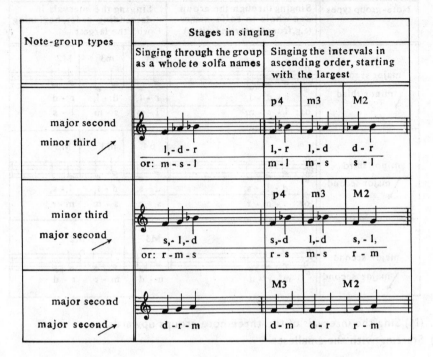

Note-group types	Stages in singing	
	Singing through the group as a whole to solfa names	Singing the intervals in ascending order, starting with the largest
major second minor third ↗	l,-d - r or: m - s - l	**p4** l,-r **m3** l,-d **M2** d - r m - l m - s s - l
minor third major second ↗	s,- l,- d or: r - m - s	**p4** s,-d **m3** l,-d **M2** s, - l, r - s m - s r - m
major second major second ↗	d - r - m	**M3** d - m **M2** d - r r - m

4. (M) Practise the intervals of the four-note groups (tetrachords) in ways similar to those described under 1, 2 and 3.

a) Intervals in a downward direction, starting with the smallest:

Note-group types	Stages in singing					
	Singing the set of notes	Singing the intervals downwards, starting with the smallest				

Note-group types	Singing the set of notes	M2	m3	p4		p5
maj.2nd min.3rd maj.2nd	r - d - l,- s, or l - s - m - r	r - d l,- s, l - s m - r	d - l, m - r	r - l, s - m	d - s, l - m	r - s, l - r
maj.2nd maj.2nd min.3rd	m - r - d - l,	M2 m - r r - d 	m3 d - l,	M3 m - d	p4 r - l,	p5 m - l,
min.3rd maj.2nd maj.2nd	s - m - r - d	M2 m - r r - d 	m3 s - m	M3 m - d	p4 s - r	p5 s - d
min.3rd maj.2nd min.3rd	d'- l - s - m	M2 l - s d'- l	m3 	p4 s - m d'- s		m6 l - m d'- m

b) Intervals in a downward direction, starting with the largest.

c) Intervals in an upward direction, starting with the smallest.

d) Intervals in an upward direction, starting with the largest.

(cf. pp. 52—53 points 1—3)

Practising the intervals of the pentatonic set of notes within a major sixth range

1. (M) Sing the pentatonic intervals within the d—l major sixth.

a) Starting from above and moving downwards, beginning with the smallest:

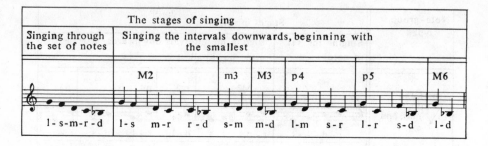

The stages of singing									
Singing through the set of notes	Singing the intervals downwards, beginning with the smallest								
	M2		m3	M3	p4		p5		M6
l - s - m - r - d	l-s	m-r	r-d	s-m	m-d	l-m	s-r	l-r	s-d	l-d

b) Downwards, starting with the largest.

c) Upwards, starting with the smallest.

d) Upwards, starting with the largest.

2. (M) Similarly practise the intervals into which the s,—m major sixth can be divided.

a) Downwards, starting with the smallest.

b) Downwards, starting with the largest.

c) Upwards, starting with the smallest.

d) Upwards, starting with the largest.

For example, 2 d):

The stages of singing									
Singing through the set of notes	Singing the intervals upwards, beginning with the largest								
	M6	p5		p4		M3	m3	M2	
s,- l,- d - r - m	s,-m	s,-r	l,-m	s,-d	l,-r	d-m	l,-d	s,-l,	d-r	r-m

The intervals of the complete pentatonic system

s, l, d r m s l d' r' m' s'

Major second

d - r   r - m   s - l

and its inversion completing
the octave:

Minor seventh

r - d'   m - r'   l - s'

56

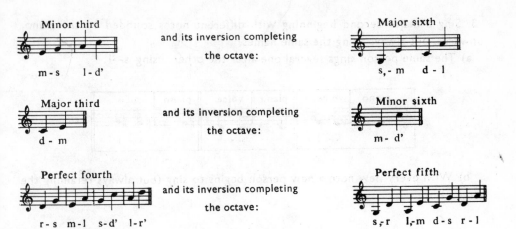

| Minor third | and its inversion completing | Major sixth |
| m - s   l - d' | the octave: | s, - m   d - l |

| Major third | and its inversion completing | Minor sixth |
| d - m | the octave: | m - d' |

| Perfect fourth | and its inversion completing | Perfect fifth |
| r - s   m - l   s - d'   l - r' | the octave: | s, - r   l, - m   d - s   r - l |

Forms of practice for the various interval types

MAJOR SECOND

1. (M) Sing a major second upwards — from a certain given starting note — with any of its names which occur in pentatony. Then using the same major second sing the other pentatonic names to it as well, and at the same time determine the pitch of "d".

e. g. from F:

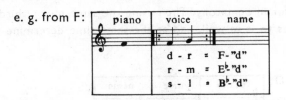

piano	voice	name
	d - r	= F-"d"
	r - m	= E♭-"d"
	s - l	= B♭-"d"

2. (M) Practise the downward major second in the same way.

e. g. from E:

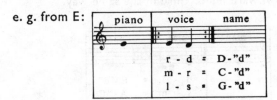

piano	voice	name
	r - d	= D-"d"
	m - r	= C-"d"
	l - s	= G-"d"

3. Sing a major second beginning with different notes sounded on the piano, upwards, but always using the same names.

a) The same person sings several one after the other, using s—l:

b) With every new note a new person begins to sing (but always retaining the same name):

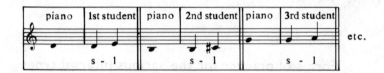

Use methods a) and b) to practise the two other major second names, too: d—r and r—m.

4. Use the practice forms given in 3. for downward major seconds as well, based on the same principles.

MINOR THIRD (See p. 57)

1. (M) Sing a minor third upwards — from a given starting note — with any of its names which occur in pentatony. Then using the same minor third sing the other pentatonic names to it as well, and at the same time determine the pitch of "d".

e. g. from D:

2. (M) Practise the downward minor third in the same way.

e. g. from E:

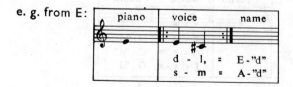

3. Sing a minor third beginning with different notes sounded on the piano, upwards, but always using the same names.

a) The same person sings several one after the other, using m—s:

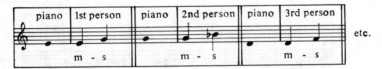

b) A different person sings from each new given note (but always using the same names):

Use methods a) and b) to practise the other minor third name as well: l,—d.

4. Use the practice forms given in 3. for downward minor thirds as well.

MAJOR THIRD (See p. 57)

As a first step connect the practising of the major third to the minor thirds, which have by now been sung a great deal and in many different ways: the ascending major third should be related to the d—l, minor third, and the descending major third to the m—s minor third. In this way the following practice forms evolve:

1. Sing the d—l,—d—m melodic phrase with which we practise the upward major third:

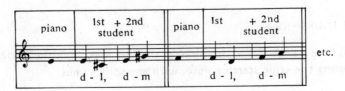

2. Divide the exercise between two students so that one sings only the minor third softly and the other sings only the major third more loudly:

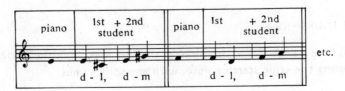

After three or four phrases the two students should exchange roles.

3. In similar ways practise the downward major third with the melodic progression m—s—m—d.

a) One person performing:

b) The same but divided between two people (also with exchange of roles):

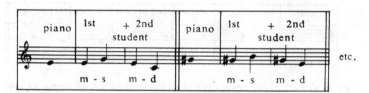

4. Leave out the preparatory minor third and sing the major third on its own, upwards, starting from different notes.

a) One person singing several one after the other:

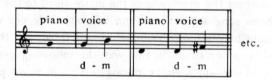

b) Different students continuing one after the other:

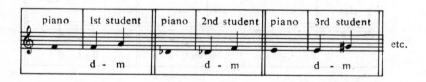

5. Practise the downward major third in ways similar to those given under 4.

PERFECT FOURTH (See p. 57)

1. (M) Sing a perfect fourth upwards, then its inversion, the perfect fifth downwards, using the same starting note, with any solfa names:

Then sing through the same pair of intervals using all the names occurring in pentatony, and at the same time determine the pitch of "d":

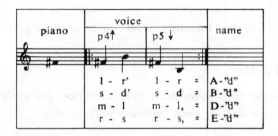

2. (M) Practise the downward perfect fourth + upward perfect fifth progression in the same way.

e. g. from E:

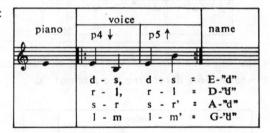

3. Sing a perfect fourth upwards, beginning on different notes sounded on the piano, but always using the same names.

a) One student sings several one after the other, using m—l:

b) With every new starting note a new person sings, but always using the same names:

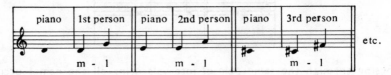

etc.

Practise in the ways used in a) and b) with the other perfect fourth names, too: s,—d; r—s; l,—r.

4. Sing downward perfect fourths in ways similar to those given under 3.

PERFECT FIFTH (See p. 57)

1. (M) Sing a perfect fifth upwards, then its inversion, the perfect fourth downwards, using the same starting note, with any solfa names:

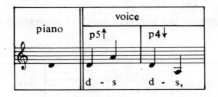

Then sing through the same pair of intervals using all the names occurring in pentatony, and at the same time determine the pitch of "d":

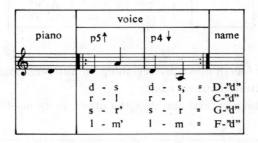

2. (M) Practise the downward perfect fifth + upward perfect fourth progression in the same way.

e.g. from G:

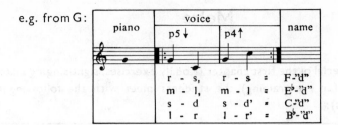

piano	voice		name
	p5 ↓	p4 ↑	
	r - s,	r - s	= F-"d"
	m - l,	m - l	= E♭-"d"
	s - d	s - d'	= C-"d"
	l - r	l - r'	= B♭-"d"

3. Sing a perfect fifth upwards, beginning on different notes sounded on the piano but always using the same names.

a) One person sings several one after the other, using s,—r:

piano	voice	piano	voice	piano	voice
	s, - r		s, - r		s, - r

etc.

b) With every new starting note a new student sings, but always using the same names:

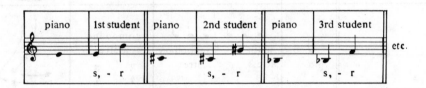

piano	1st student	piano	2nd student	piano	3rd student
	s, - r		s, - r		s, - r

etc.

Practise the other perfect fifths in similar ways: r—l; d—s and l,—m.

4. Sing the exercises in 3. using the downward fifth.

Metre

In the musical material of the first chapter (Kodály exercises, sight-singing material, musical material for ear training) the students meet with the following time signatures (metres):

Time signature	Metrical unit of the bar	Stress relationships between the metrical units of the bar	Kinds of metre	
			type	conducting
$\frac{2}{4}$	♩	♩ ♩	simple duple (even)	
$\frac{3}{4}$	♩	♩ ♩ ♩	simple triple (uneven)	
$\frac{4}{4}$ C	♩	♩ ♩ ♩ ♩ main stress / secondary stress	compound metre $\frac{2}{4}$ + $\frac{2}{4}$	
$\frac{6}{4}$	♩	♩ ♩ ♩ ♩ ♩ ♩ main stress / secondary stress	compound metre $\frac{3}{4}$ + $\frac{3}{4}$	
¢ $\frac{2}{2}$ alla breve	♩	♩ ♩	simple duple (even)	
$\frac{3}{2}$	♩	♩ ♩ ♩	simple triple (uneven)	
$\frac{4}{2}$	♩	♩ ♩ ♩ ♩ main stress / secondary stress	compoud metre $\frac{2}{2}$ + $\frac{2}{2}$	
$\frac{3}{8}$	♪	♪ ♪ ♪	simple triple (uneven)	

SIGHT-SINGING

The melodies given below are quotations from musical literature, the melodic line of which moves within the range of the Kodály exercises so far sung from staff notation — that is, in pentatony within the range of a sixth.

Of the forty-nine melodies sixteen are in the bass clef. Since the bass clef has not played any part in the Kodály material it is absolutely necessary that before singing these quotations, the students should practise note-finding singing from staff using the range of notes of the given melody written in the bass clef. (For example, the notes of the eighth extract:

In the course of this sort of practice the teacher should make the students sing all the melodic patterns within the range of notes as thoroughly as possible so that the students will gradually become accustomed to reading in the bass clef as well.

Before singing the individual melodies we have to make the students consciously aware of the metre, and the corresponding way of beating time, the set of notes used, and the solfa name of the first note. The key signature used for the melodies is adapted in every case to the given range of notes, thus the position of "d" is determined by the major third (d—m) in the pentatony. For example in the third extract:

At the individual examples the composer's name, the work's title and — if transposition has been used — the original pitch are given.

The extracts should be sung using solfa names and accompanied by beating time, in group and individual performance alike. In the end the singing can be nothing but faultless.

65

The melodies which do not include a major third — that is, those which can be interpreted in two ways within pentatony — should be sung to both solfa possibilities. For example, the first quotation might end with either "l" or "m", etc.

Unison Extracts from the Musical Literature

1. BARTÓK: BLUEBEARD'S CASTLE. (or.: from F)

2. BRITTEN: PETER GRIMES. I. (or.: from G)

3. LISZT: VIA CRUCIS. (or.: from C)

(Concerning the $\frac{3}{2}$ time signature see p. 64)

4. BARTÓK: BLUEBEARD'S CASTLE. (or.: from C)

5. BRITTEN: PETER GRIMES. I. (or.: from B♭)

6. BORODIN: THE SLEEPING BEAUTY. (or.: from F)

7. LISZT: SEPTEM SACRAMENTA. (or.: from E♭)

(Concerning the $\frac{4}{2}$ time
signature see p. 64)

8. BARTÓK: BLUEBEARD'S CASTLE. (or.: from A♭)

9. BARTÓK: 44 DUOS.

10. KODÁLY: PSALMUS HUNGARICUS.

11. BARTÓK: BLUEBEARD'S CASTLE.

a)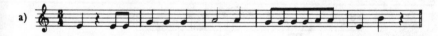

(or.: from E)

b)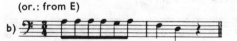

(or.: from E)

c)

(or.: from C♯)

d)

12. LISZT: REQUIEM (FOR ORGAN). (or.: from C)

13. BARTÓK: BLUEBEARD'S CASTLE.

a)
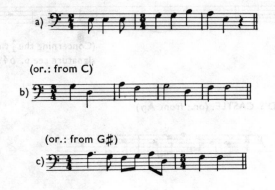

(or.: from C)

b)

(or.: from G♯)

c)

(or.: from D♯)

d)

14. GAY—BRITTEN: THE BEGGAR'S OPERA I. (or.: from B♭)

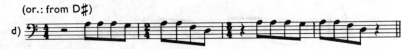

15. KODÁLY: TWO SONGS, OP. 5.

16. LISZT: SEPTEM SACRAMENTA. (or.: from F♯)

(See p. 64)

17. MUSSORGSKY: BORIS GODUNOV I.

18. DEBUSSY: TROIS CHANSONS DE CHARLES D'ORLEANS I. (or.: from F♯)

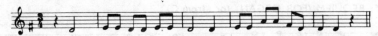

19. GRETCHANINOV: CHILDREN'S SONGS, OP. 47, NO. 1. (or.: from A)

20. BARTÓK: BLUEBEARD'S CASTLE.

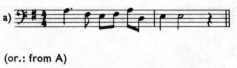

a)

(or.: from A)

b)

21. LISZT: CANTICO DEL SOL. (or.: from A)

22. BRITTEN: PETER GRIMES II. (or.: from C)

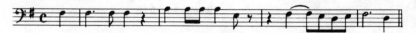

23. LISZT: MISSA CHORALIS. KYRIE. (or.: from D)

24. BARTÓK: BLUEBEARD'S CASTLE. (or.: from G)

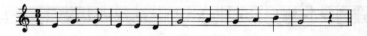

25. SAINT SAËNS : ORATORIO DEL NOËL, OP. 12, NO. 2. (or.: from A)

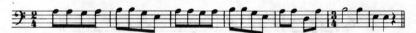

26. DELIBES: LAKMÉ I. (or.: from C#)

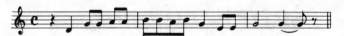

27. RAKHMANINOV: THE SONGS OF GRUSIA. (or.: from E)

28. LISZT: TU ES PETRUS.

(See p. 64)

29. GAY—BRITTEN: THE BEGGAR'S OPERA I. (or.: from G)

(Concerning the $\frac{6}{4}$ time signature p. 64)

30. BARTÓK: BLUEBEARD'S CASTLE. (or.: from C)

31. MUSSORGSKY: BORIS GODUNOV III. (or.: from F)

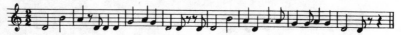

32. HONEGGER: SIX POÉSIES DE JEAN COCTEAU. (or.: from C)

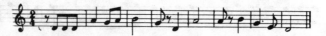

33. MUSSORGSKY: BORIS GODUNOV III. (or.: from C)

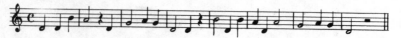

34. BRITTEN: PETER GRIMES I. (or.: from E)

35. BARTÓK: BLUEBEARD'S CASTLE (or.: from D)

36. BRITTEN: PETER GRIMES I.

(or.: from A)

a)

(or.: from E♭)

b)

37. LISZT: PATER NOSTER. (or.: from C)

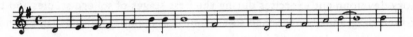

38. LISZT: MARIENGARTEN. (or.: from A)

39. LISZT: ORGAN-MASS. KYRIE. (or.: from B)

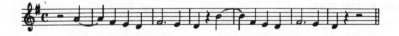

40. DELIBES: LAKMÉ. (or.: from F♯)

41. BARTÓK: THE WOODEN PRINCE. (or.: from C)

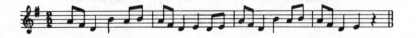

71

DEVELOPMENT OF MUSICAL MEMORY AND EAR

The development of musical memory is a task of prime importance, for the actual musical memories which live on in our consciousness — particularly those which became stored away by means of singing — are most important means towards the development of inner hearing. For this very reason it is necessary to start the memory development exercises during the first stages of solfege studies and these must then be gradually deepened so that musical memory will not lag behind the other areas in development of ability.

In this first chapter memory and ear training can scarcely be separated from each other, for until the students do not reach a certain stage in singing ability, "hearing" is still not automatic but merely the result of analysing the actual musical memory. At the beginning the students can realize the written form of heard melodies only if they consciously know the rhythmic and melodic patterns in them. Therefore the students should be asked to attempt the written forms of only those melodies which they know certainly and of the rhythmic and melodic elements of which they have a clear idea.

In these first stages of music dictation, just as in later stages, it is really our memory which is dictating to our capacity for musical recognition. We have therefore to take advantage of every opportunity for the development of musical memory and for training it as thoroughly and in as many ways as possible.

Memorizing from Staff Notation

At the same time as beginning singing the 333 Elementary Exercises, learning by heart should also be started, in the following ways:

1. The last motif (two or three bars), and later the second half of the melody

72

(four or six bars), from one of the exercises in the material for the lesson should be memorized using singing to solfa names, after singing aloud the whole melody through several times.

2. Once the students can cope with this easily they should be asked to learn melodies of similar size after singing aloud them through only once.

Those students who memorize more easily a) should learn the shorter parts with a freely chosen ostinato, which is a good preparation for two-part learning by heart, and b) should learn not only parts of melodies but whole melodies.

3. After a certain time memorizing by no more than inner hearing can be asked for — that is, without singing aloud, using only the music as seen; possibly some parts might be marked off and then the students given the chance to choose freely from among them. In this way it becomes possible for the better students to deal with more exercises within a given time without disturbing the weaker ones.

4. Finally, learning by heart should be extended to complete melodies — not, however, going beyond the eight-bar limit.

STAGES IN CHECKING THE MELODIES LEARNED

a) Singing to solfa names accompanied by beating time. (Those who have learned a melody with ostinato should perform it in this way.)

b) Solfa singing + hand-sign accompaniment.

c) Writing of the solfa names with rhythm values in the note book. For example the second half of melody № 39:

$$\frac{2}{4}\ \text{♩♩♩♩}\ |\ \text{♩♩♩}\ |\ \text{♩♩♩♩}\ |\ \text{♩ \}}\ \|$$

d d r d   l, l, d   r r d r   l,

d) As a control exercise a volunteer can write the melody on the blackboard at the pitch given in the original staff notation, likewise from memory.

e) Finally the melody should be sung (also with solfa names) in chorus from the blackboard.

Memorizing by Hand-Signs

This newer form of developing inner hearing should only be started once the students have had sufficient experience in solmization singing to the teacher's hand-signs, so that one can count on the sequence of the hand-signs evoking the memory of the already familiar melodic patterns in the students. This method of practising can be introduced in the following way:

BY USING THOROUGHLY FAMILIAR MATERIAL

a) From the two-bar or three-bar motifs memorized during the preceding lessons one should be recalled and used — after giving the pitch of the original starting note — with rhythmic, silent hand-sign outline; the students should then repeat the same melodic section with solfa singing accompanied by beating time.

b) After faultless singing a new one should be shown and then checked in a similar way.

c) As double checking, both should be sung by the same person. If this proves unsuccessful, the motifs should be shown once more by the teacher.

d) Once c) has been successfully dealt with, the melody sections should be written down (in the note-book) in staff notation using the same "d" system — depending on the pitch of the starting note.

e) As a joint control exercise individual volunteers should write the various extracts on the blackboard.

USE OF NEW MATERIAL

The stages suggested under 1. a)—e) should be used in relation with the motifs of exercises which belong to the known range of notes but which have perhaps not yet been actually sung — possibly even half-melodies.

Melody Memorizing by Ear (Melody Dictation)

Unaccompanied unison pentatonic melodies

EASY $\frac{2}{4}$ MELODIC SECTIONS
(Music material on page 379.)

Once students gained some experience in memorizing from the music and by hand-signs and in writing down of these well known melodic sections, it is possible to begin the memorizing of melodies by ear with them, using gradual stages. This kind of exercise represents an essentially more difficult undertaking for the students since here they can only orientate by means of hearing, as every visual assistance is omitted.

ASPECTS IN MEMORIZING BY EAR

1. A melodic section should always be dictated which is easier than the degree of difficulty of the exercises and musical extracts which are being sung at the time, for the students cannot recognize musical material the singing of which has not yet been innervated.

2. Work should be begun by using quite short (two-bar) details with easy phrases and rhythms.

3. Depending on the stage of development of the students, the extracts should be sounded once, twice or several times.

4. Ways of checking progress:

a) Solfa singing accompanied by beating the metric unit.

b) Solfa singing accompanied by beating time.

c) Slow tempo singing accompanied by hand-signs.

d) Writing down the tune in staff notation at the original pitch in the note-book.

e) As a further control, one of the students should write the dictated tune on the blackboard which should then finally be sung together by the group.

MORE DIFFICULT TUNES
(Music material on page 385.)

This musical material is more differentiated as regards both metre and rhythm. Memorizing by ear is therefore to be modified to a certain extent:

1. At the first encounter, the students should observe the metre and name it.

2. When the tune is played through the second time, its final note should be established and the starting note should be evoked by relating it to this last note. (If necessary the teacher plays through the melody once more.)

3. Once the metre and opening note have become conscious, the learning of the melody can be carried out in the course of one or several further performances.

4. Suggested phases of checking progress:

a) Solfa singing accompanied by beating time.

b) Conscious naming of the rhythmic elements of individual bars.

c) Singing again accompanied by beating time.

d) Writing down the tune in staff notation at the original pitch in the note-book.

e) One of the students whose writing is faultless writes the tune on the blackboard and it is sung from that by the whole group.

Pentatonic melodies with accompaniment
(Music material on page 386.)

The quotations from musical literature given here move within a pentatonic range of notes and melodic patterns not exceeding the sixth. The material of the accompaniment, on the other hand, does go beyond the framework of pentatony. Because of this the recognition of even the simplest melodic phrase can represent some difficulties.

Learning the melodies by heart, writing them down and checking the process should be carried out in the stages given above (More difficult tunes, p. 75 1—4).

Interval Recognition

The intervals of three-note pentatonic groups

1. The teacher selects one trichord (see p. 48) and plays its intervals — in any order — starting from the same note, either the lowest or the highest, while the students write down the intervals heard, using numbers and the appropriate qualification. For example the trichord d—l,—s, from the lowest note, E:

2. The teacher plays the intervals again so that the students can check their writing of them or fill in any they have missed out.

3. Following this, the students name the various intervals while they are being played once again: perfect fourth, minor third.

4. After group checking (point 3.) the students sing the intervals in both directions (first from the fixed note and then from the changing notes).

a) With interval names:

b) With the appropriate solfa names:

The intervals of the other two pentatonic trichords (r—d—l, = l—s—m and m—r—d) should be practised in the same way. For example, the r—d—l, group, with G as the highest note:

1. Recognition.

2. Individual checking.

3. General group checking with naming the intervals.

4. After general control the students sing the intervals (first from the fixed note and then from the changing notes).

a) With interval names:

b) With solfa names:

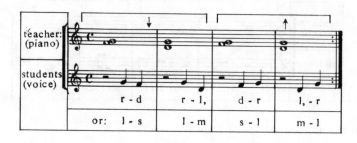

The intervals of four-note pentatonic groups

Recognition of the intervals of the pentatonic tetrachords should be practised in phases similar to those given above. For example, the intervals of the m—r—d—l, tetrachord with B as highest note:

1. Recognition.

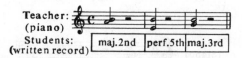

2. Individual checking.
3. General group checking, with naming the intervals.
4. After general control the students sing the intervals (first from the fixed note, then from the changing notes).

a) With interval names:

78

b) With solfa names:

teacher:
(piano)

students:
(voice)

m - r   m - l,   m - d   r - m   l,- m   d - m

Recognition of the intervals of the other pentatonic tetrachords (l—s—m—r = r—d—l,—s,; s—m—r—d and d'—l—s—m) should be practised in the same way.

Rhythm-Dictation
(Music material on page 388.)

On the basis of many years' experience, correct hearing of melodic elements—precisely because of melodic characteristics — would seem easier than making the rhythm of melodic phrases conscious and the ability to record them. For this very reason ear training exercises which demand only rhythm recording are a very necessary form of practice. If we neglect this form of rhythmic training at the beginning it is very difficult to make compensation for it later.

SUGGESTED STAGES IN PRACTICE:

1. The teacher plays the selected section on the piano while the students establish the metre and number of bars. (If the extract is longish, the teacher should play it once again after the metre has been determined.)
2. After another performance — now accompanied by the students beating time — they name the sequence of the melody's rhythm values within the individual bars.
3. After going through the rhythm of the melody precisely orally, the students should write the rhythm down.
4. The rhythm should be written on the blackboard by a volunteer.
5. Then the teacher plays the musical extract once more so that the students can become consciously convinced of the identity of the written and aural rhythmic patterns.

PLANNING SUGGESTION

If the material of each individual chapter is distributed over the minimal fifteen teaching lessons mentioned in the Introduction, the parallel progress of the various aspects in Chapter I will evolve as follows (the page numbers refer to the present book).

(see p. *80*)

The material for the individual lessons — especially from the sixth onwards — seems almost too much. But the planning suggestion also takes the "intensive home study" mentioned in the Introduction into consideration and this inevitably assumes responsibility for part of the work.

A double purpose is served by homework: on the one hand it removes the time-consuming process of individual practising from the work done in class together, and on the other hand — since the material already prepared in class comes as repetition — it encourages the consolidation of already acquired knowledge. In the interest of achieving this latter goal only material which has been suitably prepared in class should be set as homework.

Homework should always be set concretely and divided into various points and the checking of it should be included as an organic part of the following lesson.

From the eighth lesson onwards — when all the kinds of musical activity appearing in the chapter become connected with the teaching process — special care must be directed to proper distribution of the time allotted to each lesson. If this is neglected, some tasks may be allowed a disproportionately large amount of time and because of this some essential details may be omitted from other parts of the lesson.

Suggestion for time distribution within a lesson of 55 minutes:

Checking of homework	The new material in the lesson			
	Kodály exercises and memorizing from staff notation	Technical exercises and theoretical material	Memory and ear training (memorizing by ear and by hand-signs, interval recognition, rhythm dictation)	Sight-singing
20 mins.	(5-) 10 mins.	5 mins.	15 mins.	5(-10) mins.

This suggested plan may naturally be altered flexibly and if necessary once a given group of students are well known to the teacher.

CHAPTER II

(The staff notation material in the chapter uses C, C sharp and C flat as "d")

KODÁLY MATERIAL

Unison Pentatonic Melodies

MATERIAL IN STAFF NOTATION: 333 ELEMENTARY EXERCISES

The combined range of notes in the four exercises (325, 328, 329, 330) is:

Each of the melodies goes beyond the sixth range of the exercises sung so far: these move within the framework of an octave (8), a ninth (9) or a tenth (10). In spite of the larger range the only new addition to the already familiar intervals is the upward octave, the intonation of which can present no difficulty after the "Let Us Sing Correctly" exercises.

The key of the exercises is "l" or "r" pentatonic. Among the melodic motifs there appear many fourths and fifths, and for this reason it is necessary to devote special attention to these in the course of the note-finding exercises using staff notation. The fourths and fifths are as follows:

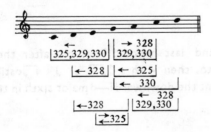

The note-finding exercises which precede melody singing — adapting to the Kodály material in the chapter — should be carried out within the framework of the s,—m' range, in both the G and the F clefs:

85

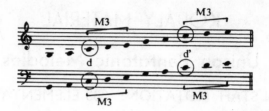

Repetition of musical elements already learned

♪ ♩. = 329

First of all sing the melody without the pauses and using a ♩ ♪♪♪ ostinato. Once the ♪ ♩. rhythm pattern in bars 2 and 6 is precise, the ostinato can be omitted and the singing may then be accompanied with no more than beating time, so that the notes with a pause mark on them can, with their formal delay, assume an appropriate role in the melody.

d—l MAJOR SIXTH = 325

The note "l" in the melody is given such an exposed role that it is easy to remember it as a principal note when it comes to singing the major sixth motif:

New musical elements

♩. ♪ ♪ ♩. = 330

   1. Sing the first and last melodic lines one after the other, first with a
⁴₄♫ ♩ ♫ ♩ ostinato, then with a ⁴₄♫ ♩ ♩ ♩ ♫ ostinato. In this particular melodic environment the downward l—d major sixth in the last line is very easy to intonate correctly:

identical cadential phrases

2. Only once the task given in 1. above has been carried out successfully should the complete melody be sung through — likewise with the ostinatos given above as accompaniment.

r—r' OCTAVE LEAP = 330, 328

In both cases it is between the last note of the first line and the first note of the second line that the octave leap occurs:

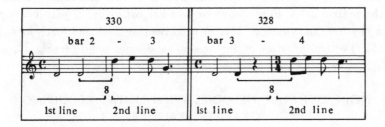

After the long "r" final note, starting again an octave higher with a note coming on the main metrical stress is secure and easy to intonate within the given "r" pentatonic tonality.

ALTERNATION OF $\frac{4}{4}$ AND $\frac{3}{4}$ = 328

Sing the melody a) beating the metric units, b) with alternating $\frac{4}{4}$ ♩ ♩ ♩ ♫ and $\frac{3}{4}$ ♩ ♩ ♫ ostinato, and c) with beating time.

MATERIAL USING SOLFA LETTERS: PENTATONIC MUSIC I—IV

The melodies in the Pentatonic Music volumes are not notated in notes written on staves but in solfa letters in conjunction with rhythm signs. The solfa letters strictly speaking replace hand-signs but without the spatial relations of the latter. Singing based on letter signs presupposes innervation of pentatonic patterns to such a degree that even when the spatial factor is removed they still evoke in us the sound of phrases notated in solfa letters. The melody listed here extends from the d-r-m pentatonic trichord to the d—l and s,—m range: its intervals therefore move within the framework of the major sixth.

87

Repetition of musical elements already learned

EASY MELODIES
(I/1, 2, 5; IV/1; I/7, III/22, 25, IV/29; I/9, 10, 11, 12, 36, II/1, 29, III/1, 2, 3, IV/3, 4, 7.)

The melodies can be sung at any pitch desired. Practising methods — like those for the 333 Elementary Exercises — must be varied, many-sided, so that simultaneously with melody singing the students' capacity for concentration and other musical abilities will develop as much as possible. Practise the melodies a) with beating the metric units, b) with one or two-bar ostinatos, c) with beating time, d) with a rhythm canon (see p. 26), e) in answering back and forth form (see p. 27, point 5), f) with alternation of singing aloud and inner singing (see p. 36, point 3).

MORE DIFFICULT MELODIES WITH MOTIFS REQUIRING SEPARATE PRACTICE

♪♪ ♩ = III/4

Practise the melody a) with the two-part rhythm accompaniment: 2/4 ♩ ♪ ♪ ♪ , b) beating the metric units, c) with a 2/4 ♪ ♩ ♪ ostinato and then a 2/4 ♪ ♩ ♪♪ ostinato, d) beating time.

♪ ♪♪ ♩ = IV/5

1. Practise this with the following ostinatos:
a) 2/4 ♩ ♪♪ ♩ b) 2/4 ♪ ♩ ♪ c) 2/4 ♪ ♪♪ ♩
2. Singing with beating time.

♪ ♪♪ ♩ AND ♪♪ ♪ ♩ = III/5, 30

III/5

1. Accompany the first and third motifs with a 2/4 ♪♪ ♩ ostinato, and the second and fourth motifs with a 2/4 ♩ ♪♪ ostinato.

2. Sing the whole melody to the accompaniment of a 2/4 ♪ ♩ ♪ ostinato.
3. Beat time while singing the melody.

III/30

1. Practise with these ostinatos: a) 2/4 ♩ ♪♪ ♩ b) 2/4 ♪ ♩ ♪ c) 2/4 ♪♪♪ ♪

2. Accompany with beating time.

¢ ($\frac{2}{2}$)= II/43, III/17, 19, II/31, 43

II/43

1. Sing the melody with the following two-part rhythm accompaniment divided between left and right hands a) in slow tempo, b) in fast tempo.

2. One group of students plays the ¢ ♩ ♩ rhythm accompaniment while another group beats the ♩ unit.

3. Repeat with the group roles exchanged.

4. Omit the rhythm accompaniment. Everyone sings and beats the ♩ metric unit.

5. Only the teacher gives the unit beat while the students sing the melody and conduct in duple time (see p. 64).

III/17

Practise this a) with beating the ♩ unit and b) beating duple time.

III/19

1. The students should sing, first in groups and then individually, the following pairs of bars:

bar 3 + bar 1   bar 7 + bar 5

a) giving the ♩ unit beat, b) beating duple time.

2. Once the above melodic progression has been carried out successfully, sing the original melody a) with giving the unit beat and b) beating time.

II/31

1. In the penultimate bar a difficult melodic phrase goes with the repeated ¢ ♩ ♩ ♫ ♩ rhythm pattern. In the interests of secure intonation of the lower "l" practise the following pair of bars ¢ (notation) with the two-part rhythm accompaniment: ¢ (notation) first of all in a slow tempo and then gradually increasing the tempo, always paying careful attention to the purity of the note "l".

2. Sing the whole melody with slow beating of the metric unit.

3. Perform it in a faster tempo, beating two along with it.

ALTERNATION OF $\frac{2}{4}$ AND $\frac{1}{4}$ = II/17

The practising methods are the same as for singing melody of similar metre in Chapter I (see p. 30). Once these methods have proved successful the form of performance used in connection with even stepping should be used. This becomes really most useful when the singing is from memory and is given at least one — but preferably three — repetitions.

SEQUENTIAL FOURTHS IN SUCCESSION (l—m—s—r) = III/26

Here the difficulty is caused not by the sequence itself but by its melodic continuation onto "d". In preparation practise the following sequence of motifs:

d—l MAJOR SIXTH UPWARDS = III/20

In the melody the stressed initial "d" and the repeated "l" coming as the highest note likewise in a stressed position make a secure preparation for the intonation of the d—l sixth in the fourth bar. The first note in each bar should be given a vigorous accent:

s—m MAJOR SIXTH UPWARDS = IV/10

The "m" top note of the upward major sixth is suitably prepared by the very exposed principal note "d", which also determines the tonality. Difficulty is more likely to be caused by the intonation of the note "s" because after the phrase it easily becomes flat. For this reason practise the following melody variants in preparation:

New musical elements

♩. ♪ ♪ ♩.= I/54

Recommended practice procedure:

1. One group of students sings the first half of the melody giving also the metric unit, while the other group taps a two-bar ⁴⁄₄ ♫ ♩ ♩ ♫ |♩ ♫ ♩ ♩ ‖ ostinato (without singing).

2. Exchange of group roles.

3. Everyone sings this part of the melody to the ostinato accompaniment.

4. One group sings the second half of the melody, beating the unit, while the other group taps a ⁴⁄₄ ♩ ♫ ♩ ♫ |♩ ♫ ♩ ♩ ‖ ostinato as accompaniment (without singing).

5. Exchange of group roles.

6. Everyone sings the second half of the melody with the ostinato.

7. A volunteer sings the whole melody to the accompaniment of the two different ostinatos connected with the two halves of the melody. The remainder of the students follow their colleague's singing by beating time.

8. Everyone sings the melody, meanwhile beating time.

9. Those who can should sing the melody by heart, accompanying themselves with beating time.

♫ ♩.= I/66

1. Take the second and third lines of the melody separately and practise them with the variants given in the following diagram, meanwhile tapping a ²⁄₄ ♩ ♫ ostinato to the singing:

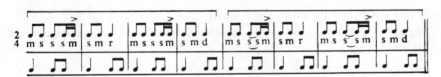

2. The students sing these two lines in their original form and beat time as well while the teacher gives the ostinato alone.

3. Finally they perform the whole melody in a similar way.

♫ ♩ ♪= IV/9

1. Practise the following pairs of bars slowly beating the metric unit, in groups and individually:

91

2. The students sing the whole melody, giving the unit beat.

3. Only the teacher beats the unit, while the students sing and beat time.

4. Finally a volunteer tries three-part performance: he gives the unit beat with the left hand, beats time with the right hand and at the same time sings the melody using solfa names.

DIMINUTION = II/15

After repeating itself, the first line, which moves evenly in quarters and interrupts itself only at the end, appears in rhythmic values diminished by half — that is, in diminution:

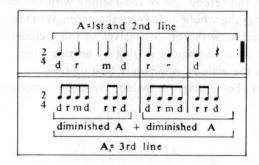

$\frac{6}{8}$ TIME = IV/6

(Concerning the $\frac{6}{8}$ time signature see p. *138*.)

1. Sing the melody in slow tempo, beating 6 in the bar (in groups and individually):

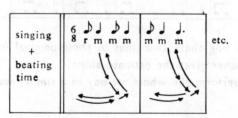

2. Practise it with a two-part $\frac{6}{8}$ rhythm accompaniment in the fastest tempo possible.

92

3. One group of students provides the above rhythm accompaniment while singing and the other group accompanies their singing with duple time-beating taking the ♩. value given in the metronome indication as a basis:

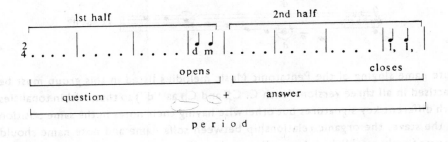

4. The same as above but exchanging the group roles.

5. The rhythm accompaniment is provided by the teacher alone, while the students all sing the melody with beating duple time.

QUESTION — ANSWER IN THE MELODY (PERIOD) = I/13, II/9, 28, 10.

I/13 and II/9

The open (relatively more open) first half of the melody is answered by the closed (more closed) second half. For example I/13:

II/28 and 10

The formal motif of opening and closing occurs twice in the melody and thus the complete form is produced by two periods together. For example, II/28:

93

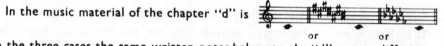

```
2  . . .|. . .|rdr|m |. . .|. . .|rdr|d |. . .|. . .|. . .|rrr|. . .|. . .|. . .|ddd|
4 |question:    opens+answer:    closes| |question:    opens+answer:    closes|
         1st period                              2nd period
```

Melodies practising singing with note names

(I/3, 8, IV/2, I/6, III/18, 21, 23, 24, 27, 28, 29.)

After appropriate practice of the note names and of note name singing to hand-signs (see p. *112* and *116)* singing the easier melodies in Pentatonic Music to note names can be begun. Since these melodies are not given in staff notation but in solfa letters, they can be sung with "d" at any pitch, not only in solfa but using note names too.

In the music material of the chapter "d" is

In the three cases the same written notes belong to the "d" system differing only in their key signature:

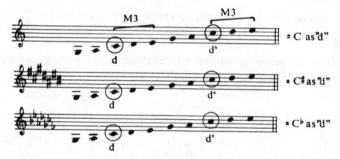

Note name singing of the Pentatonic Music melodies listed in this group must be practised in all three versions (with C, C♯ and C♭ as "d") so that, within tonalities with different key signatures but otherwise having their notes in the same position on the stave, the organic relationship between solfa name and note name should become firmly established. Naturally it is the "d" system without any key signature that is to be used first with the students. We should only move on to note name practice in C sharp "d" system and in C flat "d" system once no difficulty is presented by use and intonation of names without accidentals.

94

FORMS OF PRACTISING NOTE NAME SINGING

SOLFA + NOTE NAME SINGING ALOUD

1. Solfa singing of the selected melody, accompanied by beating the metrical unit, at the absolute pitch corresponding to the given "d" system.

2. Note name singing in the given "d" system, with beating the unit.

3. Note name singing accompanied by beating time.

These ways of singing should succeed each other continuously so that the two kinds of names and their corresponding sound can become fixed as deeply as possible in the students' consciousness and inner ear.

For example, the practising of melody I/3 in the system using C as "d":

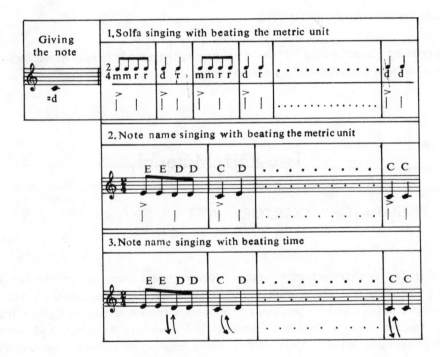

SILENT SOLFA + NOTE NAME SINGING ALOUD

1. After being given the note "d", the students work out the solfa singing silently, helped only by their own inner hearing.

2. On the basis of the idea they thus gain of the melody they then sing it aloud using note names only.

95

After being given the note "d", the students sing with note names a) the notes occurring in the melody and then b) the complete melody itself.

For example melody I/8 in Pentatonic Music in the system using C as "d":

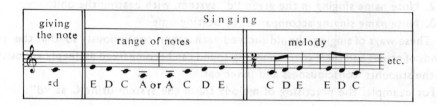

SIGHT-SINGING WITH NOTE NAMES

After being given the note "d" the students sing the melody to note names straight away without any introductory preparation.

Two-Part Material

PREPARATORY EXERCISES: "LET US SING CORRECTLY"
(№ 35, 36, 37, 38, 39, 42, 43, 44)

In this chapter there are considerably fewer exercises from the volume Let Us Sing Correctly than there were in the first chapter. Partly because the exercises are more difficult and longer, and partly because the easier two-part pieces from the volumes Fifteen Two-Part Exercises, 77 Two-Part Exercises, and Bicinia Hungarica also appear. Thus only an occasional exercise from Let Us Sing Correctly should be included in the material for a lesson. If new or less usual harmonies appear in an exercise it is very useful to repeat the already sung succession of intervals at the next lesson. The singing should be carried out in the by now familiar way (see p.44). For example in the case of exercise 36:

1. Note-finding practice to hand-signs using the set of notes l,—d—m—l—d' at the pitch of C as "d".

2. Two-part singing of the exercise.

Each exercise should be sung several times, individually and in groups, so that the students can hear the intervals which sound together as often as possible. For example, a) group singing, with exchange of parts, too; b) individual singing by two students, likewise with exchange of parts; c) two other individual students, with exchange of parts; d) group singing once more, with exchange of parts.

Since in this way the same succession of intervals is heard eight times each student is given the possibility to practise consciously and intensively the intonation of these intervals and observation of their sound.

TWO-PART WORKS

Pentatonic range of notes

Before singing the two-part exercises, careful attention must be devoted to note-finding practice from staff notation in order to give adequate preparation for the reading and intonation of new kinds of melodic motifs which move over a larger range. The set of notes to be used in such practice is:

FIFTEEN TWO-PART EXERCISES/2

1. The students sing the upper part as a group and then individually.
2. The students sing the soprano part and the teacher adds the alto part.

97

3. The students practise the alto part with the melody of the first bar of the soprano:

soprano + alto
continuous singing

4. The first bar of the soprano is sung by the teacher alone and the students enter with the first note of the alto:

teacher   students

5. The teacher continues with the soprano after the first bar while the students sing the alto.

6. The students divide themselves into two groups and perform the exercise in two parts, exchanging parts as well.

7. Two individuals sing the piece (also exchanging parts).

BICINIA HUNGARICA I/17

In the first half of the composition the theme is in the soprano, and in the second half it is in the alto. The two halves of theme — ending on "l", thus it is a "l" pentatonic melody — correspond precisely to one another, only the first half begins from "m" and the second half from "l".

1st half: etc.

2st half: etc.

With the exception of the note "m", in the second half there is a repetition of the first half a fifth lower (fifth-changing theme). The note "m" which is an exception corresponds with the upper "d" of the first half in the fifth-answer:

In this pentatonic, fifth-changing melody, therefore, since in pentatony there is no lower fifth to correspond to "d", this upper "d" is answered by the "pentatonic sixth" below it, that is the note "m".

98

Suggested stages in learning the exercise:

1. The students sing the fifth-changing theme in groups and then individually, accompanying by beating the metrical unit.

2. Once they know the theme well, they should perform it again while the teacher adds the accompanying part (thus, in the first half the alto, and in the second half the soprano).

3. After these preparatory activities they can turn to practising the accompanying part of the first half of the melody.

a) The teacher sings the first two bars of the theme and the students echo him with the accompaniment an octave lower:

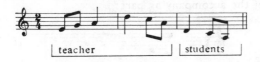

b) Likewise the second motif and its accompaniment:

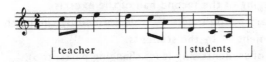

c) Join the two motifs together using the same method singing:

d) Leaving the echo method, teacher and students sing the first four bars in their original form.

e) Practise the third motif together with the second:

4. Two-part singing of the first half of the exercise.

a) The teacher gives the theme while the students provide the accompaniment,

b) Two groups of students sing the eight bars (exchanging parts too).

5. Bring together the accompanying part of the second half of the melody with the first bar of the second half of the theme.

a) The students begin the singing with the theme, and the accompanying part is given as a continuation of that:

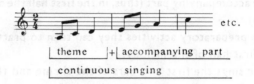

b) The teacher sings the opening bar of the theme and the students only enter at the first note of the accompanying part:

6. Two-part singing of the second half of the exercise.

a) The lower part — the theme — is performed by the teacher, the upper part — the accompaniment — by the students.

b) Two groups of students sing it (exchanging parts, too).

7. Performance of the whole piece, beating time as well.

a) One group sings the upper part right through, and the other group the lower part right through.

b) The same with the groups exchanging parts.

c) Similar two-part singing by two individuals.

77 TWO-PART EXERCISES /26

The melody is constructed from the different rhythm variations of the melodic motifs using the notes s,—d—m , and form a period:

After one bar the lower part gives the same melody an octave lower, thus producing an octave canon. Precise imitation is modified only in the last bar, for the sake of the cadence.

The ♫ ♩. rhythm pattern in the fourth and eighth bars of the theme is a simpler but less usual form of the ♫♩ ♩ notation.

Once the students have thoroughly practised the various sequences of the main notes s,—d—m in the course of preparatory note-finding activity. they can start learning the exercise itself.

1. Soprano and alto sing their own parts right through — beating the quarter metrical unit all the time — beginning at the same time:

2. They sing as required by the original music — at the distance of one bar from each other, that is — but with the alto singing the musical material of the upper part in the first bar one octave lower:

3. Finally they sing the two-part exercise with the alto's original start of one bar's rest.

BICINIA HUNGARICA IV/132

In the "d" pentatonic theme — which has a descending melodic line — there is a tonal fifth change: the s—d' main fourth in the first bar is answered by the main fifth d—s. From the third bar there is precise correspondence between the two halves of the melody at the fifth, but once more with the characteristic pentatonic sixth:

There are two melodic motifs which require special preparation (on the basis of the range of notes written on the blackboard):

   a) The 🎵 melodic progression in the seventh bar of the theme, after the 🎵 main notes which have been sounded many times before it. It represents a special problem that whereas the pairs of eighths (🎵) were always combined with note repetition in bars 1—6, here this eighth movement is combined with note change and precisely with the m—s—d' motif, differing from the m—!—d' main notes. In note-finding exercises, therefore, series of motifs similar to the following should be sung: d—s—m—l—d'—l—m—s—d'—s—m—l—m—s—d' etc.

   b) The s—m' major sixth phrase in the upper part, interrupted by a rest. Preparatory melody, for example: d—m—l—s—m—l—d'—s—m'—d'—l—s—m'—r'—d' etc.

After this — since no rhythm difficulties are presented — it is possible to start learning the exercise. The stages are:

   1. The students sing the theme right through, beating the metric unit.

   2. The teacher accompanies the students by singing the accompanying part (in the first half the lower part, and in the second half the upper part).

   3. The students sing the upper part a) in unison b) with the teacher singing the lower part. If the s—m' major sixth interrupted by a rest causes difficulty in singing together, try the following as an intermediate solution to bar 9:

   4. Prepare the entry of the lower part.

   a) Get the students to sing the following pairs of patterns:

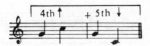

at various pitches, and then

b) the sequence  from bar 1 of the exercise:

piano	singing	piano	singing	piano	singing	
	s - s - d - d		s - s - d - d		s - s - d - d	etc.

c) Practise this last exercise with answering singing:

teacher	student	teacher	student	
s - s	d - d	s - s	d - d	etc.

5. The students sing the lower part, beating the metric unit, while the teacher a) sings the first notes of the theme during the rest, and then b) sings the whole of the upper part.

6. Two-part performance, beating time. (In groups and individually.)

BICINIA HUNGARICA IV/125

The lower fifth-changing part of the "d" pentatonic theme once again includes the pentatonic sixth.

As melodic preparation it is necessary to give intensive practice to the

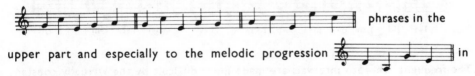 phrases in the

upper part and especially to the melodic progression 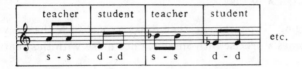 in

the lower part. For example s—m—r—m—r—l,—s—m etc.

After appropriate preparation:

1. Sing the theme right through, beating time.

2. The teacher accompanies the students singing the theme by singing the other part.

3. Practise the accompanying part in the following way:

4. Two-part performance.

a) The students sing the upper part and the teacher the lower part.

b) Exchange parts.

c) Two student groups perform it — exchanging parts, too.

d) Two individual students perform it in this way.

5. Try the following as new forms of performance: During the singing of the upper part a) tap the rhythm of the lower part, and b) play the lower part on the piano, or on any string instrument.

BICINIA HUNGARICA IV/135

The fifth-changing "l" pentatonic theme has a tonal fifth change which from the third bar becomes a precise fifth-answer, once more with the pentatonic sixth:

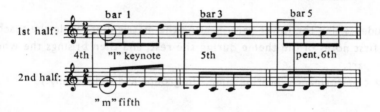

In the musical material of the exercise the 4th and 5th intervals have a very important role:

The frequent 4th—5th intervals are made more difficult by the virtually constant rolling eighth rhythm values, the movement of the melody. A lot of time must be spent on preparatory note-finding exercises, or else the singing of the melody will be very insecure.

After suitable preparation:

1. The students sing the theme right through, accompanying themselves by beating the metrical unit, both in groups and individually.

2. The teacher adds the accompanying part to the theme.

3. Practise the entry of the lower part.

a) The students sing the following two bars beginning at various pitches:

b) Practise this in answering form:

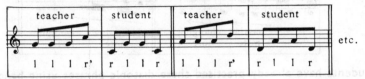

4. With a similar start the students sing the whole of the accompanying part of the first half of the melody.

5. Practise the accompanying part of the second half of the melody with singing in the first two notes of the theme.

a) Without the first tie:

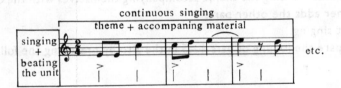

b) In the original form, likewise accompanied by beating the metrical unit.

6. Two-part performance.

a) The students sing the upper part (beating the unit), the teacher the lower part.

b) Exchange parts.

c) Two groups of students sing the exercise.

d) Two individuals perform it.

FURTHER RECOMMENDED EXERCISES: Bicinia Hungarica II/71, IV/123; 77 Two-Part Exercises/51; Bicinia Hungarica IV/131, 129, 155, 138, 133; Fifteen Two-Part Exercises/1; Bicinia Hungarica IV/140, 157, 167.

Pentatonic theme with diatonic accompaniment

77 TWO-PART EXERCISES/46

In the material accompanying the "l" pentatonic theme the notes "t" and "f" occur alike — "t" as a passing note and lower changing note, "f" only as an upper changing note:

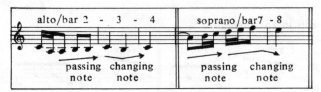

The students have already practised these diatonic phrases using hand-signs (see p. 117). Now it is primarily through note-finding singing from staff notation that we have to establish the d—t,—d , l,—t,—d and m—f—m phrases.

The stages used in learning this exercise are:
1. Theme singing.
a) Unison introducing of theme, with a ♪♩ ♪ ostinato.
b) The students sing the theme accompanying themselves with the ostinato while the teacher adds the other part.
2. Part singing.
a) Prepare the joining of bars 4—5 in the alto by practising the following pair of motifs:

b) The melodic start in the soprano's sixth bar is helped by practising this melodic progression:

c) In the final phrase [music] of the accompanying part the note "s" may well be insecure. Prepare for this with the following pentatonic motifs:

3. Two-part performance in the usual way.

Diatonic range of notes

BICINIA HUNGARICA II/92

The major folksong theme has an A A⁵, A⁵,, A structure. The second line provides a tonal fifth change to the first line:

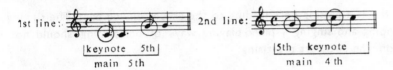

The new melodic elements and their practice:
1. "f" as passing note.
During the note-finding exercises practise the following phrases:

2. The phrase with a leap from "t" in the cadence of the fifth change melody:

Practise the following sequence of closing motifs from the first, second and fourth lines of the theme:

107

3. The l,—f minor sixth interval which is alien to pentatony.

a) For clear intonation of this minor sixth it is necessary to connect the already practised m—f—m pattern with the m—l, perfect fifth, e.g. l,—d—m—f—m——l,—f—m—r—m—l,—f—m—d—l, etc.

b) From the accompanying part take the pair of bars containing this minor sixth:

and get the students to sing it in groups and then individually.

After this kind of preparation learn the exercise in the familiar way. (Theme singing; part singing; two-part performance.) In singing the theme take care with the

last note of the third line (A⁵): This final F does not belong to

the theme but is a passing note leading to the accompanying part. The singing + rhythm tapping and singing + piano playing ways of performing should not be omitted from the two-part practising.

FURTHER SUGGESTED EXERCISE: Bicinia Hungarica II/86.

Range including altered notes

BICINIA HUNGARICA I/42a

In this exercise in the major mode the diatonic range is enlarged by the lower changing note "fi". Note-finding practice should be carried out on the basis of the following, using the complete range of notes:

In the course of preparation practise the note "fi" only as a changing note, e.g. d—m—s—fi—s—m—d—s—fi—s—l—s—f—m—r—s—fi—s—d etc.

After suitable preparation the students can sing the exercise straight away in two parts.

Of the two altered notes in the music "si" is the easier to intonate since it appears as a lower changing note. The altered passing note "fi" requires more thorough preparation.

Write the notes used in the exercise on the board:

and get the students to sing various melodic progressions using this set of notes, e. g. l—si—l—m—d—l—si—l—m—l—s—fi—s—f—m—fi—s—f—m—d—l,—l—
—m—fi—s—f—m etc.

The motifs in the first three lines of the theme move within the framework of the harmonic minor. The ♩♪♩ |♪♪♩ cadential progression in the last line, however, transforms the music material in a phrygian character.

The ♫♩· rhythm pattern appears several times in the exercise. Practise these bars with a ⅔ ♫♩ ♫♩ |♫♩ ꞌ ♪ | ostinato, giving a strong accent on the first note of the ♫♩· rhythm pattern:

FURTHER RECOMMENDED EXERCISES: 66 Two-Part Exercises/17;55 Two-Part Exercises/3.

THEORETICAL INFORMATION AND TECHNICAL EXERCISES

The Names of the Notes

It is an indispensable part of solfa studies — particularly for musicians who only later become acquainted with the relative method — that the relationship between the solfa names and the absolute staff notation names within the various tonalities should become conscious, and then, through this, automatic. Precisely for this reason once the students have reached a certain level in the sphere of solfa singing and possess a degree of security in it, we must then also make note name practice an organic part of the studies.

The altered note names in use in English speaking countries are unfortunately not well suited to singing purposes (e.g. G sharp, F flat, etc.). This is the reason behind the trend which has been spreading in the last few years whereby, leaving behind the traditional expressions such as F sharp, B flat, etc., singing practice has evolved for itself new altered note names. These are produced by the addition of certain endings to the diatonic note names, as follows:

1. The note names altered by a ♯:

C sharp = C♯; pronounced **cease**
D sharp = D♯; pronounced **dease** (like "cease" with the changed 1st letter)
E sharp = E♯; pronounced as in **eastern**
F sharp = F♯; pronounced as in **feas** (without the letter "t")
G sharp = G♯; pronounced **geese**
A sharp = A♯; pronounced **ace**
B sharp = B♯; pronounced as in **beast** (without the letter "t")

2. The note names altered by a ♭:

C flat	= C♭; pronounced **cess**
D flat	= D♭; pronounced as in **desk** (without the letter "k")
E flat	= E♭; pronounced as in **escalator**
F flat	= F♭; pronounced as in **festival**
G flat	= G♭; pronounced **guess**
A flat	= A♭; pronounced **ice**
B flat	= B♭; pronounced as in **best** (without the letter "t")

3. In double alteration (x and ♭♭) the endings are doubled, e.g.

F♯   C♭♭

pronounced: feas + eas   ces + es   etc.

Making the note names conscious

Innervation of the above kind of new names for altered notes can be helped forward in several ways.

1. Pointing to them in various orders, read the individual notes in the middle line together with their corresponding ♯ and ♭ variations:

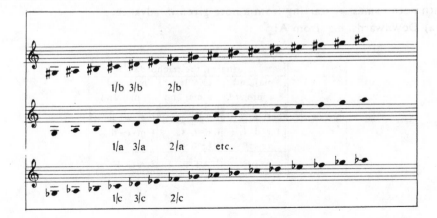

111

2. Read the given notes of the middle line together with their ♭ and ♯ variations:

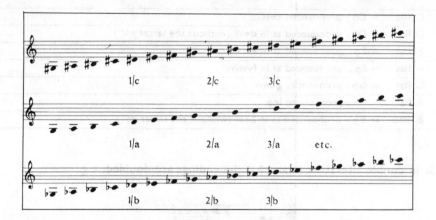

3. Practise reading as given in 1. and 2. in the F clef as well.

4. Give the fifth-pillar sequence of sharps with these new names: F♯ C♯ G♯ D♯ A♯ E♯ B♯.

5. And the fifth-pillar sequence of flats: B♭ E♭ A♭ D♭ G♭ C♭ F♭.

As soon as the evocation of these names no longer presents any difficulty, they can be gradually included in the singing exercises.

Note name singing of pentatonic trichords and tetrachords

1. (M) The students sing the various types of pentatonic trichords to solfa, then with note names — starting from a note given in advance.

a) Downwards, e.g. from A:

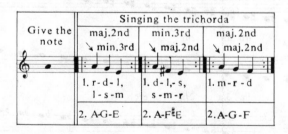

Give the note	Singing the trichorda		
	maj.2nd ↘ min.3rd	min.3rd ↘ maj.2nd	maj.2nd ↘ maj.2nd
	1. r-d-l, l-s-m	1. d-l,-s, s-m-r	1. m-r-d
	2. A-G-E	2. A-F♯-E	2. A-G-F

112

b) Upwards, e.g. from D:

Give the note	Singing the trichords		
	maj.2nd min.3rd ↗	min.3rd maj.2nd ↗	maj.2nd maj.2nd ↗
	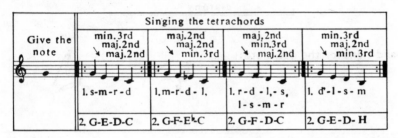		
	1. m-s-l l,-d-r	1. r-m-s s-l-d'	1. d-r-m
	2. D-F-G	2. D-E-G	2. D-E-F♯

The teacher should give increasingly difficult starting notes so that the possibility of singing all the ♯ and ♭ versions can arise.

2. (M) Practise the tetrachords in the same way.

a) Downwards, e.g. from G:

Give the note	Singing the tetrachords			
	min.3rd maj.2nd ↘ maj.2nd	maj.2nd maj.2nd ↘ min.3rd	maj.2nd min.3rd ↘ maj.2nd	min.3rd maj.2nd ↘ min.3rd
	1. s-m-r-d	1. m-r-d-l,	1. r-d-l,-s, l-s-m-r	1. d'-l-s-m
	2. G-E-D-C	2. G-F-E♭-C	2. G-F-D-C	2. G-E-D-H

b) Upwards, e.g. from E:

Give the note	Singing the tetrachorda			
	1. d-r-m-s	1. l,-d-r-m	1. s,-l,-d-r r-m-s-l	1. m-s-l-d'
	2. E-F♯-G♯-B	2. E-G-A-B	2. E-F♯-A-B	2. E-G-A-C

113

Range of Notes, Hand-Signs

Diatony

Part of the musical material in the chapter already moves beyond the pentatonic framework. The new "t" and "f" notes extend pentatony into seven-degree diatony — a seven-part perfect fifth chain:

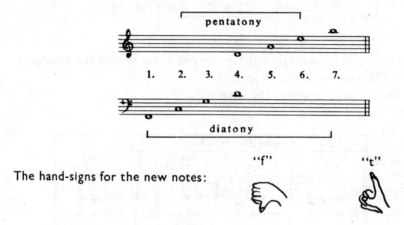

The hand-signs for the new notes:

Orientation within the diatonic system — as within pentatony — is helped by singing with solfa to hand-signs and then from staff notation.

Alteration

Both in the Kodály material and in the extracts for sight-singing there appear altered notes — that is, notes with accidental being outside the given key signature. For this reason it is necessary to become familiar with the altered versions of the solfa names as well:

diatonic name	♯ form	♭ form
d	di, pronounced **dee** (as in deed)	none, because below "d" there comes a minor 2nd
r	ri, pronounced **ree** (as in reed)	ra, pronounced as in **rascal**
m	none, because above "m" there is a minor 2nd	ma, pronounced as in **master**
f	fi, pronounced **fee** (as in feed)	none, because below "f" there comes a minor 2nd
s	si, pronounced **see** (as in seed)	none, because in the baroque and Viennese classical styles the dominant in the major tonality is not flatted
l	li, pronounced **lee** (as in leer)	lo, pronounced **law**
t	none, because above "t" there is a minor 2nd	ta, pronounced as in **Tartar**

MAKING THE ALTERED SOLFA NAMES CONSCIOUS THEORETICALLY

The teacher writes on the blackboard the letter sign for the seven solfa names and puts a ♯ above the names which can be altered upwards (d, r, f, s, l) and a ♭ below those which can be altered downwards (r, m, l, t).

Following this he points to the accidentals written up in any order while the students determine the solfa name of the signs pointed to one by one.

If, for example, the teacher points to the sharp above "r" the students should answer "ri"; if he points to the flat below "l", they should answer "lo", etc.

Task of singing to hand-signs within the pentatonic range of notes

SOLFA SINGING

The musical material of the first chapter made the intonation of the fourth, fifth and sixth intervals within the range s,—m and d—l conscious in the students. At the same time there was an attempt through singing to hand-signs to evolve receptivity towards the pentatonic set of notes over a larger range. In the course of this it was not the large interval leaps that we practised with the students but the easily intonated melodic progressions using the adjacent pentatonic notes.

It is the task of this second chapter:

a) to practise the fourth, fifth and sixth intervals of the extended s,—m' range;

b) to prepare the intonation of pentatonic sevenths (l,—s; r—d'; m—r' and s—l,; d'—r; r'—m); and

c) to make the students feel the melodic connection between the third-tenth relation: l,—d and l,—d'; d—m and d—m'.

For example, here is a series of notes for a):

d—r—m—d—l,—r—s,—d—m—s—l—m—s—r—m—d—r—s—m—l—d'—s—l—r'—d'—s—l—m—r—l,—s,—d (that is, the practising of fourths);

a series of notes for b):

l,—s,—d—m—s—d—l,—s—m—r—s—l,—d (practising of the l,—s seventh)

a series of notes for c):

l,—d—m—r—l,—m—r—s—l—m—l—d'—l—m—d'—l—m—r—l,—d'—l (that is, to practise the tenth l,—d') etc. etc.

NOTE NAME SINGING

The teacher gives a pentatonic melody not moving beyond the octave by hand-signs and the students sing this back to him using the note names of the pentatonic system with C as "d".

The teacher's hand-sign melody	d r m d r s m l m r s d r l,d m l,m r d	etc.
The students' singing	C D E C D G E A E D G C D A C E A E D C	
Actual pitch		

Task of singing to hand-sign within the diatonic range of notes

SOLFA SINGING

Practice of the notes characteristic of diatony, "t" and "f" (for their hand-signs see page 114), using the following stages:

116

	"t"	"f"
a) As changing note	d—t,—d	m—f—m
b) As passing note	l,—t,—d d—t,—l,	s—f—m m—f—s
c) "t" or "f" arrived at by a leap, and their melodic resolution	d—m—r—t,—d d—m—s—t,—d d—s—m—t,—d etc.	m—d—r—f—m s—m—d—f—m m—d—l,—f—m etc.
d) "t" or "f" arrived at by a second and left with a leap	m—d—t,—r—d d—t,—m—r—d m—d—t,—s—d d—l,—t,—s,—d etc.	m—f—r—s—d m—f—r—t,—d s—m—f—t,—d s—f—r—m—d etc.

NOTE NAME SINGING

The teacher gives an easy diatonic melody by hand-signs and the students sing it back to him using the note names of the diatonic system without key signature. For example:

The teacher's hand-sign melody	d m f r s m d t, d r s, t, d f m r s t, d	etc.
The students' singing	C E F D G E C B C D G B C F E D G B C	
Actual pitch		

Keys and Modes

Of the keys of the seven-degree diatonic system it is the major starting from "d" and the minor starting from "l" which are the most frequent in art music.

117

The major and its relative minor

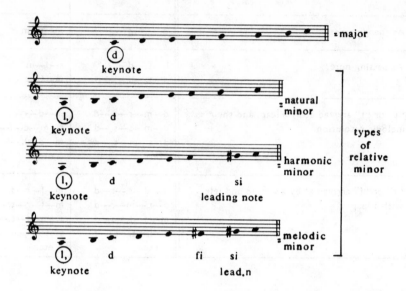

The natural minor agrees in sound with the aeolian mode (see p. 200). In spite of this it is necessary to make some distinction between the two keys. With reference to folk music and the Renaissance style we speak of aeolian tonality whereas in the case of similar melodic progressions — generally moving downwards — in art music after the Renaissance we use the term natural minor.

FORMS OF PRACTISING FOR THE MAJOR

1. (M) Sing the major scale to solfa in ⌒ direction in even metrical units, accompanying by beating 2, 3, 4 or 6, at any pitch. (For beating six in a bar see page 64 and 138.)
For example, in $\frac{6}{8}$:

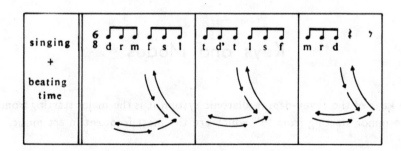

2. (M) Practise the exercise given in 1. using note names as well, singing successively in C♭, C and C♯ major.
For example, in $\frac{3}{4}$:

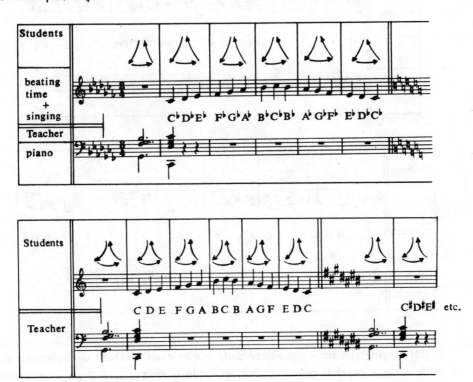

3. (M) Combine solfa singing with a certain rhythm pattern and accompany with beating time. For example with the rhythm pattern $\frac{2}{4}$ ♪ ♩ ♪ :

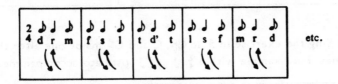

4. (M) Practise the exercise in 3. with note names as well, in C♭, C and C♯ major. For example with the rhythm pattern $\frac{3}{4}$ ♩. ♪♫ :

5. (M) Singing the scale melody to solfa and in even metrical units, accompany it with various rhythm ostinatos. For example with a ♪♩ ♪♩. ♪ ostinato:

Singing + ostinato	4/4 ♩ ♩ ♩ ♩ d r m f ♪♩ ♪♩. ♪	♩ ♩ ♩ ♩ s l t d' ♪♩ ♪♩. ♪	♩ ♩ ♩ ♩ t l s f ♪♩ ♪♩. ♪	♩ ♩ ♩ ♩ m r d ♪♩ ♪♩. ♪

6. (M) Sing the exercise in 5. in C♭, C and C♯ major one after the other using note names. For example with a 2/4 ♪♩ ♫ ostinato accompaniment:

120

FORMS OF PRACTISING FOR THE MINOR

1. (M) Sing to solfa, in ⌒↘ direction, in even metrical units the natural, harmonic and melodic minors one after the other, accompanying the singing by beating 2, 3, 4 or 6 in the bar. The pitch chosen for the starting note, "l", remains identical throughout. For example, beating $\frac{4}{4}$:

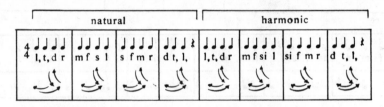

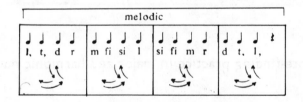

2. (M) Practise as described in 1. using the note names of A minor and at that pitch.

3. (M) Combine the solfa singing accompanied by beating time with a certain rhythm pattern and practise all three minors in that way. For example, with the rhythm pattern $\frac{3}{4}$: ♪ ♩. ♪ :

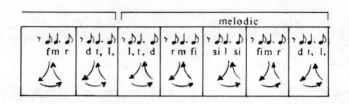

4. (M) Practise the way of singing given in 3. in A minor using note names.

5. (M) Singing the scale melodies to solfa and in even metrical units, accompany them with a rhythm ostinato. For example the ostinato $\frac{4}{4}$ ♪ ♩. ♩ ♪ :

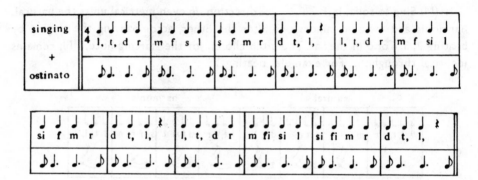

6. (M) Sing the exercise given in 5. in A minor using note names.

Note-finding practice in major and harmonic minor

MAJOR

1. Note name singing from solfa letters.
Write on the board the solfa letters of the major key from "s" to "r":

s, l, t, **d** r m f s l t **d'** r'

tonic

and pointing to the order of these solfa letters characteristic of the major tonality, get the students to sing them in C major with note names, at the absolute pitch of the given "d". For example:

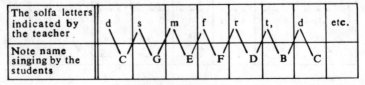

122

2. Solfa singing from degree numbers.

Giving the number 1 to the tonic, write on the board the degree figures for every note within the s —r range (using Roman figures for those under "d"):

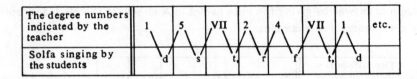

V   VI   VII   **I**   2   3   4   5   6   7   **8**   9

tonic

d

and pointing to these figures in any order get the students to sing the appropriate notes to solfa names. For example:

The degree numbers indicated by the teacher	1	5	VII	2	4	VII	1	etc.
Solfa singing by the students	d	s	t,	r	f	t,	d	

3. Solfa + note name singing from degree numbers.

Once note name singing from solfa letters and note name singing from degree numbers appear to be sufficiently secure, these two processes can be combined: the teacher points to the degree numbers and the students sing the various steps in the scale, first to solfa and then straight away using the C major note names (at the given absolute pitch). For example:

The degree numbers indicated by the teacher	5	3	1	6	2	7	8	etc.
Solfa+ note name singing by the students	s/G	m/E	d/C	l/A	r/D	t/B	d/C	

4. Note name singing from degree numbers.

Use the form of practice given in 3. but omit the solfa singing: the students sing the note names straight away from the degree numbers. For example:

The degree numbers indicated by the teacher	8	5	3	6	4	2	VII	5	1	etc.
Note name singing by the students	C'	G	E	A	F	D	B	G	C	

123

1. Solfa singing from letters.

Since the minor key is still unusual we have first to evolve its novel sound in the minds of the students. For this reason as a first stage practice of solfa singing using letters only should be carried out in the range si —r (at the A minor pitch):

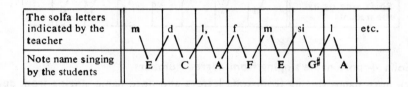

si, l, t, d r m f si l t d' r'
tonic

2. Note name singing from solfa letters.

The teacher points to the solfa letters written on the board in any order and the students answer by giving the note names in A minor (at the pitch appropriate to the given note). For example:

The solfa letters indicated by the teacher	m	d	l,	f	m	si	l	etc.
Note name singing by the students	E	C	A	F	E	G#	A	

3. Solfa singing from degree numbers.

Since the tonic in the minor is "l", the number I is in this case to represent the note "l".

The degree numbers written on the board:

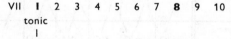

VII I 2 3 4 5 6 7 8 9 10
tonic
l

The singing should be given at the A minor pitch here, too. Take care with the leading note: VII and 7 = "si"!

The degree numbers indicated by the teacher	1	3	5	7	8	4	3	6	etc.
Solfa singing by the students	l,	d	m	si	l	r	d	f	

4. Solfa + note name singing from degree numbers.

The singing is again at the A minor pitch, based on the degree numbers written on the board (VII—10). For example:

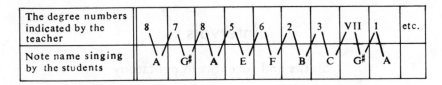

The degree numbers indicated by the teacher	1	6	5	VII	1	5	7	8	etc.
Solfa+note name singing by the students	l,/A	f /F	m/E	si,/G#	l,/A	m/E	si/G#	l/A	

5. Note name singing from degree numbers.

Use the way of practising given in 4. but omit the solfa singing. For example:

The degree numbers indicated by the teacher	8	7	8	5	6	2	3	VII	1	etc.
Note name singing by the students	A	G#	A	E	F	B	C	G#	A	

The pentatonic modes using C as "d"

(M) Give the note C as "d" and get the students to sing the "s", "l", "d", "r" and "m" pentatonic modes to solfa, then straight away to note names, all accompanied by beating duple time.

a) Singing in ⟶ direction:

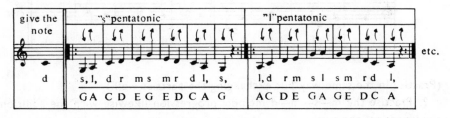

give the note	"s"pentatonic	"l"pentatonic	
d	s, l, d r m s m r d l, s,	l, d r m s l s m r d l,	etc.
	GA CD EG ED CA G	AC DE GA GE DC A	

b) Singing in ⟍ direction:

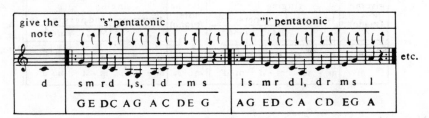

give the note	"s"pentatonic	"l"pentatonic	
d	s m r d l,s, l d r m s	l s m r d l, d r m s l	etc.
	GE DC AG AC DE G	AG ED CA CD EG A	

125

Since the range of the above exercises extends from "s," to "m'" the students with deeper voices should sing only the "s" and "l" pentatonic modes, leaving the "d", "r" and "m" pentatonic modes for those with higher voices.

In individual singing the work should be divided between five different students. The order in which they sing — that is, who is to sing the "s" pentatonic mode, who the "l" mode, etc. — should be decided in advance so that the continuity of the singing is assured.

Intervals

Sixths and sevenths in pentatony

MINOR SIXTH

Since the minor sixth is the inversion of the major third (see p. 57), it should be practised in association with that interval.

1. Extend the d—l,—d—m pair of intervals sung in answering form when practising the major third, as follows:

(Practise in the same way but exchanging the parts as well.)

2. Practise the m—s—m—d melodic progression likewise with the addition of the inversion, the sixth:

(Also with exchange of parts.)

3. Omit from the forms of practice in 1. and 2. the introductory minor third.

a) Singing of minor sixth upwards:

piano	singing		piano	singing	
	M3 ↓	m6 ↑		M3 ↓	m6 ↑
m	m - d	m - d'	m	m - d	m - d'

etc.

b) Singing of minor sixth downwards:

piano	singing		piano	singing	
	M3 ↑	m6 ↓		M3 ↑	m6 ↓
d	d - m	d - m,	d	d - m	d - m,

etc.

4. Divide the exercise in 3. between two individuals.

a) Singing of minor sixth upwards:

piano	singing		piano	singing	
	1st person M3 ↓	2nd person m6 ↑		1st person M3 ↓	2nd person m6 ↑
m	m - d	m - d'	m	m - d	m - d'

etc.

b) Minor sixth downwards:

piano	singing		piano	singig	
	1st person M3 ↑	2nd person m6 ↓		1st person M3 ↑	2nd person m6 ↓
d	d - m	d - m,	d	d - m	d - m,

etc.

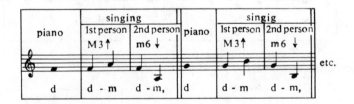

Exchange parts during practice as well.

MAJOR SIXTH

The major sixth is the inversion of the minor third (see p. 57), and so it is to be practised with the help of this already familiar interval.

1. (M) Sing a minor third downwards and then its inversion, using the same starting note, the major sixth upwards, with any appropriate solfa names. Then

sing the same pair of intervals using their other names within the pentatonic system:

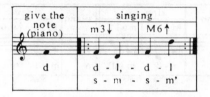

Repeat this from different starting notes.

2. (M) Practise the sequence of the upward minor third and the downward major sixth as well:

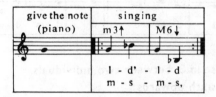

Repeat this at other pitches, too.

3. (M) Divide the exercises in 1. and 2. between two individuals.

a) Major sixth upwards:

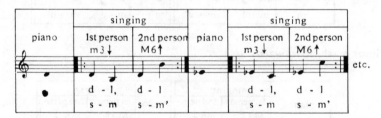

b) Major sixth downwards:

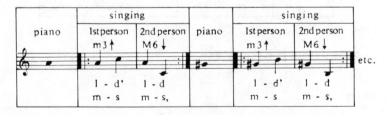

To be practised with exchange of parts, too.

The minor seventh is the inversion of the major second (see p.56), and so it should be practised in conjunction with that interval.

1. (M) Starting from any given note sing one of the pentatonic major seconds downwards and then, from the same starting note, its inversion — the minor seventh upwards:

give the note (piano)	singing	
	M2 ↓	m7 ↑
	r - d - r - d'	

and follow this by singing this same pair of intervals with all the other names possible within pentatony:

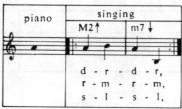

piano	singing	
	M2 ↓	m7 ↑
	r - d - r - d'	
	m - r - m - r'	
	l - s - l - s'	

Repeat this exercise at various pitches.

2. (M) In a similar way practise the major second upwards together with the minor seventh downwards:

piano	singing	
	M2 ↑	m7 ↓
	d - r - d - r,	
	r - m - r - m,	
	s - l - s - l,	

Start from different notes.

3. (M) Use the forms of practising given in 1. and 2. but divide them between two individual students.

a) Minor seventh upwards:

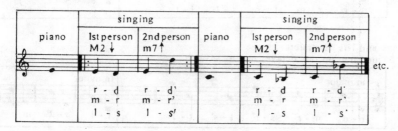

piano	singing		piano	singing	
	1st person M2 ↓	2nd person m7 ↑		1st person M2 ↓	2nd person m7 ↑
	r - d	r - d'		r - d	r - d'
	m - r	m - r'		m - r	m - r'
	l - s	l - s'		l - s	l - s'

etc.

b) Minor seventh downwards:

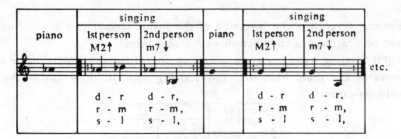

piano	singing		piano	singing	
	1st person M2↑	2nd person m7↓		1st person M2↑	2nd person m7↓
	d - r	d - r,		d - r	d - r,
	r - m	r - m,		r - m	r - m,
	s - l	s - l,		s - l	s - l,

etc.

The students should also exchange parts.

The interval types of the major and harmonic minor keys

Minor second

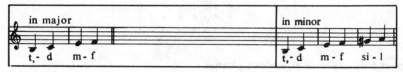

in major — t,- d   m - f

in minor — t,- d   m - f   si - l

and its inversion
making up the octave: major seventh

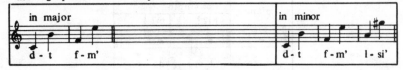

in major — d - t   f - m'

in minor — d - t   f - m'   l - si'

Major second

in major — d - r   r - m   f - s   s - l   l - t

in minor — l,- t,   d - r   r - m

and its inversion
making up the octave: minor seventh

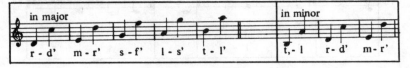

in major — r - d'   m - r'   s - f'   l - s'   t - l'

in minor — t,- l   r - d'   m - r'

130

Augmented second   and its inversion
                    making up the octave : diminished seventh

in minor

f - si

in minor

si - f'

Minor third

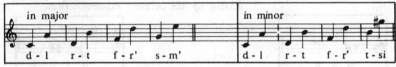

in major	in minor
l,- d t,- r r - f m - s	l,- d t,- r r - f si - t

and its inversion
making up the octave: major sixth

in major	in minor
d - l r - t f - r' s - m'	d - l r - t f - r' t - si

Major third

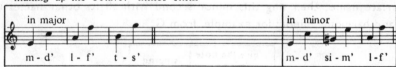

in major	in minor
d - m f - l s - t	d - m m - si f - l

and its inversion
making up the octave: minor sixth

in major	in minor
m - d' l - f' t - s'	m - d' si - m' l - f'

Perfect fourth

in major	in minor
d - f r - s m - l s - d' l - r' t - m'	l,- r t,- m d - f m - l

and its inversion
making up the octave: perfect fifth

in major	in minor
f - d' s - r' l - m' d - s r - l m - t	r - l m - t f - d' l - m'

131

Augmented fourth

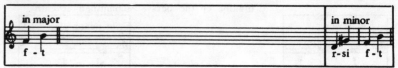

f - t ⏐ in minor ⏐ r - si ⏐ f - t

and its inversion
making up the octave: diminished fifth

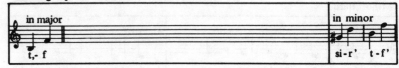

t, - f ⏐ in minor ⏐ si - r' ⏐ t - f'

Diminished fourth ⏐ **and its inversion**
⏐ **making up the octave : augmented fifth**

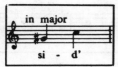
si - d'

d - si

Forms of practising the various interval types

SECONDS (List on page *130*)

1. (M) Give a starting note and sing a minor second from it upwards with any appropriate name; then sing this minor second with all its other names in the major and harmonic minor; for example, from G:

give the note (piano) ⏐ singing
m - f
t, - d
si - l

Following this establish which major and harmonic minor keys the variously named minor seconds starting from G occur in:

m - f = E♭ major, C minor
t, - d = A♭ major, F minor
si - l = A♭ minor

132

2. (M) Practise in the same way the downward minor second, too; for example, from D:

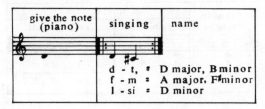

give the note (piano)	singing	name
	d - t,	= D major, B minor
	f - m	= A major, F#minor
	l - si	= D minor

3. (M) Sing a major second upwards as in 1.; for example, from E:

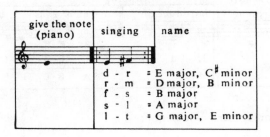

give the note (piano)	singing	name
	d - r	= E major, C# minor
	r - m	= D major, B minor
	f - s	= B major
	s - l	= A major
	l - t	= G major, E minor

4. (M) Practise in the same way with downward major second; for example, from F:

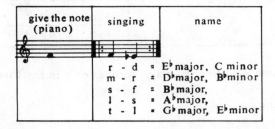

give the note (piano)	singing	name
	r - d	= E♭ major, C minor
	m - r	= D♭ major, B♭ minor
	s - f	= B♭ major,
	l - s	= A♭ major,
	t - l	= G♭ major, E♭ minor

5. (M) Give the keynote and then sing the minor seconds as they follow each other within the tonality, to solfa and then to note names (in C major and A minor).

a) In the ascending major:

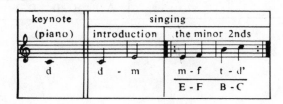

keynote (piano)	singing	
	introduction	the minor 2nds
d	d - m	m - f t - d'
		E - F B - C

133

b) In the descending major:

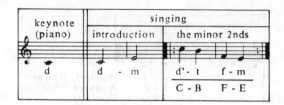

keynote (piano)	singing	
	introduction	the minor 2nds
d	d – m	d'- t f - m C - B F - E

c) In the ascending harmonic minor:

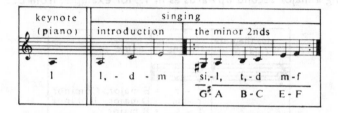

keynote (piano)	singing	
	introduction	the minor 2nds
l	l, – d – m	si,- l, t, - d m - f G♯- A B - C E - F

d) In the descending harmonic minor:

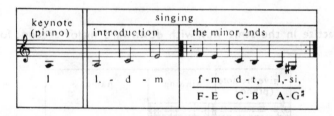

keynote (piano)	singing	
	introduction	the minor 2nds
l	l. – d – m	f - m d - t, l,- si, F - E C - B A - G♯

6. (M) In the same way, sing the major seconds only in the harmonic minor (in A minor).

  a) In the ascending minor:

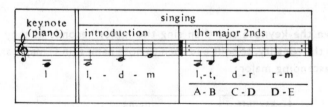

keynote (piano)	singing	
	introduction	the major 2nds
l	l, – d – m	l,- t, d - r r - m A - B C - D D - E

b) In the descending minor:

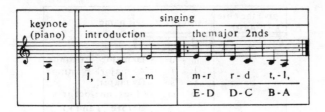

keynote (piano)	singing	
	introduction	the major 2nds
l	l, - d - m	m-r r-d t,-l,
		E-D D-C B-A

THIRDS (List on page *131*)

1. (M) Sing minor thirds as in 1. on page *132*; for example, from E:

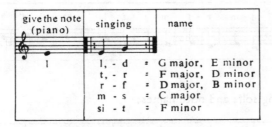

give the note (piano)	singing	name
l	l, - d = G major, E minor	
	t, - r = F major, D minor	
	r - f = D major, B minor	
	m - s = C major	
	si - t = F minor	

2. (M) In a similar way practise minor thirds downwards, too; for example, from A:

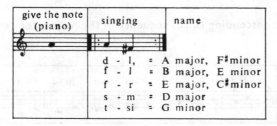

give the note (piano)	singing	name
	d - l, = A major, F#minor	
	f - l = B major, E minor	
	f - r = E major, C#minor	
	s - m = D major	
	t - si = G minor	

3. (M) Sing the major thirds as described for the minor thirds (see 1. and 2. above).

a) Upwards, for example, from E:

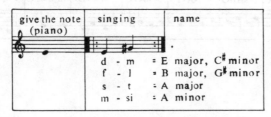

give the note (piano)	singing	name
	d - m = E major, C#minor	
	f - l = B major, G#minor	
	s - t = A major	
	m - si = A minor	

135

b) Downwards, for example, from F:

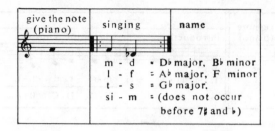

give the note (piano)	singing	name

m - d   = Dᵇ major, Bᵇ minor
l - f   = Aᵇ major, F minor
t - s   = Gᵇ major.
si - m = (does not occur before 7♯ and ♭)

4. (M) Sing an ascending thirds sequence in the major (at C major pitch).
a) To solfa:

Singing	d - m r - f m - s f - l s - t l - d' t - r' d'
Actual pitch	

b) Singing using solfa and note names:

d-m-C-E | r-f-D-F | m-s-E-G | f-l-F-A | s-t-G-B | l-d'-A-C | t-r'-B-D | C

5. (M) Sing the descending thirds sequence in the major, too (at C major pitch)
a) To solfa:

Singing	d'- l t - s l - f s - m f - r m - d r - t, d
Actual pitch	

b) Using solfa and note names:

d'-l-C-A | t-s-B-G | l-f-A-F | s-m-G-E | f-r-F-D | m-d-E-C | r-t,-D-B | C

6. (M) Sing the minor thirds as they come in the major key, to solfa, and then to note names, after giving the keynote.

a) In C major, ascending:

b) In C major, descending:

7. (M) Practise the major thirds in ways similar to those given in 6.

a) In C major, ascending:

b) In C major, descending:

Metre

In chapter II the following new time-signatures occur:

Time signature	Metrical unit	Stress relationships between the metrical units in the bar	The time signature's	
			type	form of beating time
$\frac{6}{8}$	♪	main stress ┊ secondary stress	compound $\frac{3}{8} + \frac{3}{8}$	
$\frac{2}{8}$	♪		simple duple (even)	

SIGHT-SINGING

Unison Extracts from the Musical Literature

MATERIAL IN STAFF NOTATION

(The key signatures of the extracts are 7♯, 7♭, or none.)

PRACTICE

1. Perform the melodies to solfa but at the correct pitch given in the staff notation.

2. Within a single lesson all the extracts sung should have the same key signature for the sake of secure and clear intonation.

3. Before beginning to sing the quotations the students should be fully aware of the time signature, key, and the solfa name of the first note.

4. The singing should be accompanied by beating time.

5. During practice there should be alternation of group and individual work so that all the students can take part in the active work.

Pentatonic range

42. STRAVINSKY: THE WEDDING. (or.: from E)

(Concerning the $\frac{7}{8}$ time
signature see p. 138.)

43. KODÁLY: PSALMUS HUNGARICUS.

139

44. KODÁLY: TE DEUM.

45. KODÁLY: PSALMUS HUNGARICUS.

(Concerning the ⁶⁄₈ time
signature see p. *138*.)

46. LISZT: O HEILIGE NACHT.

47. GAY—BRITTEN: THE BEGGAR'S OPERA III.

48. LISZT: O HEILIGE NACHT. (or.: 1♭)

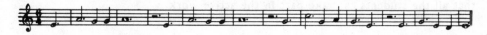

49. PUCCINI: TURANDOT II.

50. KODÁLY: A SONG OF FAITH. (or.: 1♭)

51. GLINKA: BARCAROLA. (or.: 1♭)

(Concerning the ⁶⁄₈ time
signature see p. *138*.)

52. KODÁLY: HYMN TO KING STEPHEN. (or.: 1♯)

53. KODÁLY: TE DEUM.

54. BARTÓK: BLUEBEARD'S CASTLE. (or.: from E)

55. KODÁLY: TE DEUM. (or.: from E)

56. BARTÓK: BLUEBEARD'S CASTLE. (or.: 1♭)

57. STRAVINSKY: THE RITE OF SPRING. (or.: 3♯)

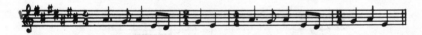

58. BARTÓK: BLUEBEARD'S CASTLE. (or.: from D♯)

59. RAKHMANINOV: THE SONGS OF GRUSIA. (or.: 2♯)

60. LISZT: ZUR TRAUUNG. (or.: 5♯)

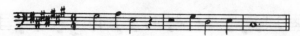

61. BARTÓK: BLUEBEARD'S CASTLE. (or.: 3♯)

62. LISZT: DIE HEILIGE CÄCILIA. LEGENDE. (or.: 3♭)

63. BRITTEN: PETER GRIMES II. (or.: 4♭)

64. KODÁLY: SIXTEEN SONGS, OP. 1. (or.: 3♭)

65. DELIBES: LAKMÉ I. (or.: 4♭)

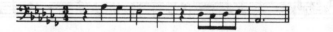

66. WAGNER: DAS RHEINGOLD I. (or.: 4♭)

67. BARTÓK: BLUEBEARD'S CASTLE. (or.: 3♭)

68. BRITTEN: PETER GRIMES II. (or.: 4♭)

Diatonic range

69. HANDEL: CH'IO MAI VI POSSA.

70. CESTI: I CASTI AMORI D'ORONTEA

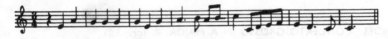

71. BEETHOVEN: STRING QUARTET IN C MINOR, OP. 18, NO. 4. II.

72. BEETHOVEN: MASS IN C MAJOR, OP. 86. GLORIA.

73. MOZART: COSÌ FAN TUTTE. I.

74. T. A. ARNE: THE MAIDEN'S COMPLAINT.

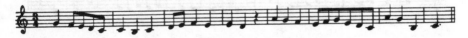

75. HANDEL: ISRAEL IN EGYPT. II.

76. J. DOWLAND: AWAKE, SWEET LOVE.

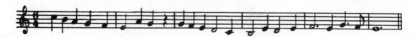

77. A. SCARLATTI: BELLEZZA, CHE S'AMA. (or.: 3♯)

78. J. HAYDN: MASS IN B FLAT MAJOR. BENEDICTUS. (or.: 1♯)

79. HANDEL: CONCERTO GROSSO IN A MAJOR. II. (or.: 3♯)

80. J. S. BACH: THE WELL-TEMPERED CLAVIER. II. (or.: 3♯)

81. MOZART: COSÌ FAN TUTTE. I. (or.: 2♯)

82. G. B. BONONCINI: PER LA GLORIA. (or.: 1♯)

83. MOZART: COSÌ FAN TUTTE. II. (or.: 1♯)

84. HANDEL: MESSIAH. II. (or.: 3♭)

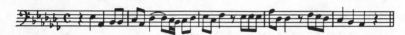

85. HANDEL: ISRAEL IN EGYPT. I. (or.: 3♭)

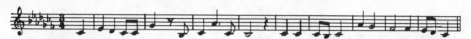

86. LULLY: PROSERPINE. II. (or.: 1♭)

The grace notes are omitted from the Lully quotations because proper performance of these would often present technical difficulty.

87. BEETHOVEN: SONATA IN A FLAT MAJOR, OP. 110. FUGUE. (or.: 4♭)

88. LULLY: ATYS. II.

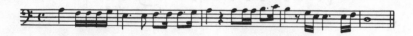

Dorian melody. (See the church modes on page *200*.)

89. LULLY: PROSERPINE. IV. (or.: 1♭)

90. VIVALDI: CELLO SONATA IN F MAJOR. (or.: 3♭)

91. VIVALDI: CELLO SONATA IN F MAJOR. (or.: 1♭)

EXTRACTS IN SOLFA LETTERS

In this group only diatonic melodies appear. Practise singing them to note names in the range of notes without key signature, and try out several different ways as with the Pentatonic Music melodies (page 94).

92. FARNABY: SOME TIME SHE WOULD. (or.: 1♯)

93. J. S. BACH: DU FRIEDENSFÜRST, HERR JESU CHRIST. CHORALE. (or.: 3♯)

94. J. S. BACH: MACH'S MIT MIR, GOTT, NACH DEINER GÜT'. CHORALE. (or.: 2♯)

95. J. S. BACH: GOTT DER VATER WOHN' UNS BEI. CHORALE. (or.: 2♯)

96. J. S. BACH: THE WELL-TEMPERED CLAVIER. I. (or.: 6♭)

97. J. S. BACH: O HAUPT VOLL BLUT UND WUNDEN. CHORALE. (or.: 1♭)

98. HANDEL: ISRAEL IN EGYPT. II. (or.: 1)

147

99. LULLY: AMADIS.

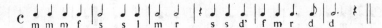

C m m m f │ s s l m r │ s s d' │ f m r d │ d

100. A. E. M. GRÉTRY: L'AMANT JALOUX.

3/8 l, m m │ s f m │ d l, t, │ t, r d t, l, │ l, ‖

Material in Several Parts

(All the extracts are given in the system with C as "d" that is, without key signature.)

PRACTICE

1. Perform the melodies to solfa but at the correct pitch given in the staff notation.

2. Before beginning to sing the quotations the students should be fully aware of the time signature, the key, and the solfa name of the first note or notes.

3. The singing should be accompanied by beating time.

4. The canons should only be performed in several parts once the melody is known precisely and securely by everyone. Canons using more than two parts should have the number of parts gradually increased.

5. Practise the extracts in 2, 3 and 4 parts first of all part by part and begin singing the parts together — likewise putting them together gradually — once the parts are known well.

6. Group and individual singing should be alternated in the course of practice so that all the students can take part in the active work.

101. CANON FROM THE 18TH CENTURY.

102. RHAU: ICH HAB' HEIMLICH ERGEBEN MICH. BICINIUM. (or.: 1♭)

103. CH. PRAETORIUS: CANON.

104. RHAU: VON EDLER ART. BICINIUM. (or.: 1♭)

105. PRAETORIUS: CANON.

106. GUMPELZHEIMER: CANON.

107. CHERUBINI: CANON.

108. RHAU: FRÖHLICH WILL ICH SINGEN. BICINIUM. (or.: 1♭)

109. CHERUBINI: CANON.

110. MOZART: THE MAGIC FLUTE. OVERTURE. (or.: 3♭)

111. J. S. BACH: HEUT' TRIUMPHIERET GOTTES SOHN. CHORALE.

112. ISAAC: MADRIGAL.

DEVELOPMENT OF MUSICAL MEMORY

Memorizing a Unison Melody

From staff notation

For this purpose the unison sight-singing extracts are used (see pages 139—145). Apart from pentatonic melodies, those using the diatonic range should also be memorized, but selecting those which are rhythmically easy so that the students can concentrate on the melodic phrases. The immediate aim is that they should store away among their musical memories as much as possible from the novel patterns in a relatively short time. An appropriately developed musical memory makes it possible later for observation of unknown melodies to become conscious and speedy hearing.

STAGES IN CHECKING THE MEMORIZED MELODY

1. Singing the melody to solfa, accompanying it by beating time, at the pitch given in the staff notation.
2. Solfa singing + hand-sign melody illustration.
3. Note name singing accompanied by beating time, in the given "d" system.
4. Writing the material down in staff notation.
5. Note name singing from the exercise book, accompanied by beating the metrical unit. (Control.)

From solfa letters

The material is selected from the sight-singing melodies in solfa notation (see pages 146—148). These melodies are without exception diatonic.

Checking on the memorizing of these extracts is carried out as in the case of quotations memorized from staff notation (see above). Note name singing and writing in staff notation should be carried out using only C as "d".

From hand-signs

Suitable extracts can once more be found among the sight-singing material, primarily among the rhythmically easy extracts in which the characteristic diatonic notes also appear and the singing of which has already been carried out faultlessly from the music at one of the earlier lessons.

PRACTISING PROCEDURE

1. The short rhythmic hand-sign melody given by the teacher is sung by the students to solfa, accompanied by beating time (with C as "d").
2. Once the singing is faultless the teacher gives a new extract and asks for the same procedure as before.
3. As repetition the students sing both a) to solfa, b) to note names, with C as "d". (If necessary, the teacher shows the hand-signs for the melodies once more to the students.)
4. Once this has been carried out successfully the students write down the two melodic progressions in staff notation.
5. Control singing (from their exercise books) to note names, accompanied by beating the metric unit.

Memorizing of Two-Part Material

Once the students have acquired a certain amount of practice in the memorizing of unison melodies, it is time to start memorizing two-part extracts. To begin with select quite short and easy extracts so that productive results should in no way be prevented by the music material being too extensive or the sequence of the musical elements being not perfectly clear.

SUGGESTED METHOD OF PRACTISING

1. The students sing the selected extract in two parts.
2. They memorize one of the parts determined by the teacher silently, to solfa.
3. Those who can do so sing it accompanied by beating time.
4. After a few individual performances, the students sing it from memory as a group.

5. They then learn and sing the other part in a similar way.

6. They go through the part learned first again (from memory), then do the same with the second so that they will clearly remember both.

7. Two groups of students perform the extract in two parts from memory, and then exchange their parts.

8. Two individuals sing it in a similar way.

9. Faultless solfa singing should be followed by note name singing. a) First they sing the two parts separately. b) They perform the extract in two parts, as a group and in pairs.

10. Individuals perform the learned extract by singing one part to solfa and playing the other (simultaneously) on the piano.

11. Once several students have succeeded in performing it in two parts faultlessly, everyone writes down the extract in the correct rhythm and in the given key.

12. As control, sing what has been written down a) part by part and b) in two parts together, to note names.

Within one lesson no more than one two-part extract should be memorized because this learning process — particularly to begin with — requires great concentration and a lot of time.

THE TWO-PART EXTRACTS

113. D. SCARLATTI: "STUDIO" IN F MAJOR. (or.: 1♭)

114. MOZART: 12 DUOS. NO. 5. (K. 487) (or.: 1♯)

115. KODÁLY: BICINIA HUNGARICA. IV/125.

116. J. S. BACH: TWO-PART INVENTION IN A MINOR.

117. KODÁLY: BICINIA HUNGARICA. IV/123.

118. HANDEL: MESSIAH. I. (or.: 3♯)

119. MOZART: AIR. (K. 15ᵃᵃ) (or.: 3♭)

120. KODÁLY: BICINIA HUNGARICA. IV/132.

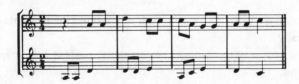

121. HANDEL: FUGUE IN G MAJOR. (or.: 1♯)

157

EAR TRAINING

Recognition of Intervals

The intervals of pentatony within the sixth range

In chapter I recognition by ear of the m—d' minor sixth has already been encountered in connection with practising the pentatonic tetrachords (see pages 78—79). But since the major sixth did not occur among the intervals of the tetrachords the students had no opportunity to come to a suitably clear distinction between the sounds of the two different sixths. For this reason it is absolutely necessary that we relate the interval recognition exercises of the pentatonic tetrachord within the m—d' framework with the pentatonic range of notes within the d—l and s,—m major sixths.

Procedure for ear training is here the same as it was for the trichords and tetrachords (see pages 76—79).

Fox example, here are the intervals in the s,—m framework in the order fifth, third, sixth, second, with G as the highest note:

1. Recognition. Teacher: (piano)

Students: (writing)

p5	M3	M6	M2

2. The teacher plays once more the intervals while the students control their writing individually.

3. Control as a group with naming the intervals: perfect 5th, major 3rd, major 6th and major 2nd.

4. Singing (starting first from the fixed note, then from the other one).

a) With interval names:

perf. 5th   maj. 3rd   maj. 6th   maj. 2nd   perf. 5th

b) With solfa names.

Or, for example, the intervals within the m—d' framework in the order fourth, third, sixth, with C# as the lowest note:

1. Recognition.

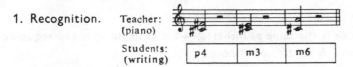

2. Individual checking.
3. Group checking.
4. Singing (starting first from the fixed note, then from the other).
a) With interval names,   b) With solfa names.

(Cf. points 1—4, page *158.*)

The intervals of pentatony within the seventh range

The intervals within the range of the frameworks l,—s , r—d' and m—r' should also be practised in the above way but in an order whereby the interval of a seventh does not precede the interval which is one degree smaller then itself.

The intervals existing in the groups of notes with a seventh range are as follows:

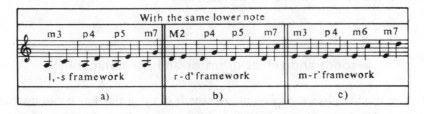

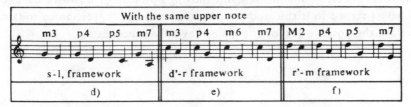

The order of the interval sequence selected for ear training purposes — taking the above basic principle into consideration — can be arranged in many different ways by the teacher. For example, here are some possibilities offered by b) above:

Ear training procedure is the same as hitherto — for example d) in the sequence 3rd, 5th, 7th, 4th, with A as the upper note:

1. Recognition.

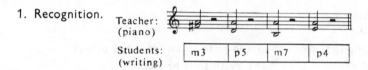

Teacher: (piano)

Students: (writing)

| m3 | p5 | m7 | p4 |

2. Individual checking.
3. Group checking.
4. Singing (starting first from the fixed note, then from the other one).
a) With interval names.   b) With solfa names.
(Cf. 1—4, page *158*)

etc.   etc.

This is virtually an inexhaustible practice form with which — among other things — it is possible to assist certain recognition of the two most easily mistaken intervals, the perfect 4th and the perfect 5th.

Seconds and thirds in major and harmonic minor

1. The teacher gives the two minor seconds of the major key on an instrument in any tonal order, with a melodic line moving upwards or downwards, and after they have listened to it the students sing the melodic progression to solfa names. There are the possibilities for the major key minor seconds:

	upwards	downwards	
a)	m—f — t—d'	d'—t — f—m	c)
b)	t,—d — m—f	f—m — d—t,	d)

The four sequences can, for example, be given as follows by the teacher: c)—b)—d)—a). The practical realization of this:

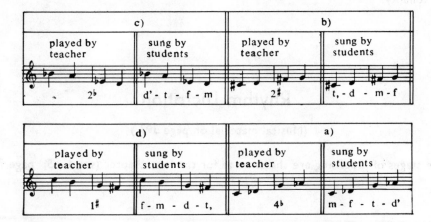

c)		b)	
played by teacher	sung by students	played by teacher	sung by students
2♭	d' - t - f - m	2♯	t, - d - m - f

d)		a)	
played by teacher	sung by students	played by teacher	sung by students
1♯	f - m - d - t,	4♭	m - f - t - d'

2. Apply this same way of practising to the minor seconds occurring in the harmonic minor as well.

The possibilities for melodic variation are:

	upwards	downwards	
a)	si,—l,—t,—d—m—f	f—m—d—t,—l,—si,	d)
b)	t,—d—m—f—si—l	l—si—f—m—d—t,	e)
c)	m—f—si—l—t—d'	d'—t—l—si—f—m	f)

For example the sequence of melodic progressions a)—f)—b):

161

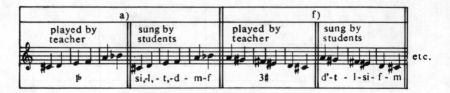

a)		f)	
played by teacher	sung by students	played by teacher	sung by students
♭	si,-l, - t,-d - m-f	3♯	d'-t - l-si- f - m

etc.

3. Practise similarly the recognition of the various sequences of major and minor thirds, in the major key, using both upward and downward melodic progressions alike. (Cf. 1., page *160*)

The above exercises play an important role primarily in the forming of a feeling for tonality.

Rhythm Dictation

(Musical material on page *393.*)

The stages of practising are the same as for the first chapter (see 1—5, page *79*)

Melody Dictation

(Musical material on page *396.*)

In the material for melody memorizing by ear only six pentatonic extracts occur. Most of the extracts are diatonic in range. These melodies contain considerably more difficult musical elements then the pentatonic extracts which have appeared so far and so this melody dictation must be preceded by various kinds of preparatory work.

THE PREPARATORY STAGES

1. On the piano, or any other instrument, the teacher plays the series of notes containing the characteristic phrases of the melody selected for ear training pur-

poses, using even rhythmic values — and the students sing back the individual notes to solfa.

If, for example, the melody goes like this:

then in the course of preparation the following series of melodic patterns might be used:

In this case the dialogue between instrument and singing evolves as follows:

Piano (teacher)									etc.
Singing (students)	ɣ d ɣ r	ɣ m ɣ d	ɣ s ɣ f	ɣ m ɣ r	ɣ d ɣ t,	ɣ d ɣ f	ɣ m ɣ r		

2. The teacher sings the preparatory phrases to solfa and the students answer him by singing to note names. For example:

Teacher's sol-fa singing	s	f	m	r	t,	d	f	m	t,	d	
Actual pitch											etc.
Student's note name answer	G	F	E	D	B	C	F	E	B	C	

3. The teacher gives the melodic patterns by using hand-signs and the students answer him by singing to note names. For example:

Teacher's hand-sign melody	m r d m s f m r d r t, d f m r s t, r d etc.
Students' note name singing	E D C E G F E D C D B C F E D G B D C etc.
Actual pitch	

(Cf. Note name singing, p. 117.)

After preparation —

1. Perform the melody together with its accompaniment, making the students pay attention to a) the range ot notes (pentatonic or diatonic) and b) the solfa names of the last note.

(If they are unable to establish these points at the first hearing, play it again.)

2. While performing the melody again (more than once if necessary) a) the students should give the solfa name of the first note, b) they should determine the time signature and c) establish whether the melody begins on a stressed or unstressed part of the bar.

3. After clearing up these details it is possible to begin the solfa memorizing by ear of the motifs of the melody — or all of it.

4. The students sing the learned melody a) to solfa and accompanied by beating time, and b) to note names, accompanied by beating the metric unit.

5. After faultless performance of this kind has been achieved, clarify the rhythm pattern of each bar.

6. Once this process of working to make the elements conscious has been completed, the students write down the melody — together with the rhythm — in their exercise books, at the given pitch.

7. When all the students are ready they sing the melody written down, to note names accompanied by beating the metric unit.

8. If the melody has an accompaniment, the final performance should be singing by the group with beating time, together with the accompaniment.

Bach Chorale Extracts

(Music material on page 401.)

It would be difficult to find more suitable and at the same time more beautiful musical material to encourage development of concentration on the bass. Perform these four-part extracts on the piano and ask the students to concentrate on the bass. The quotations should be included in the ear training and memory development procedures, similarly to melody dictation:

1. During the first hearing ask the students to pay attention to the closing and opening notes of the bass part. (Play the extract again if necessary.)

2. Through another hearing the students should establish the time signature and whether the starting of the musical material is stressed or unstressed.

3. Once these points have been cleared up the extracts should be played several times so that the students can memorize by ear the bottom part, with conscious concentration on the bass.

4. Volunteers sing by heart, to solfa accompanied by beating time. (Girls naturally singing an octave higher than boys.)

5. Once solfa singing has been carried out successfully by everyone, note name singing follows, likewise accompanied by beating time.

6. After faultless singing as a group, the students write down the bass part in the F clef at the given pitch.

7. When they have finished writing, they sing it from their exercise books, to note names.

8. Finally comes group performance: the teacher plays the four parts and the students sing the bass progression they have written.

The preparatory stages described on pages *162—163* can — if it appears necessary — also be used before dictation of the chorale extracts. In that case the piano part of the instrument — voice dialogue (point 1, page *162*) should sound in the register of the chorale's bass part.

PLANNING SUGGESTION

(See the diagram at the end of the book.)

As the diagram shows, the material for study in this chapter is so many-sided that there is no time to include all the practice forms in each lesson. When putting together the material for individual lessons, however, we must always keep in mind that there can be no solfege lesson without singing from music (Kodály material, sight-singing), ear training, memory training and conscious technical practice. Which part of the material or which practice form represents these four main branches of the studies within individual lessons, which musical quotation the teacher uses to develop the various abilities, or what is to be repeated from what has already been studied — all this also depends on the degree of the students' knowledge at the actual time. But in spite of this the organic and logical connection between the individual lessons can never be allowed to disappear.

Without systematic and varied homework — and regular checking of it — the work will not bear lasting results. For the development of the musical abilities it is not just the amount of time devoted to it that counts, but regular repetition in practice is also indispensable.

CHAPTER III

(The staff notation material in the chapter uses F or F# as "d")

KODÁLY MATERIAL

Unison Pentatonic Melodies

MATERIAL IN STAFF NOTATION: 333 ELEMENTARY EXERCISES

Matters of formal and melodic interest

The 25 melodies listed here (275, 276, 277, 279, 280, 283, 284, 286, 287, 288, 289, 292, 293, 294, 297, 310, 311, 313, 314, 318, 319, 320, 321, 323, 324) do not go beyond the degree of difficulty of the exercises sung in chapter II. Since the range of their notes is connected to the major third F—A, they play an extremely important part in the development of secure orientation in the new "d" position.

The note-finding practice which precedes melody singing should be carried out in the r,—l range in both the G clef and the F clef:

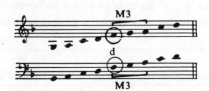

Apart from two exceptions all the exercises are in "l" pentatony, and for this reason their melodic progression and cadential phrases have a novel effect. With regard to rhythm patterns there is nothing new. At the same time, however, their formal construction and their melodic structure are extraordinarily varied and multicoloured. When we come to singing the melodies, a few minutes should be devoted to formal analysis of them, because in these motifs many musical elements are to be found which point in the direction of folk music and art music.

Sing the melodies to solfa and practise them in the already familiar ways — with giving the metrical unit, rhythm ostinato, beating time, rhythm canon, in answering form, and with alternation of inner singing and singing aloud.

DESCENDING FIFTH CHANGE
(284, 310, 313, 314, 318, 319, 323)

The four-line folksong-structure melodies display the following types of form:

$A^5 A^5, A A = 318, 319$

The cadence notes of the lines of the melody reach the final note by descending gradually:

$A^5 A^5 A, A = 310, 323$

Of the fifth-changing second half of the melody's closing phrases that of the third line turns back to the cadential pitch of the first half-melody, thus opening up the third line vigorously and in this way virtually connects it with the fourth line. For example, exercise 310:

$A^5 B^5 A B = 314$

$A B^5 A, B = 284$

$A^5 A B A = 313$

DOME-SHAPED FIFTH CHANGE
(277, 280, 320)

All these melodies are built into organic form from one kind of musical material. Their melodic structure:

A A⁵ A,⁵ A = 320

The third line— a return to A , as it were— differs from the basic motif only in its last note:

A A⁵ A,⁵ A, = 277, 280

As opposed to the real fifth changes which have appeared so far, melody 277 produces a tonal fifth change:

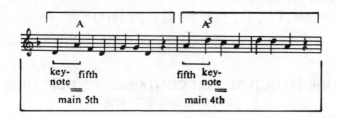

PERIOD (QUESTION-ANSWER)
(276, 284)

Melody 284:

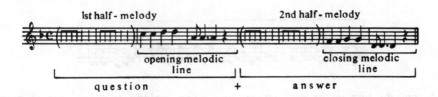

171

Melody 276:

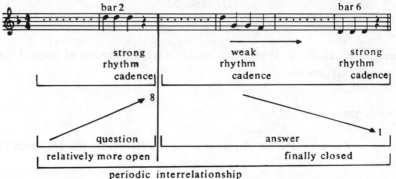

The equal rank rhythm cadences of bars 2 and 6 divide the form asymmetrically. The peculiarities of the melody's two kinds of rhythm cadence:

a) In the strong (masculine) rhythm cadence the last note is more stressed than the one immediately preceding it.

(Other examples: $\frac{2}{4}$ ♩ ♪ ‖ $\frac{2}{4}$ ♫♩ ‖ $\frac{3}{4}$ ♩♪♪ ‖ $\frac{3}{4}$ ♫♩ ‖ $\frac{4}{4}$ ♪♩. ♩♪ ‖ etc.)

b) In the weak (feminine) rhythm cadence the last note is less stressed than the one immediately preceding it.

(Other examples: $\frac{2}{4}$ ♩ ♩ ‖ $\frac{2}{4}$ ♩ ♫ ‖ $\frac{3}{4}$ ♩ ♩ ‖ $\frac{4}{4}$ ♩ ♩♪ ‖ etc.)

LINE STRUCTURE (SELF-CONTAINED MELODIC LINE)
(277, 279, 280, 292, 320)

In the exercises quoted the first line or the first two lines of the melody are heard as a self-contained formal unit:

Each melodic line might well appear in a given melody as a line which brings the form to an end, that is, as a final line.

172

DESCENDING FOURTH CHANGE
(289, 321)

In the melodic structures $A^4 A^4$, A,, A, (No. 321) and A B^4 C B (No. 289), in the lower fourth-changing lines the note "m" of the A^4 and B^4 material is answered by "d", since within the pentatonic range "m" has no lower fourth to correspond to it. (Cf. the pentatonic sixth in the fifth-changing melodies, pages *98, 102, 103, 104*.) For example:

TWO-SECTION FORM (FORMAL UNIT CONSISTING OF TWO PERIODS)
(286, 287, 293, 297, 311)

In these melodies the opening-closing occurs twice. For example:

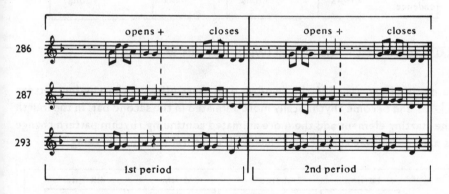

etc.

FORM-CREATING RHYTHM CHARACTERISTICS
(277, 279, 280, 294, 313, 324)

RHYTHMIC CONDENSATION

In melodies 277, 279 and 313, the third line retains the number of bars occurring in the other lines but — either wholly or partly — changes to rolling eighths and virtually "runs" into the last line of the melody. Thus the third and fourth lines merge into an indivisible formal unit.

For example in exercise 277:

1st line	2nd line	3rd line	+ 4th line
4/4 ♩♩♩♩ | ♩♩♩♩ ‖	♩♩♩♩ | ♩♩♩‖	♩♩♩♩ | ♫♫♫♫	♩♩♩♩ | ♩♩♩‖
rhythm cadence: strong	strong	weak →	strong

NARROWNESS OF RHYTHM

The third line of melody 280 tightens up the cadential rhythm pattern of the other lines, and shortens it in time. As a result of this the third line becomes a bipodic one — with only two stresses in its musical material — and in this way the quality of its rhythm cadence also changes:

1st line	2nd line	3rd line	+	4th line
2/4 ♩♩ | ♫♩ | ♩‖	♩♩ | ♫♩ | ♩‖	♩♩ | ♫♫		♩♩ | ♫♩ | ♩‖
rhythm cadence: strong	strong	weak →		strong

FORMAL EXCHANGE OF POSITION BETWEEN RHYTHM PATTERNS

In the music of exercise 324 the two-bar lines start off with the rhythm pattern 2/2 ♩ ♩ | and become rhythmically more animated in the second bar. In the fourth line the starting element and the more animated continuing rhythm pattern change places and in this way the melody ends with a natural rhythmic braking:

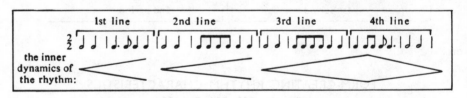

174

THE THIRD FORMAL ELEMENT BRINGING SOMETHING NEW
OR CONTRASTING
(277, 279, 288, 292, 294, 311, 313)

The contrasting motif appears in the rhythm or melodic line of the third formal element.

'POINTS OF INTEREST IN DIMENSIONS
(275, 276, 280, 314, 319)

a) Tripodic melodic lines (with three stresses, three bars): 275, 319.
b) Asymmetric inner division: 276 (see page 172).
c) Heteropody (lines containing different numbers of bars within the same melody): 280 (see page 174) and 314.

SEQUENTIAL MELODY FORMATION
(283, 284)

The sequential elements of the melodies:

No. 283				No. 284	
bar 2	bar 4	bar 5	bar 7	3rd melodic line	
correspondence of closing phrases	correspondence of opening elements			basic idea	+ pentatonic third sequence
fifth-changing cadential element	sequential start				

175

MATERIAL USING SOLFA LETTERS: PENTATONIC MUSIC I—IV

Repetition of musical elements already learned

¢	III/15
Alternation of $\frac{3}{4}$ and $\frac{4}{4}$:	I/88.
Alternation of $\frac{2}{4}$ and $\frac{4}{4}$:	II/27.

In the melodies there are musical elements which are in fact familiar but which nevertheless require a great deal of further repetition for practical realization of them to be managed with facility.

The melodies should be sung to solfa, making use of the customary forms of practice.

New elements

SEVENTH UPWARDS = IV/24

The l,—s minor seventh appears twice — first between the first and second lines, and then between the second and third lines. In both cases the melodic antecedents provide very thorough preparation.

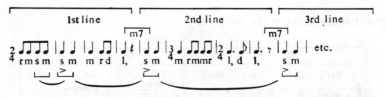

Accompany the exercise mainly with beating time.

4 → 4 IN SUCCESSION = IV/18

Practise the following progression a few times:

Singing the original melody should only begin once intonation in these six bars is perfectly secure both in individual and in group performance.

ALTERNATION OF $\frac{3}{8}$ AND $\frac{2}{8}$ = IV/25

The essence of this change in metre — just as with the alternation of $\frac{3}{4}$ and $\frac{2}{4}$ — lies in the alternation of triple and duple bars. For this reason they should be practised mainly with beating time and with an alternating ostinato (e.g. $\frac{3}{8}$ ♩.♫ and $\frac{2}{8}$ ♫).

MELODY BEGINNING WITH AN UPBEAT = III/12

(= That an unaccented start which does not exceed the time value of the metrical unit.)

1. In the music mark the motif endings (bar 2: $\frac{4}{4}$ ♩ ♫ ♩· ♫ ‖ ; bar 4:
$\frac{4}{4}$ ♩ ♩ ♩· ♫ ‖bar 6:$\frac{4}{4}$ ♩ ♫ ♩· ♫ ‖) , and sing the melody with repetition and accompanied by beating time.

2. Practise — likewise beating time — in answering form as well, in as many ways as possible: with two individuals or two groups; with alternation of solo-tutti or tutti-solo.

The teacher should see to it that the students should take breath only at the ends of the motifs — in accordance with the marks indicated.

TRIPLET (♫♩) = IV/13

Performance of this melody is rendered difficult by the alternation of ♩♫, ♫♩ and ♫♩ rhythm patterns. Practise, continuously and in a fast tempo, the following pairs of bars:

Once the difference between the ♩♫, ♫♩ and ♫♩ rhythm patterns becomes clear and precise, the whole melody should be sung accompanied by beating the metrical unit, giving sharp accent on the first melodic notes in each unit:

177

Easy melodies for practising note name singing

(II/16, 24, 53, 56; III/9, 10, 16; IV/14, 15, 16, 17, 19, 20, 22, 23.)

The melodies listed here are simple from the rhythmic and melodic points of view and thus are suitable for practising with note names.

The music material in this chapter has as "d":

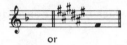

or

In both cases the same written notes belong to the "d" system and only differ in their key signature:

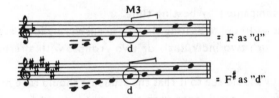

= F as "d"

= F♯ as "d"

The students must practise singing the melodies to note names in both versions. The note names belonging to the system with F♯ as "d" should, however, only be practised after certain orientation has been gained in the range using F as "d".

WAYS OF PRACTISING SINGING TO NOTE NAMES

Singing of melodies should be started once the students can cope with note name practice from hand-signs (see page *191*) without difficulty.

SOLFA + NOTE NAME SINGING ALOUD

(For a detailed description see page *95*.)
For example, the melody of II/24 in Pentatonic Music using F as "d":

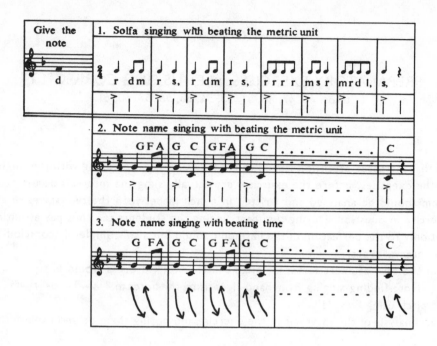

SILENT SOLFA + NOTE NAME SINGING ALOUD

(For a detailed description see page 95.)

RANGE OF NOTES + MELODY NOTE NAME SINGING

(For a detailed description see page 96.)
For example, the melody of III/9 in Pentatonic Music using F# as "d":

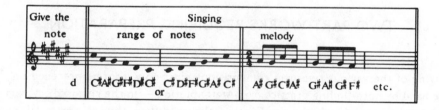

SIGHT-SINGING TO NOTE NAMES

(See page 96.)

179

Two-Part Material

PREPARATORY EXERCISES: "LET US SING CORRECTLY"
(Nos. 46, 47, 48, 51, 53, 54, 55, 56, 57, 60, 61.)

So that increased attention is paid to conscious observation along with the singing of the exercises, before the exercises are actually sung the intervals occurring in them should be analysed and written in pencil in between the two staves of the exercise in question. During two-part singing the students can thus pay attention not only to the perfection of the harmonic sound but also, completely consciously, the interval types.

In the case of exercise 46, for example, the work process would be:

1. Note-finding singing from hand-signs using the notes m,—s,—l,—d—r—m , at the pitch using F as "d".

2. Analysis of the intervals in the exercise and noting them down in the music:

3. Two-part singing. (See page 44, under 3.)

TWO PART WORKS REQUIRING PREPARATION

Singing of the various two-part compositions must now, too, be preceded on the one hand by note-finding practice from staff notation — in the given "d" system — and on the other hand by a brief analytical survey (key, thematic material, more difficult melodic motifs or rhythm patterns, etc.).

In this chapter the general procedure for learning the exercises is no longer given in detail — those details requiring special attention or representing difficulty are pointed out, to be accompanied with the suggested ways of practising.

In studying the exercises an increasingly important part should be played

— mainly as homework — by the two-part forms of performance carried out by one person. (See page *104*, under 5.)

Pentatonic range of notes

The exercises generally have no key signature because in the pentatonic range of notes containing the major third F—A the note B♭ ("f") does not appear.

Note-finding singing from staff notation should be practised in the G and F clefs within the r,—l range:

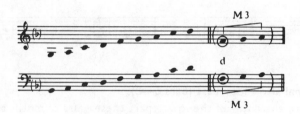

BICINIA HUNGARICA I/7

1. Its key is "l" pentatonic.
2. The first bar alto entrance can be prepared by practising the following pair of bars:

3. In the theme's cadential phrase ( ) the note "s" is frequently uncertain. Perfect intonation of it can be encouraged by singing the following sequence:

cadential phrase

BICINIA HUNGARICA I/15

1. Its key is "l" pentatonic.
2. The first three bars of the soprano melody are imitated, at a distance of one bar, by the alto a fifth lower:

3. In the  melodic progression of the lower part the note "r" (G) is usually flat. Practise the following — in a slow tempo:

a)

b)

c) the original alto's four bars (bars 5—8).

4. To prepare the entry of the lower part these pairs of motifs should be sung:

BICINIA HUNGARICA I/19

1. This is a "l" pentatonic theme, with A A⁵ B C structure.

2. In the soprano's upper fifth-changing motif the initial note "s" will only be clear if the students are capable of hearing securely the motif s—l—m , as a tonal melodic unit, in the tonality of "l" pentatonic. For this reason the following should be practised:

3. On account of the rhythm patterns ♪ ♩. and ♩. ♪ the theme should be sung with beating the metric unit.

4. So that the alto's octave imitation will sound clearly, practise the imitative progression in bars 3—4:

182

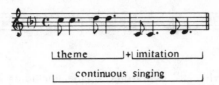

theme +imitation

continuous singing

BICINIA HUNGARICA 1/20

1. This theme has a A A^5 B C structure, in "l" pentatonic, with a tonal fifth change in the second line:

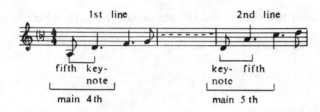

fifth key-
note

key- fifth
note

main 4th

main 5th

2. Take the melody's opening phrase and its variants separately and sing them accompanied by beating the metrical unit in the following sequence, paying careful attention to secure note-finding and precise rhythm:

theme +accompaniment

continuous singing

3. The alto entry in bar 4 is also difficult. Practise these bars a few times:

BICINIA HUNGARICA 1/23

1. A theme with an A^5 B^5 A B structure, in "s" pentatonic.
2. The alto entry imitating the first motif of the theme can be prepared by singing the following melodic progressions:

a)

b)

BICINIA HUNGARICA 1/26

1. The structure of this "l" pentatonic theme, including a pentatonic sixth, is
A⁵ B⁵ A B.

notes in the 1st half:

notes in the 2nd half: pentatonic
                            sixth

2. Practise both the theme and the accompanying part, which is broken up by

rests, with this two-part rhythm accompaniment:

77 TWO-PART EXERCISES/70

1. The soprano's last motif requires special attention after the melodic progressions moving on the main notes s—m—d. The following should be sung as
preparation:

2. The final motif in the alto part can also cause problems.

a) Practise the following serie of phrases with beating the metrical unit:

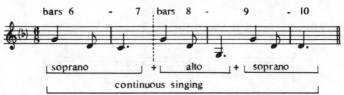

bars 6   -   7   bars 8 -   9   - 10

soprano   +   alto   +   soprano

continuous singing

b) Practise the alto's final motif in conjunction with the soprano's similar material, giving the units to it and later beating time:

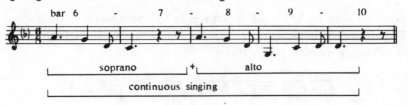

bar 6   -   7   -   8   -   9   -   10

soprano   +   alto

continuous singing

Pentatony + "t"

55 TWO-PART EXERCISES/26

1. Among the notes of "l" pentatonic there now appears an upward passing note "t" (in the first bar of the alto).

2. The pentatonic patterns of the exercise are perfectly familiar. But in spite of this both parts need intensive practice separately because of the continuous interval movement. It is particularly advisable to sing through the alto several times, both in groups and individually.

3. Since the soprano has a very high tessitura this exercise cannot be practised with exchanging the parts. In order to spare the voices of those singing the soprano, the first few two-part performances should be organised so that the teacher accompanies the group singing the alto part by playing the upper part on the piano (or other instrument) and the sopranos join in the two-part singing only once the altos can manage their own part faultlessly with the piano accompaniment.

77 TWO-PART EXERCISES/33

1. The notes used in the upper part:

final note

They can be put into solfa in two dif-   a)   s'   r'   l   m = B♭ as "d"

ferent ways: b)   d'   s   r   l, = F as "d"

Since it is primarily the note A that joins this group of notes in the lower part (= F—A major third), the second solfa possibility is the realistic one. This appears to be reinforced by the final note D.

2. Before singing the upper part practise the following pairs of phrases:

3. Prepare the last four bars of the lower part by using the following variants:

a)

b)

c)

185

Practise variants a) and b) many times — in groups as well, but primarily individually — so that the cadential motif will fit securely into the tonality. The help given by the note "d" should only be dispensed with (see variant c) once the students can hear and intonate the cadential motif clearly.

Diatonic range of notes

Note-finding practice from staff notation should now be carried out using the complete diatonic range of notes.

77 TWO-PART EXERCISES/43

1. The "l" pentatonic theme should be sung through first without tying the tied notes, accompanied by beating the metrical unit. Once this is managed successfully in a fast tempo, practise it with the original tied notes — likewise with giving the unit.

2. The diatonic accompanying part does not contain any kind of melodic difficulty. The rhythm, however — mainly because of the syncopation chain through two bars (bars 8—9) — requires careful attention. As preparation:

a) Sing bars 7—9 of the soprano part (possibly an octave lower if desirable) without the tied notes being tied and beating the unit by alternating the left and right hands and giving a strong accent on the unit beat marked by the left hand, which sounds on the stressed part of the bar:

b) Practise in a similar way but with the original tied notes.

77 TWO-PART EXERCISES/45

Under the "l" pentatonic theme there is a diatonic accompaniment. The note "t" appears in already familiar and practised phrases. The part of the alto's first motif which moves down to "f" is, however, novel:

In the pentatonic melodies sung hitherto the melodic progressions 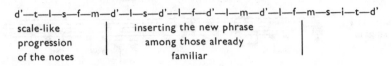 and 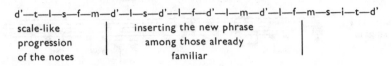 have frequently been encountered. Thus the new diatonic progression 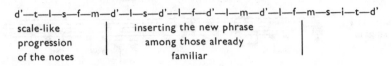 can best be prepared by combining it with the two familiar pentatonic phrases. Carry out therefore note-finding practice similar to the following on the basis of the range using one flat:

d'—t—l—s—f—m—d'—l—s—d'--l—f—d'—l—m—d'—l—f—m—s—l—t—d'

scale-like progression of the notes	inserting the new phrase among those already familiar	

Range including altered notes

77 TWO-PART EXERCISES/35

1. The diatonic range is extended by use of the note "fi". Thus in the preparatory work, too, this range of notes should be used:

2. In singing the exercise the altered note "fi" does not cause any problem since it comes in the most easily intonated form, as a changing note. But serious preparatory work is required by the theme's first two motifs, and the alto imitation which has the effect of a tonal answer to the first motif.

a) The theme's first motif is essentially two successive fourths:　Practise therefore the following pairs of melodic patterns:

Once this last fourth sequence is securely intonated by the students, they can begin slow practice of the original motif.

b) In the alto imitation the theme's notes　are answered by

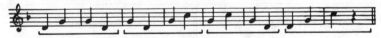 as if there were a tonal answer in the key of G. But here we are in a tonality with D as keynote (D "l" pentatonic + D aeolian, coloured by "fi"), and so this fourth-fifth correspondence sounds unusual. For this reason practise the following progressions as preparation:

187

The four bars should be sung in their original form only once the above have been carried out successfully.

3. In the theme's second motiv difficulty may be caused by the leap to lower "l" because of the motif's ninth range:

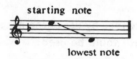

Sing the following pair of motifs a few times:

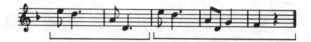

TWO-PART PIECES WHICH CAN BE SUNG AT SIGHT

Pentatonic range	Pentatony + "t"
77 Two-Part Exercises/1	Bicinia Hungarica I/31
Bicinia Hungarica I/2, 3, 4	77 Two-Part Exercises/18
77 Two-Part Exercises/2	
Bicinia Hungarica I/5	**Diatonic range**
77 Two-Part Exercises/5	77 Two-Part Exercises/1
Bicinia Hungarica I/6	Bicinia Hungarica I/33
77 Two-Part Exercises/6, 7	
15 Two-Part Exercises/3	**Range including altered notes**
Bicinia Hungarica I/8, 9, 10, 12, 14, 16, 22	Bicinia Hungarica I/42, b

The twenty-three exercises listed here can be used by the teacher as two-part sight-singing material on the basis of what has been learned so far. Naturally making the key and time signature conscious, and the establishing of the position of "d" and at the same time the name of the first note are all indispensable here, too. The two-part singing should be accompanied by beating time or giving the metrical unit, guided by the teacher, so that the two parts will progress together in time.

Melody with Piano Accompaniment

Modulating musical material

EPIGRAMS/5

The formal construction of the melody is:

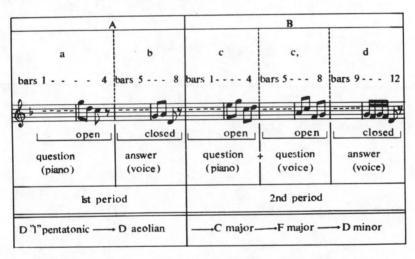

(The order of keys refers to the whole of the music material.)

In the thematic material pentatonic phrases dominate. Suggested places for changing "d":

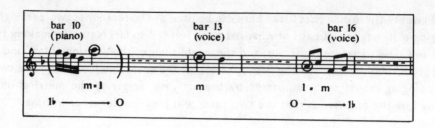

THEORETICAL INFORMATION AND TECHNICAL EXERCISES

Range of Notes, Hand-Signs

Pentatony

SOLFA SINGING TO HAND-SIGNS

Practise the pentatonic interval progressions of 4 + 4, 4+ 5, 5 + 4 and 5 + 5.

Here, for example, is a melody practising the 4 + 4 progression: l,—d—m—r—
—l,—r—s—m—r—d—r—s—d' —l—s—r—m—l—r'—d'—l—d'—s—r—m—d—s—
—r—l,—d—s,—l, or a melody with the 5 + 5 progression: d—s—d'—d—s—r'—d'
—l—m—r—s—l—r—s,—d—m—r—l—m'—r'—d' etc.

NOTE NAME SINGING TO HAND-SIGNS

The teacher's pentatonic hand-sign melody is answered in note names by the students using the pentatonic range of notes connected with F or F♯ as "d". For example, here is a sequence at the pitch using F as "d":

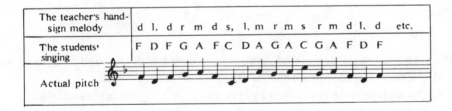

The teacher's hand-sign melody	d l, d r m d s, l, m r m s r m d l, d etc.
The students' singing	F D F G A F C D A G A C G A F D F
Actual pitch	

Diatony

SOLFA SINGING TO HAND-SIGNS

Practise reaching the diatonic notes "t" and "f" from any note within the octave upwards and downwards alike. For example:
d—m—s—t,—d—l,—f—t,—d or d'—l—t—d'—l—f—r—t—d'—m—f—r—d—s,—f
—t,—d etc.

191

NOTE NAME SINGING TO HAND-SIGNS

The teacher gives an easy diatonic hand-sign melody and the students sing it using the note names of one flat or six sharps key signature. For example, a sequence using F♯ as "d":

The teacher's hand-sign melody	d m r s, d f, m, l. s, t, d f m t, d etc.
The students' singing	F♯ A♯ G♯ C♯ F♯ B A♯ D♯ C♯ E♯ F♯ B A♯ E♯ F♯
Actual pitc	

Diatony + alteration

SOLFA SINGING TO HAND-SIGNS

Of the altered versions of the solfa names, "fi" and "ta"—as the characteristic altered notes in melodic progressions modulating towards the dominant and subdominant respectively — are given new hand-signs. These are:

fi   ta

The students should sing melodic patterns coloured with "fi" and "ta" in which
  a) the two altered notes occur as changing or passing notes,
  b) the altered note is reached by leap and is given a melodic resolution.
   For example: d—m—s—fi—s—m—fi—s—d'—l—f—m—r—t,—d—ta,—l,—r—t, —s,—d etc.

SOLFA SINGING FROM STAFF NOTATION

Extend the range of notes in the key signature using 1♭ and 6♯ for note-finding practice from staff notation with the most common altered notes (di, fi, si, ri, ta, lo).
  a) In the G clef:

or:

b) In the F clef:

or:

In this form practice, too, the altered notes should be sung as changing notes, passing notes, and altered notes reached by a leap and followed by resolution.

For example: d—m—ri—m—s—t,—d—ta,—l,--f—r—t,—d—s—lo—s—fi—s—f —m—r—m—di—r—f--t,—d etc.

SOLFA — NOTE NAME SINGING IN ANSWERING FORM

The teacher sings to solfa, and at the pitch using F or F♯ as "d" melodic patterns which include altered notes and the students answer with note names. For example the melody d—ta,—l,—t,—d—m—fi—s—m—di—r—t,—d with F as "d":

The teacher's solfa singing:	d	ta,	l,	t,	d	m	fi	s	m	etc.
Actual pitch:										
Students' note name answer:	F	E♭	D	E	F	A	B	C	A	

or, the melody d—lo,—s,—t,—d—m—l,—si,—l,—r—d using F♯ as "d":

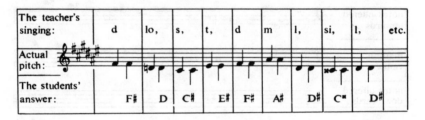

The teacher's singing:	d	lo,	s,	t,	d	m	l,	si,	l,	etc.
Actual pitch:										
The students' answer:	F♯	D	C♯	E♯	F♯	A♯	D♯	C✱	D♯	

(See page 111 for the names of notes altered by a double sharp or a double flat.)

Keys and Modes

The pentatonic modes with F and F# as "d"

(M) After the note "d" has been given, the students should be asked to sing any of the pentatonic modes ("d", "r", "m", "s" or "l" pentatonic) upwards or downwards to solfa, and then immediately afterwards to the note names appropriate to the given "d".

For example, "m" pentatonic upwards, with F as "d":

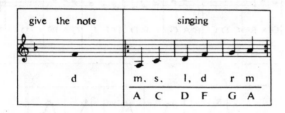

give the note	singing
d	m, s, l, d r m
	A C D F G A

or "r" pentatonic downwards, with F# as "d":

give the note	singing
d	r d l, s, m, r,
	G# F# D# C# A# G#

etc.

Major and minor keys with one flat or six sharps

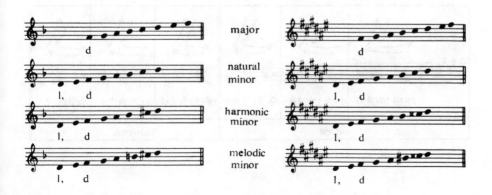

195

1. (M) Sing the natural, harmonic and melodic D minor — D♯ minor — in the direction, moving in even metrical units and accompany this continuous singing with beating time in 2, 3, 4, or 6. For example, the D minor types, in $\frac{3}{4}$ time:

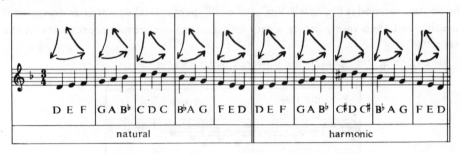

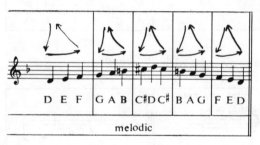

(Cf. 1—2 on page *121*.)

2. (M) Use note name singing accompanied by beating time in conjunction with a certain rhythm pattern and practise the three types of minor in this way.

For example, the D ♯ minor types with the rhythm pattern $\frac{4}{4}$ ♪♩ ♪♩ ♩ :

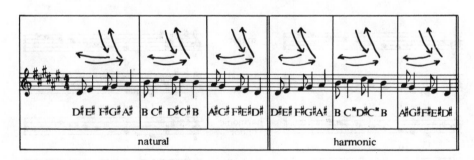

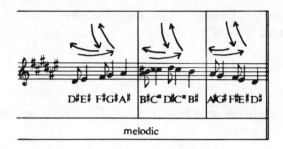

melodic

(Cf. 3—4 on pages *121—122*)

3. (M) Accompany the continuous singing in even metrical units with a rhythm ostinato.

For example, the D minor types with the ostinato ♩. ♪♫♩ ♪ :

| D E F G | A B♭C D | C B♭ A G | F E D | D E F G | A B♭ C♯ D |

| C♯ B♭ A G | F E D | D E F G | A B C♯ D | C♯ B A G | F E D |

(Cf. 5—6 on page *122*)

Note-finding exercises in major and harmonic minor

IN F MAJOR

1. Note name singing from solfa letters within the range r—l' (𝄞 ━━).

2. Solfa + note name singing from degree numbers in the range II—6
(𝄞 ━━).

3. Note name singing from the above degree numbers.
(Cf. 1, 3, 4 on pages *122—123*)

IN F♯ MAJOR

The practice stages are the same as for F major. The pitch is naturally to be adapted to the names of the notes.

IN D MINOR

1. Note name singing from solfa letters within the range r—l' (♯),
(Leading note = si!)

2. Solfa singing from degree numbers, in the range IV—8 (♯).
3. Solfa + note name singing from the above degree numbers.
4. Note name singing from the degree numbers.
(Cf. 2—5 on pages *124—125*)

IN D♯ MINOR

The practice stages are the same as for D minor. The pitch is to be adapted to the names of the notes in the 6 sharps system.

Dual fifth pillar

The fifth pillar is produced by depicting the major keys and their relative minor keys in ascending — or descending — fifth-order:

5	C sharp major	A sharp minor	7♯	
5	F sharp major	D sharp minor	6♯	
5	B major	G sharp minor	5♯	
5	E major	C sharp minor	4♯	
5	A major	F sharp minor	3♯	
5	D major	B minor	2♯	
5	G major	E minor	1♯	
5	C major	A minor	0	
5	F major	D minor	1♭	
5	B flat major	G minor	2♭	
5	E flat major	C minor	3♭	
5	A flat major	F minor	4♭	
5	D flat major	B flat minor	5♭	
5	G flat major	E flat minor	6♭	
5	C flat major	A flat minor	7♭	

ascending (+) direction (dominant direction)

descending (−) direction (subdominant direction)

ORIENTATION IN THE FIFTH PILLAR

The individual members of the fifth pillar are at a distance of one or several fifths. If this fifth-distance is in the ascending line then the relationship is in the "plus" (+) direction. If, on the other hand, it is in the descending line then the relationship between the keys is in the "minus" (—) direction. For example, B flat major ⟶ D major = +4 fifths distance; B minor ⟶ G minor = a distance of —4 fifths; B flat minor ⟶ G major = a distance of +6 fifths, etc.

Church modes (Model keys)

In the Renaissance style, and also in the Bach chorale melodies, folksongs and twentieth century works — melodies or whole works in the dorian, phrygian, mixolydian or aeolian modes are often to be encountered. These belong to the modal key group, and, as the "modes" of the diatonic system, they are connected to the same key signature system:

PRACTISING THE MODES

(M) Sing those modes with a perfect fifth — except the ionian and aeolian — to solfa, beginning from the same pitch, as follows:

a) Moving in even quarters, accompanying with beating time in 2, 3, or 4. For example, the dorian, lydian, phrygian and mixolydian in succession, beating triple time:

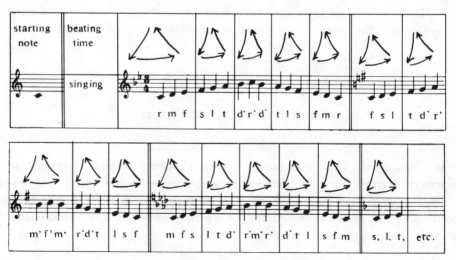

b) In even quarters with a $\frac{2}{4}$, $\frac{3}{4}$ or $\frac{4}{4}$ rhythm ostinato. For example, the mixolydian, dorian, phrygian and lydian in succession with the ostinato $\frac{4}{4}$ ♩. ♪ ♫ ♩ :

c) In various — $\frac{2}{4}$, $\frac{3}{4}$ or $\frac{4}{4}$ — rhythm patterns, accompanied by beating time as appropriate. For example, the lydian, dorian, mixolydian and phrygian in succession with the rhythm pattern $\frac{2}{4}$ ♪ ♩ ♫ :

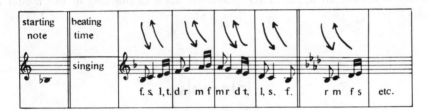

MAKING THE KEY SIGNATURES FOR THE CHURCH MODES CONSCIOUS

Quite apart from singing the modes it is also necessary for the students to be able to take in their key signatures, their belonging to the given tonal system quickly, and to see clearly the interrelationship between the modes, since the music of the Renaissance style uses these modes exclusively.

In making the process conscious there are two stages, which complement each other.

1. The teacher names the mode and its key signature and the students give the name of the keynote of the mode. For example:

a) Teacher: Which is the mixolydian with two sharps?
   Student: A mixolydian. (That is the mode beginning from the note "s" in the system with two sharps.)
b) Teacher: Which is the lydian with five flats?
   Student: G flat lydian. (That is the mode beginning from "f" in the system which has five flats.)

etc.

201

2. The teacher names the mode and its keynote and the students determine the key signature of the mode. For example:

a) Teacher: What is the key signature for F# dorian?

   Student: 4 sharps. (Since the dorian starts from "r", the named note, F# is the note "r" in the system required; and if F# is "r", then "d" will be E; therefore we are in the system using the key signature of 4 sharps.)

b) Teacher: What is the key signature for C phrygian?

   Student: 4 flats. (Since the phrygian starts from "m", the given C is "m" in the system required; if C is "m", then "d" is Ab; therefore we are in the key signature of 4 flats.)

etc.

These practice forms should be returned to from time to time so that the students will have an opportunity to become used to thinking in the model key system.

Intervals

Thirds in the harmonic minor

1. (M) Sing a sequence of thirds in D harmonic minor to solfa.
a) Ascending:

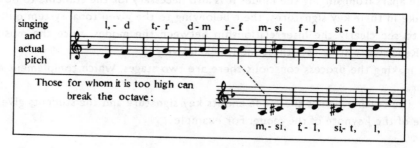

b) Descending:

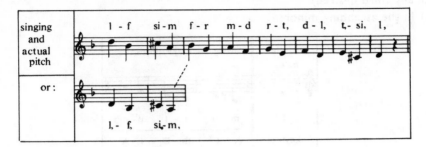

2. (M) Practise the sequences in 1. using solfa + note name singing as well. For example, descending:

3. (M) Sing the sequences given above (1. and 2.) in D♯ harmonic minor, too.

4. (M) After giving the keynote D, practise only the minor thirds as they come in order in the tonality, first to solfa, then to note names, beginning with any minor third.

a) In the ascending harmonic minor:

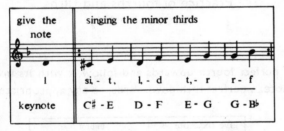

b) In the descending harmonic minor:

5. (M) In a similar way sing only the major thirds in D harmonic minor (beginning with any third desired).

a) In the ascending minor:

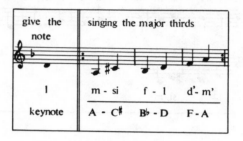

give the note	singing the major thirds
l	m - si f - l d'- m'
keynote	A - C♯ B♭ - D F - A

b) In the descending minor:

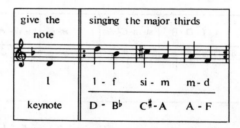

give the note	singing the major thirds
l	l - f si - m m - d
keynote	D - B♭ C♯-A A - F

6. (M) Practise the exercises in 4. and 5. in D♯ harmonic minor as well.

Practice of fourths and fifths
(List on page *131*)

1. (M) Sing a perfect fourth upwards and follow it with its inversion from the same starting note, a perfect fifth downwards, to any appropriate solfa names:

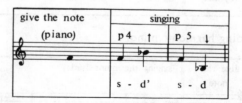

give the note (piano)	singing	
	p 4 ↑	p 5 ↓
	s - d'	s - d

Then sing this same pair of intervals using all solfa name possibilities of the major and harmonic minor keys:

```
           p4 ↑        p5 ↓
    s  -  d'      s  -  d
    l  -  r'      l  -  r
    t  -  m'      t  -  m
    d  -  f       d  -  f,
    r  -  s       r  -  s,
    m  -  l       m  -  l,
```

Following this, establish which major keys and which harmonic minor keys the perfect fourth (and perfect fifth) sung from the given starting note F to the various solfa names appear in:

```
    s  -  d'      s  -  d  ·  B♭ major
    l  -  r'      l  -  r  =  A♭ major,  F minor
    t  -  m'      t  -  m  =  G♭ major,  E♭minor
    d  -  f       d  -  f, =  F  major,  D minor
    r  -  s       r  -  s, =  E♭ major
    m  -  l       m  -  l, ·  D♭ major,  B♭ minor
```

Repeat this sequence starting from as many different notes as possible.

2. (M) Practise the downward perfect fourth and its inversion similarly, for example, from E:

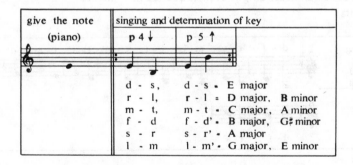

give the note	singing and determination of key		
(piano)	p 4 ↓	p 5 ↑	
d - s,	d - s · E major		
r - l,	r - l = D major,	B minor	
m - t,	m - t · C major,	A minor	
f - d	f - d' · B major,	G♯ minor	
s - r	s - r' · A major		
l - m	l - m' · G major,	E minor	

Use this exercise from various starting notes.

3. (M) Sing the sequence of perfect fifth upwards — perfect fourth downwards as in 1. For example, from D♯:

give the note	singing and determination of key	
(piano)	p 5 ↑	p 4 ↓

(musical staff notation)

d - s	d - s. • (the key signature would need 9 sharps)
r - l	r - l. • C♯ major, A♯ minor
m - t	m - t, • B major, G♯ minor
f - d'	f - d • (the key signature would need 10 sharps)
s - r'	s - r • (the key signature would need 8 sharps)
l - m'	l - m • F♯ major, D♯ minor

Sing the same progression from different starting notes.

4. (M) Similarly practise the perfect fifth downwards — perfect fourth upwards sequence. For example, starting from E♭:

give the note	singing and determination of key	
(piano)	p 5 ↓	p 4 ↑

(musical staff notation)

s - d	s - d' • A♭ major
l - r	l - r' • G♭ major, E♭ minor
t - m	t - m' • (the key signature would need 8 flats)
d - f,	d - f • E♭ major, C minor
r - s,	r - s • D♭ major
m - l,	m - l • C♭ major, A♭ minor

Sing the exercise from various starting notes.

5. (M) Practise an ascending fourth sequence in F major.

a) To solfa:

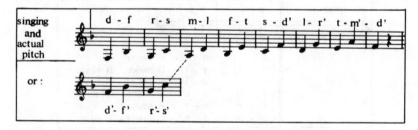

b) Singing to solfa + note names:

6. (M) Practise a descending fourth sequence, too, in F major.

a) To solfa:

b) Singing to solfa + note names:

7. (M) Sing the sequence of fourths as described under 5. and 6. but now in F♯ major.

8. (M) Sing the major key's augmented fourth in F major in the following way:

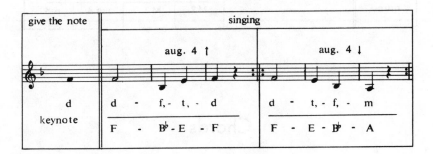

give the note	singing	
	aug. 4 ↑	aug. 4 ↓
d	d - f, - t, - d	d - t, - f, - m
keynote	F - B♭ - E - F	F - E - B♭ - A

9. (M) Practise the augmented fourth in F♯ major, too (see 8.).

The intervals of the diatonic pentachords

(Pentachord = five adjacent notes in a given system — in this case diatony.)

1. (M) Choosing any pitch sing any diatonic pentachord upwards to solfa, and

then each of the intervals from the basic note, starting with the smallest, the intervals being named afterwards. For example, the intervals of the ascending pentachord from "s":

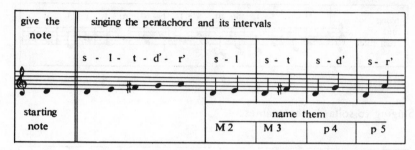

give the note	singing the pentachord and its intervals				
	s - l - t - d'- r'	s - l	s - t	s - d'	s- r'
starting note			name them		
		M 2	M 3	p 4	p 5

etc.

2. (M) Practise in similar way the intervals of descending pentachords, too. For example the descending pentachord from "t":

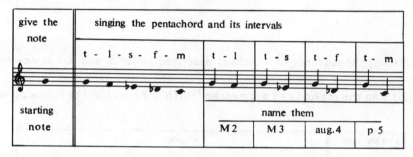

give the note	singing the pentachord and its intervals				
	t - l - s - f - m	t - l	t - s	t - f	t - m
starting note			name them		
		M 2	M 3	aug.4	p 5

etc.

Chords

In the Renaissance, but even more so in the baroque and Viennese classical styles a very important part is played by harmonic thinking. The fundamental harmony in these styles is the chord built from thirds, which in its simplest form appears as a diatonic triad. Chord singing practice should thus begin with this triad.

Triads in the major and harmonic minor keys

A triad is built on every note in both major and minor. The structure of each identical — consisting of two thirds one above the other:

Their sound is, however, different because of the different kinds of thirds used.

THE TYPES OF TRIADS

The third structure of the major key triads:

(The degree number of the chords — that is, from which degree of the scale they start — is always indicated by a Roman figure.)

The third structure of the harmonic minor key triads:

(Since the leading note of the harmonic minor is not indicated in the key signature, it must be pointed out in the degree number sign. The basic principles involved in this method of indication are as follows:

a) If the accidental comes before the lowest note in the chord then it is marked below the Roman figure. For example, the VII degree = $\text{VII}_\sharp$.

b) If it is the third from the bass that is altered, it is marked beside the Roman figure, to its right. For example, degree V = V♯.

c) If any other note in the chord is altered, an Arabic figure is written to indicate the interval between the lowest note and the altered note and the accidental is then placed beside this Arabic figure. For example, degree III = $\text{III}^5_\sharp$)

209

The four kinds of third structure occurring in the major and harmonic minor are:

a)	b)	c)	d)
↑ 3 3	↑ 3 3	↑ 3 3	↑ 3 3

a) That beginning with a major third — similarly to the major third major key — is the major triad.

b) That beginning with a minor third — similarly to the minor third minor key — is the minor triad.

c) That constructed from minor thirds — on account of its diminished fifth (see page 132) — is the diminished triad.

d) That constructed from major thirds — on account of its augmented fifth (see page 132) — is the augmented triad.

How these types occur in the major and harmonic minor:

The name of the type	Third structure	Intervals in relation to root	Where it occurs	
			in major	in harmonic minor
Major	] m 3] M 3	] M 3] p 5	I, IV, V,	V, VI
Minor	] M 3] m 3	] m 3] p 5	II, III, VI	I, IV
Diminished	] m 3] m 3	] m 3] dim. 5	VII	II, VII
Augmented	] M 3] M 3	] M 3] aug. 5	——	III

Singing exercises with the triads

1. (M) Sing the triad sequence in F major, first using solfa, then note names.

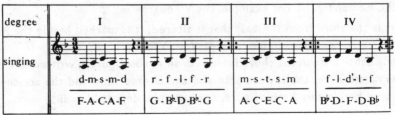

degree	I	II	III	IV
singing	d-m-s-m-d	r-f-l-f-r	m-s-t-s-m	f-l-d'-l-f
	F-A-C-A-F	G-B♭-D-B♭-G	A-C-E-C-A	B♭-D-F-D-B♭

210

V	VI	VII	
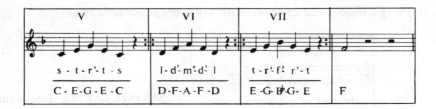			
s - t - r¹- t - s	l- d²- m²d² l	t - r¹- f² r¹- t	
C - E-G - E - C	D -F-A -F -D	E -G- B♭G- E	F

Those with high voices should start in the one-line octave and only go down an octave after III:

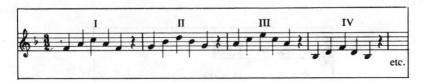

etc.

2. (M) Sing the triad sequence in D harmonic minor, too.

degree	I	II	III⁵ˢʰ	IV
singing	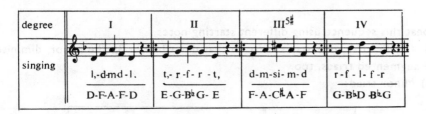			
	l,-d-m-d -l.	t, - r -f- r - t,	d-m-si- m- d	r-f - l- f -r
	D-F-A-F-D	E -G-B♭G- E	F- A-C♯A -F	G-B♭D -B♭G

V♯	VI	VII	
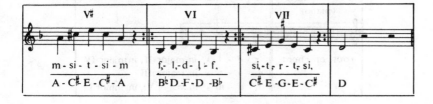			
m - si- t - si - m	f,- l,-d- l- f,	si,-t, r - t, si,	
A - C♯E -C♯-A	B♭D -F-D -B♭	C♯ E -G-E-C♯	D

If this is too high for those with lower voices they can break the octave after II:

II	III⁵ˢʰ	
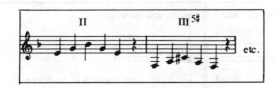		etc.

211

3. (M) Sing a major triad upwards, with any appropriate solfa names:

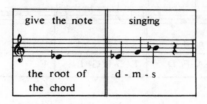

give the note	singing
the root of the chord	d - m - s

and then sing this same major triad with all the solfa names it could have in major and harmonic minor, and name the degree of the sung chord within the tonality (see page *210*):

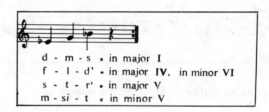

d - m - s . in major **I**
f - l - d' - in major **IV**, in minor **VI**
s - t - r' . in major **V**
m - si - t . in minor **V**

Repeat this sequence using different starting notes.

4. (M) Practise, in a way similar to that described in 3., the minor, diminished and augmented triads, too.

a) Minor triad:

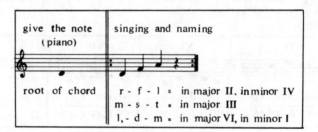

give the note (piano)	singing and naming
root of chord	r - f - l = in major **II**, in minor **IV**
	m - s - t . in major **III**
	l, - d - m . in major **VI**, in minor **I**

b) Diminished triad:

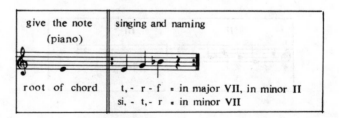

give the note (piano)	singing and naming
root of chord	t, - r - f . in major **VII**, in minor **II**
	si, - t, - r . in minor **VII**

212

c) Augmented triad:

give the note (piano)	singing tonal framework + the augm. chord	name
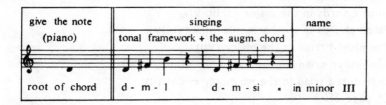		
root of chord	d - m - l d - m - si ▪ in minor	III

In this case evocation of the tonic note "I", and secure hearing of it, make pure intonation of the augmented chord's leading note "si" possible. Later, once the students are able to hear the augmented chord on its own, the introductory bar (tonal framework) determining the tonality naturally can — indeed must — be omitted from the singing.

Practise singing the above chord types from various starting notes.

5. (M) Sing the major chords as they come in order in the tonality — after giving the tonic of the key with one flat — first to solfa, then to note names.

a) Upwards in F major:

tonic (piano)	I	IV	V
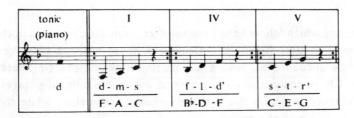			
d	d - m - s	f - l - d'	s - t - r'
	F - A - C	B♭-D -F	C - E - G

If the first chord lies too low, begin with IV:

tonic (piano)	IV	V	I

b) Upwards in D harmonic minor:

tonic (piano)	V♯	VI
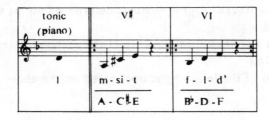		
l	m - si - t	f - l - d'
	A - C♯E	B♭-D -F

213

6. (M) Similarly practise the minor, diminished and augmented chords in the keys with one flat.

    a) Minor chords in the major (II, III, VI).

    b) Minor chords in the harmonic minor (I, IV).

    c) Diminished triad in the major (VII).

    d) Diminished triads in the harmonic minor (II, VII).

    e) Augmented triad in the harmonic minor (III).

    (Cf. page *210*.)

Singing of these series should always be begun with the triad which is most suitable for the student or group actually singing from the voice. range point of view. The essential point is that after the initial chord the others should follow in their ascending order within the tonality.

7. (M) Practise the exercises described in 1, 2, 5 and 6 in a similar way within the major and harmonic minor with a key signature of six sharps.

Chord analysis

The quotations which follow have been selected from various works in the baroque and Viennese classical styles. In the music of these extracts only root position triads will be encountered, with a few passing notes or changing notes as ornamentation. Chord analysis should be carried out in the following stages:

1. The teacher performs the quotation chosen for analysis while the students listen and follow it in the music.

2. The students name the key of the extract on the basis of sound and reading the music.

3. While the teacher performs the extract again the students accompany him by solfa singing of the lowest part — that is, the bass.

4. The students

    a) sing through all the individual chords in broken form, from the lowest note using note names;

    b) establish the degrees on this basis;

    c) name the ornamental notes alien to the chords.

5. The teacher writes the degree numbers determined during the chord analysis on the blackboard.

6. The students sing the chord sequence of the analysed quotation in different ways. (See page *216*.)

Here is an analysis of the following extract based on the above steps.

122. MOZART: THE MAGIC FLUTE. I. (or.: 1♯)

1. Performance.
2. Key: F major.
3. Second performance with singing of the bass to solfa:

$$\frac{2}{4}\text{d} \quad |\text{s,d s, } |\text{s, } |\text{d s, d }\|$$

4. Note name singing and naming of the chords:

Singing and naming	Alien notes
bar 1	
F A C . I	passing note / accented upper changing note / accented lower changing note
bar 2	
C-E-G . V F-A-C . I C-E-G . V	————
bar 3	
C-E-G . V	————
bar 4	
F-A-C . I C-E-G . V F-A-C . I	————

215

5. The teacher writes the chord progression on the blackboard:

I V I V V I V I

From the harmonic aspect the quotation consists of no more than an alternation of tonic and dominant.

6. Practice of the chords in the extract analysed.

Since in the above extract it was the same pattern which occurred all the time, it will be enough to sing the first three chords, as the others are precise repetition of them. Thus the chord progression to be sung is: I—V—I in the major.

	Stages in singing	Practical realization
Solfa singing	a) The sequence of the lowest notes in the chords sung as a separate part	d - s, d
	b) Singing the chords in broken from	d-m-s s,- t,- r d-m-s
Note name singing (in any of the key signatures practised so far; e.g. in F#major)	a) The sequence of the lowest notes in the chords sung as a separate part	F# - C# - F#
	b) Singing the chords in broken from	F# A#-C# C# E#- G# F# A# C#

Transpose the chord progression into other major keys as well — C, C# or Cb major — and sing also transforming it, that is, instead of major within the harmonic minor. The steps in the singing and the practical realization are the same as for the major. (In the minor "I" is 1!)

QUOTATIONS FOR CHORD ANALYSIS PURPOSES

123. J. S. BACH: ERMUNTRE DICH, MEIN SCHWACHER GEIST. CHORALE. (or.: 1#)

124. MOZART: THE MARRIAGE OF FIGARO. OVERTURE. (or.: 2♯)

125. MOZART: THE MAGIC FLUTE. II.

126. MOZART: THE MAGIC FLUTE. II. (or.: 2♭)

127. J. HAYDN: PIANO SONATA IN G MAJOR. III. (or.: 2♭)

In this quotation diatonic and altered changing notes occur as ornamental notes.

128. MOZART: THE MAGIC FLUTE. II. (or.: 2♯)

129. J. S. BACH: ALS DER GÜTIGE GOTT. CHORALE. (or.: 1♯)

130. MOZART: THE MAGIC FLUTE. I. (or.: 3♭)

131. HANDEL: PIANO SUITE IN G MINOR. PASSACAGLIA. (or.: 2♭)

A typical sequential progression from the baroque style, the range of which uses, with the exception of the cadential dominant, the notes of the natural minor. The last chord pattern of the authentic sequence, however, always gives the dominant — tonic progression using the leading note "si".

SIGHT-SINGING

Unison Extracts from the Musical Literature

MATERIAL USING STAFF NOTATION

Pentatonic range

132. KODÁLY: TE DEUM

a) (or.: 3♭)

b) (or.: 0)

133. BARTÓK: BLUEBEARD'S CASTLE.

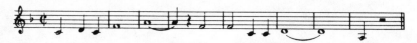

a)

b)

134. LISZT: DIE HEILIGE CÄCILIA. LEGENDE. (or.: 0)

135. LISZT: MISSA CHORALIS. KYRIE.

136. VAUGHAN WILLIAMS: THE HOUSE OF LIFE.

137. BRITTEN: PETER GRIMES. I.

138. DVOŘÁK: SONATINA IN G MAJOR, OP. 100. III. (or.: 0)

139. BARTÓK: BLUEBEARD'S CASTLE.

140. KODÁLY: TE DEUM.

a)

(or.: 1♯)

b)

(or.: 1♯

c)

(or.: 2♯)

d)

141. MUSSORGSKY: KHOVANSHTCHINA. I. (or.: 3♯)

142. KODÁLY: TWO SONGS, OP. 5.

143. LISZT: INNO A MARIA VERGINE (or.: 2♯)

144. KODÁLY: PSALMUS HUNGARICUS. (or.: 3♯)

145. STRAVINSKY: THE WEDDING. (or.: 2♯)

146. PUCCINI: TURANDOT. II. (or.: 2♭)

147. KODÁLY: TE DEUM. (or.: 4♯)

148. BORODIN: SYMPHONY IN A MINOR. II. (or.: 2♭)

149. PUCCINI: TURANDOT. III. (or.: 0)

150. VAUGHAN WILLIAMS: A PIPER.

151. KODÁLY: SEVEN SONGS, OP. 6.

152. RAVEL: L'ENFANT ET LES SORTILÈGES.

153. BRITTEN: PETER GRIMES. I. (or.: 3♯)

Diatonic range

154. MONTEVERDI: L'INCORONAZIONE DI POPPEA. I.

155. HANDEL: TAMERLANO. I.

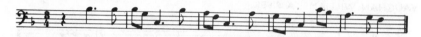

156. HANDEL: TAMERLANO. III.

157. H. PURCELL: HAIL! BRIGHT CECILIA. ODE. (or.: 2♯)

158. J. S. BACH: CANTATA, NO. 212. (or.: 1♯)

159. HANDEL: SAUL. I. (or.: 1♯)

160. HANDEL: SAUL. III. (or.: 1♯)

161. J. HAYDN: MASS IN B FLAT MAJOR. (or.: 2♯)

Range including altered notes

162. H. PURCELL: THE HISTORY OF DIOCLESIAN.

163. HANDEL: RODELINDA. I. (or.: 2♭)

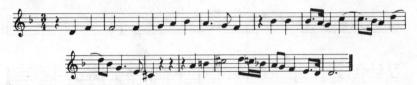

164. H. PURCELL: THE HISTORY OF DIOCLESIAN. (or.: 0)

165. J. S. BACH: CANTATA, NO. 213. (or.: 2♭)

166. LULLY: ISIS. II.

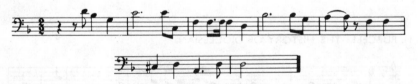

167. G. CACCINI: AMARILLI. (or.: 2♭)

226

168. MOZART: THE MAGIC FLUTE. I. (or.: 0)

169. LULLY: PHAÉTON. I. (or.: 2♭)

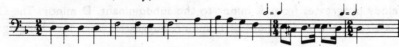

Modulating melodies

170. J. S. BACH: CANTATA, NO 112. (or.: 1♯)

The melody begins in D minor and, after the F major of bars 5 and 6, ends in A minor. The change of "d" should come at the last note of bar 6 — the tied note:

171. J. S. BACH: CANTATA, NO 208. (or.: 1♭)

The melody progresses from A minor to the subdominant, D minor. The C♯ of bar 13 is already the leading-note of D minor. Suggested place for changing "d":

172. LULLY: PROSERPINE. I. (or.: 2♭)

The music moves from D minor to A minor. The change of key occurs in bar 5:

228

EXTRACTS IN SOLFA LETTERS

The following extracts should be sung only to note names, using the key signatures with one flat or six sharps, accompanying with beating time.

173. J. S. BACH: NUN RUHEN ALLE WÀLDER. CHORALE. (or.: 4♭)

c m | d r m f s | f m m f | s s r m | d t, s, | d r m m | r m |

d r m f s | f m m f | s s r m | d t, s, | d r m f | m r d ||

174. MONTEVERDI: L'INCORONAZIONE DI POPPEA. I. (or.: 2♯)

⁶₄ m r d dd | s m f s r | d t, d r m r d t, | l, s, l, t, d d d t, | d _ _ ||

175. J. S. BACH: GOTT DES HIMMELS UND DER ERDEN. CHORALE. (or.: 4♭)

c d r m f s | d t, l, s, | l, t, d r | m f r d ‖ m m r m | f m r r d r |

l, t, d r | m f r d t, d ‖

176. LULLY: ALCESTE. II.

³₄ l' l' | m' m' f' | d' | t t d' | s | m m m | f f | s s | d ||

177. J. S. BACH: WENN MEIN STÜNDLEIN VORHANDEN IST. CHORALE. (or.: 3♯)

c d | s, l, t, d | r m r d m f | s s f m f s | f m m | f m r d r | m m d m f |

s s m f s | f m m | f m r d r | m m d r | m m l, t, | d t, l, s, s, |

d r m r m | f m r | d ‖

178. J. HAYDN: THE SEASONS. IV. (or.: 0)

t, t, t, l, t, d dd | r rr d r m mm | r m f s, l, t, d d ||

179. J. S. BACH: WER IN DEM SCHUTZ DES HÖCHSTEN. CHORALE. (or.: 3♯)

d t, d | r r d r | m f | m r d t, d | r d : d r m f |

m r d r d t, | l, t, s, s, r m | f m r d | s m m | r d t, d | r d ||

180. J. S. BACH: NUN BITTEN WIR DEN HEILIGEN GEIST. CHORALE. (or.: 3♯)

d | r r d t, | l, s, l, t, | d m f | s l s f | m r d t, l, t, | d m m |

m r m | d d r m f | m r m d | r m f m r d t, | l, s, d r m | r d t, l, |

s, l, t, | d r | d ||

181. MOZART: IL SERAGLIO. I.

m, d | f, r | s, m | l, f f t, t, s s m | m m f r s s, d ||

Material in Several Parts

182. RHAU: VOR ALL'N ICH KRÖN'. (Bicinium.)

183. RHAU: ZUCHT, EHR UND LOB IHR WOHNET BEI. (Bicinium.)

184. GIARDINI: VIVA TUTTE LE VEZZOSE.

185. PALESTRINA: CANON.

186. CALDARA: CANON.

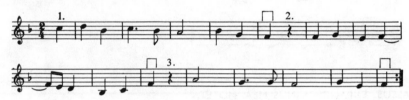

187. GASTOLDI: MOTET.

233

188. CHERUBINI: CANON.

189. LASSUS: EXPANDI MANUS MEA. MOTET.

In this motet appears the characteristic 11 degree set of notes of the so called Palestrina style. The special feature of this range of notes is that along with the 7 diatonic notes appear the leading notes of the dorian, mixolydian and aeolian modes (see page *200*) — "di", "fi", "si" — and the note "ta" which neutralises the f—t augmented fourth (or t,—f diminished fifth). In the music there is thus constant alternation of the notes d—di, f—fi, s—si and t—ta, depending on the melodic or harmonic progression of the moment. Since the music does not move outside this 11 degree framework, the "d" of the range of notes does not change either.

On this basis the above motet should be sung throughout with F as "d".

190. PALESTRINA: ET MISERICORDIA. MOTET.

This motet also uses the 11 degree range of notes mentioned above. All the altered notes of the style occur in the music — "fi", "di", "si" and "ta": sing it without changing "d".

191. MOZART: THE MAGIC FLUTE. I. (or.: 1♯)

192. J. HAYDN: CANON.

193. H. PURCELL: KING ARTHUR. II. (or.: 1♯)

In this extract the leading-notes of the relative dorian and aeolian modes ("di" and "si"), and also "ta" occur. This range of notes thus still preserves the Renaissance traditions.

194. LULLY: ISIS. PROLOGUE. (or.: 1♯)

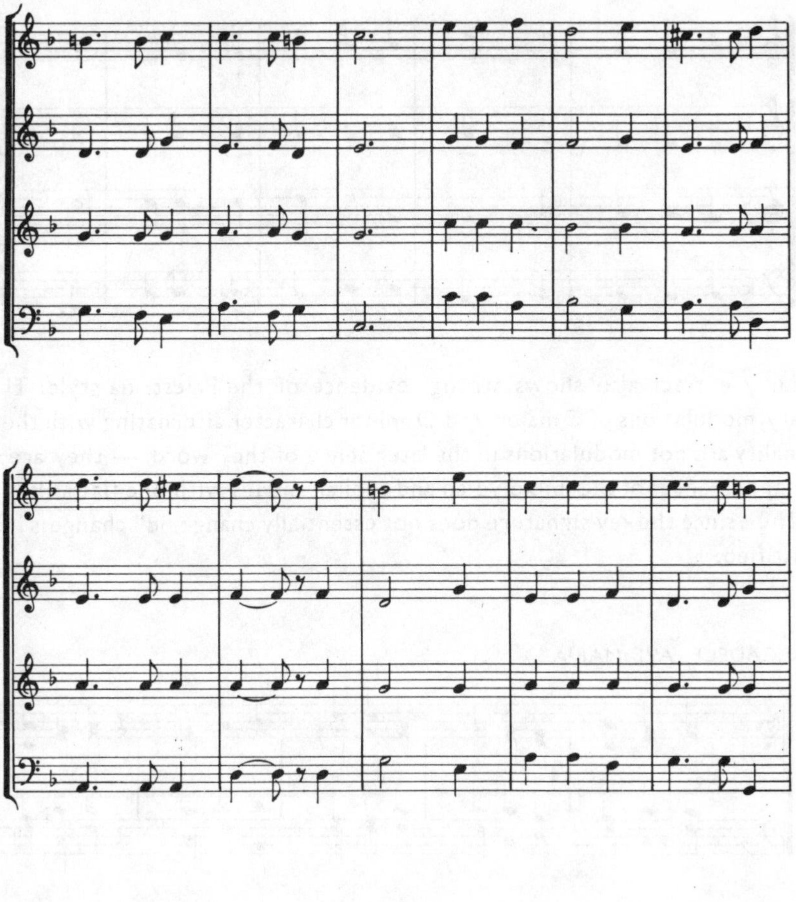

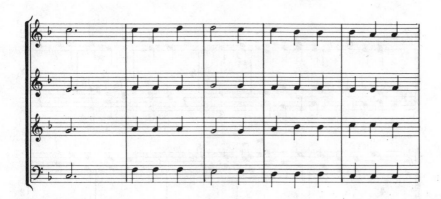

This Lully extract also shows strong evidence of the Palestrina style. The momentary modulations of C major and D minor character alternating with the F major tonality are not modulations in the later sence of the word — they are merely the appearances of the mixolydian and aeolian modes with one flat as key signature. Thus, since the key signature does not essentially change, "d" change is likewise not justified.

195. ARCADELT: AVE MARIA.

In this choral work the wavering in s—si and f—fi is here, too, a Renaissance stylistic feature. "Si" is the leading-note of the relative aeolian mode, having the same key signature, and "fi" that of the relative mixolydian. Sing the music with the same "d" throughout.

196. J. HAYDN: CANON.

DEVELOPMENT OF MUSICAL MEMORY

Memorizing and Transposing a Unison Melody

Memorizing of melodies from solfa letters and from hand-signs can now be omitted. For learning melodies from staff notation we can use the pentatonic and diatonic melodies with more difficult rhythms in the sight-singing material, and also the easier extracts which include altered notes. At this level we should still not ask the students to memorize modulating musical material.

Checking the learned melody takes the following stages:

1. Solfa singing of the memorized melody, accompanied by beating time, at the pitch given by the staff notation.

2. Solfa singing + hand-sign melody illustration (in the case of pentatonic and diatonic extracts).

3. Note name singing, accompanied by beating time, in the given "d" system.

4. Writing down the learned musical material in staff notation (likewise using the given "d" system).

5. Description and discussion of the rhythm pattern in bars where the rhythm is difficult.

6. As control, singing of the melody written down in the exercise books, using note names and accompanying with beating the metrical unit.

Once the students feel securely at home in the new key signatures — one flat and six sharps — they should try transposed singing of the melody which has been memorized, using any of the "d" systems practised so far (with C, C♯, C♭, F or F♯ as "d").

For successful **transposition** there are **two basic conditions:**

1. It is necessary to know the melody to be transposed by heart precisely, to solfa.

2. It is necessary to know exactly and consciously the key signature system ("d" system) into which we wish to transpose the memorized melody.

Transposition of the melody which has been learned should only be attempted once the students have written it down according to the original staff notation and have then checked this.

1. Repeat the melody by heart to solfa
a) at the original pitch b) at the pitch of the key chosen for transposition.
2. Following this, sing the extract with the note names of the transposition "d" system (and at that pitch), accompanying with beating time, in groups and individually until the performance is faultless.

Memorizing Two-Part Material

Sight-singing in two parts of the chosen extract (see page 155.1) can now be omitted from the learning process used so far (see page 155) and memorizing should be managed by the students with the help of no more than their inner hearing — after being given the note "d". This can only be successful if memorizing the unison melodies using F as "d" or F# as "d" has been given intensive practice.

THE TWO-PART EXTRACTS

197. KODÁLY: 77 TWO-PART EXERCISES.

d) № 71.

e) № 5.

198. MOZART: PIANO SONATA IN B FLAT MAJOR. I. (K. 333)

199. MOZART: 12 DUOS. (K. 487)

(or.: 1♯)

a) № 5.

(or.: 1♯)

b) № 5.

(or.: 3♯)

c) № 4.

(or.: 1♯)

d) № 1.

200. J. HAYDN: PIANO SONATA IN D MAJOR. III. (or.: 2♯)

201. KODÁLY: 77 TWO-PART EXERCISES. No. 35.

202. D. SCARLATTI: SONATA IN A MINOR.

203. TELEMANN: ALLEGRO. (or.: 1♯)

246

204 LASSUS: MOTET.

205. HANDEL: SAMSON. I.

206. WITTHAUER: GAVOTTE. (or.: 0)

EAR TRAINING

Recognition of Intervals

The intervals of pentatony within the seventh range

This form of practice should be continued in the way described in Chapter II (see page *159*).

Interval recognition from "Let Us Sing Correctly"

Of the exercises already sung Nos. 10, 11, 13, 16, 18, 20, 28, 32, 33 can be used for this purpose, as follows:

   1. The exercise chosen is performed by the teacher in two parts—one singing to "la-la", the other playing on the piano — while the students note down the various intervals with a figure and the appropriate description.

   2. During a second performance the students check their noting of the intervals and fill in what they omitted the first time.

   3. At the third performance the students name the individual intervals.

   4. After mutual checking (written in 3.) they sing the intervals, first upwards and then downwards: a) to solfa b) to note names. For example, exercise 20:

   1. Recognition.

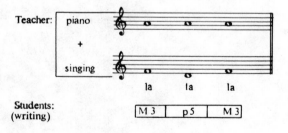

2. Individual checking.

3. Group checking, with naming: major third, perfect fifth, etc.

4. Singing, upwards, then downwards.

a) To solfa:

d - m   l,- m   d - m   m-d   etc.

b) To note names (after the teacher's naming the first note):

F - A   D-A   F- A   A- F   etc.

Thirds in major and harmonic minor keys

1. On any instrument and at any appropriate pitch the teacher plays the harmonic minor's four minor thirds in their order beginning with any particular one he chooses, with the melodic line progressing upwards or downwards; and the students, after listening to this melodic sequence, sing it from memory with the appropriate solfa names.

Possibilities for the minor thirds sequence:

	upwards	downwards	
a)	si, - t, - l, - d, - t, - r - r - f	f - r - r - t, - d - l, - t, - si,	e)
b)	l, - d, - t, - r, - r - f, - si - t	t - si, - f - r, - r - t, - d - l,	f)
c)	t, - r, - r - f, - si - t, - l - d'	d' - l, - t - si, - f - r, - r - t,	g)
d)	r - f, - si - t, - l - d' - t - r'	r' - t, - d' - l - t - si, - f - r,	h)

249

For example, b) and g) in practice:

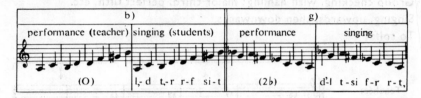

b)		g)	
performance (teacher)	singing (students)	performance	singing
(0)	l‚-d t‚-r r-f si-t	(2♭)	d‹-l t-si f-r r-t,

2. In a similar way practise the harmonic minor's major thirds, too. (These major thirds are d—m; m—si; f—l; see page *131*.)

3. If recognition of the above harmonic minor progressions is coped with confidently and with sufficient speed, this form of ear training should be used for alternating minor and major thirds in major and minor keys. For example,

   a) minor thirds in the major key, descending, starting from "r";
   b) major thirds in the minor key, ascending, starting from "f";
   c) major thirds in the major key, descending, starting from "l". In practice:

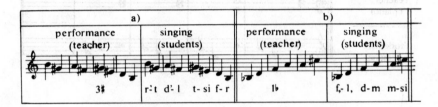

a)		b)	
performance (teacher)	singing (students)	performance (teacher)	singing (students)
3♯	r‹-t d‹-l t- si f- r	1♭	f‚-l, d-m m-si

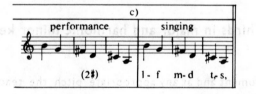

c)	
performance	singing
(2♯)	l- f m- d t‚- s,

etc.

Recognition of pairs of thirds heard together

Practise recognition by ear of the pairs of thirds which are heard one above the other within the major and harmonic minor keys $\left(\frac{m3}{M3} \quad \frac{M3}{m3} \quad \frac{m3}{m3} \quad \frac{M3}{M3}\right)$ as follows:

a) The teacher performs the above pairs of thirds in any order, in relation to a central note, which is given in advance on the piano and remains unchanged,

b) while the students analyse the thirds as they sound together, by ear, and write them down and then, after group checking, they sing the thirds with the possible appropriate solfa names in major and harmonic minor.

For example, practising the sequence $\frac{m3}{M3}$ $\frac{m3}{m3}$ $\frac{M3}{M3}$ $\frac{m3}{M3}$ $\frac{M3}{m3}$

1. Recognition. Teacher: (piano)

Students:	m 3	m 3	M 3	m 3	M 3
(writing)	M 3	m 3	M 3	M 3	m 3

2. Individual checking and filling in omissions. (If necessary the teacher plays the sequence several times.)

3. Group checking by naming the pairs of thirds: $\frac{m3}{M3}$ etc.

4. Solfa singing starting from the middle note (using all the names which can occur in the major and harmonic minor keys):

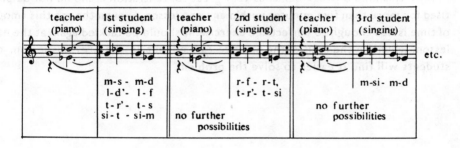

teacher (piano)	1st student (singing)	teacher (piano)	2nd student (singing)	teacher (piano)	3rd student (singing)
	m-s - m-d		r-f - r-t,		m-si- m-d
	l-d'- l- f		t-r'- t- si		
	t-r'- t-s				
	si- t - si-m	no further		no further	
		possibilities		possibilities	

etc.

Rhythm Dictation

(Musical material on page 405.)

When the time signature ¢ appears in the extracts it is necessary to draw the students' attention to the fact that the metrical unit is the half note (♩), for otherwise they will interpret the rhythm patterns in diminution (that is in $\frac{2}{4}$ instead of $\frac{2}{2}$). Apart from this the stages for practising are the same as hitherto (see page 79).

Kodály: 24 Little Canons

These exercises prepare for two-part melody dictation. The teacher plays the melody on some instrument and the students sing it in canon beginning one bar later by ear, to solfa — possibly to note names as well. With regard to this last kind of singing the melodies should be played and sung in the "d" system practised in the chapter.

Practice of canons 1, 2, 3 and 5 can be included in this chapter, at the pitch using F as "d". The canon should be sung — according to the directions to be found in the music — an octave lower than the first part played on the instrument.

At the beginning the singing in canon should be preceded by playing the whole exercise on the instrument like a unison melody so that the students can clearly hear the melody's tonality, the relationship between first and last notes, and the tonal function of the individual motifs, even before coming to the two-part work.

The second part should to begin with be sung as a group. After two or three repetitions any student can try singing the canon part as a solo. If this is not successful, we must return to group performance.

Since this kind of work demands very great concentration it should not be practised for more than five minutes within any one lesson — even though this amount of time is not enough to perfect the exercise. It should be tackled again at the next lesson, when, on the basis of the practice carried out in the previous lesson, the students will find it easier to solve the problem.

Melody Dictation

(Musical material on page 408.)

The stages in preparation are the same as they were in Chapter II (see page 162). The only difference is that whereas earlier the practice was carried out in the system with C as "d" here — in keeping with the given musical material — all the work is related to F as "d".

The procedure for melody dictation (see page 164) is to be slightly modified in its first point, since alongside the major extracts there are now minor melodies as well:

1. Perform the melody (together with its accompaniment) and ask the students to pay special attention to a) the set of notes used (pentatonic or diatonic), b) the solfa name of the final note and c) the key, if the melody is diatonic (whether it is major or minor).

Points 2—9 remain valid as described in Chapter II.

Bach Chorale Extracts

(Musical material on page 413.)

In the procedure for study and practice (see page 164) the first point is modified here, too:

1. During the first performance the students should notice a) the key of the extract (whether it is major or minor) and b) the last and the first notes of the bass part.

Points 2—8 remain unchanged.

PLANNING SUGGESTION

(See the diagram at the end of the book)

CHAPTER IV.

(The staff notation material in the chapter has B and B flat as "d")

KODÁLY MATERIAL

Unison Pentatonic Melodies

MATERIAL USING SOLFA LETTERS: PENTATONIC MUSIC I—IV

Familiar elements

RHYTHMIC OR METRIC FEATURES

I/71

In this melody a $\frac{2}{4}$ bar is inserted among the $\frac{4}{4}$ bars. Singing accompanied by an ostinato can be managed by using the first or the second half of the $\frac{4}{4}$ ostinato to accompany the $\frac{2}{4}$ bar. In this way the formal asymmetry of the melody manifests itself much more vigorously than if a new rhythm accompaniment, different from the $\frac{4}{4}$ ostinato, were taken for the $\frac{2}{4}$ bar.

Ostinatos which can be used are, for example:

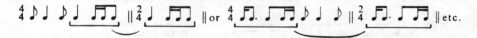

II/33

Since the lines of the melody are isorhythmic it is possible to try melody singing accompanied by the rhythm canon from memory as well, in the following stages:

a) The students sing the melody from the music and meanwhile memorize the rhythm of the isorhythmic motifs.

b) The teacher sings the melody and the students clap the rhythm canon to it from memory, at a distance of one bar.

c) One group of students sing the melody while the other group provides the rhythm canon accompaniment to it, from memory.

d) The same with the groups exchanging parts.

e) A student volunteers to sing the melody and at the same time claps or taps the rhythm canon to it.

f) The students sing the melody from memory while the teacher provides the rhythm canon.

g) A student volunteers to sing the melody from memory while another volunteer accompanies him with the rhythm canon, likewise from memory.

h) A student tries to perform the two-part exercise on his own, from memory.

i) After this has been managed successfully by several individuals, this can be carried out by the group as well, likewise from memory.

II/84

The time signature is ₵ . Practice should be accompanied first by giving the ♩ unit beat, and then by beating duple time. So that the inner stress relationships of the alla breve (₵) time signature should become conscious through the singing, care should be taken that the written third quarter — which in $\frac{4}{4}$ is given a secondary accent — remains unstressed.

III/57

In this melody, apart from the ♩ rhythmic element at the end of the motifs there are only two rhythm patterns: ♫♩ and ♫♫♩ . This feature in the rhythm makes it possible for the rhythm accompaniment to be related to the rhythm patterns in the melody and not to the metrical stress groups (that is, the bars): for example, a ♩ accompaniment to the rhythm pattern ♫♩ ,a ♫♫♩ accompaniment to the rhythm pattern ♫♫♩ , and a , ♪ accompaniment to the rhythm element ♩ . Thus the melody and its rhythm accompaniment produce the following two-part music:

melody singing + rhythm accompaniment		
$\frac{3}{4}$ ♫ ♩ ♫♫ ♩ l l d' d' l s	♫♫ ♩ ♫♫ ♩ s s s l l s m	etc.
$\frac{3}{4}$ ♩ ♫♫ , ♪	♫♫ ♫♫ , ♪	

Before two-part practising is begun it is absolutely necessary to make the connection between the melody and the accompaniment's various rhythm patterns conscious so that the students will be able to perform the rhythm accompaniment from memory without writing it down.

Two-part practice should be carried out in the following stages:

a) The students sing the melody and the teacher provides the rhythm accompaniment.

b) They exchange parts.

c) One group of students sings while the other accompanies.

d) The groups exchange parts.

e) Individual volunteers perform the tow-part exercise on their own.

f) After a few successful individual performances the two-part exercise should be given by all the members of the group together.

260

IV/80

The students should sing a) with the two part $\frac{6}{8}$ [rhythm notation] rhythm accompaniment, b) with the $\frac{6}{8}$ [rhythm notation] ostinato and c) with beating duple time on the basis of the metronome indication ($\downarrow. = 84$).

IV/86

Precise rhythmic performance of the melody here is made considerably difficult by the rhythm patterns [rhythm notation] and [rhythm notation] , and then [rhythm notation] and [rhythm notation] following each other closely. For this reason, as preparation, the following rhythm variations of bars 1—2 and 8—9 should be sung continuously and in a fast tempo, accompanied by beating the metrical unit:

a)

bars 1- 2 :	$\frac{2}{4}$ [rhythm]	[rhythm]	[rhythm]	[rhythm]	[rhythm]	[rhythm]
	l, d r m	s l s r	l,d r m	s l s r	l, d r m	s l s r
unit beat:						

b)

bars 8-9 :	$\frac{2}{4}$ [rhythm]	[rhythm]	[rhythm]	[rhythm]	[rhythm]	[rhythm]
	m s l s	r m s	m s l s	r m s	m s l s	r m s
unit beat:						

After this preparation sing the melody right through with beating the metrical unit, but the accents should not be omitted either.

IV/113

In this melody there is alternation of $\frac{3}{4}$ and $\frac{2}{4}$ bars. Here, too, we should use the kind of ostinato accompaniment in which the ostinatos associated with the two different key signatures are organically related to each other — that is, the rhythm accompaniment to the bar containing fewer metrical units is included in some form in the rhythm progression of the ostinato accompaniment of the time signature containing more units. For example:

$\frac{3}{4}$ [rhythm notation] $\frac{2}{4}$ [rhythm notation] or

$\frac{3}{4}$ [rhythm notation] $\frac{2}{4}$ [rhythm notation] etc.

(Cf. 1/71, page 259)

261

MELODIC FEATURES

The number of the melody	The melodic pattern or progression requiring practice
III/52	
II/58	
III/56	
III/59	
III/58	
II/73	
II/59	
II/77	
II/96	
IV/75	
IV/114	
II/88	
III/74	
IV/112	

Practice suggestions:

III/52

As preparation sing the following pairs of bars:

$\frac{2}{4}$ l s | m l s | l s r | m l s | l s r | m l s ‖

II/58

Sing the following pair of motifs a few times:

$\frac{2}{4}$ s l s r | m | | d¹ l s r | m | ‖

III/56

Practise this pair of motifs before singing the melody:

$\frac{2}{4}$ s s s r | m | | s s s r | d | ‖

III/59

Use this melodic progression as preparation:

$\frac{4}{4}$ m r r s | s r d | ‖

III/58

Practise the following pairs of motifs:

$\frac{2}{4}$ d m s l | m r l s | d r m l | m r l s | d r m l | r r l s | d r m m | r r l s ‖

II/73

Sing the preparatory melodic sequence in $\frac{4}{4}$:

$\frac{4}{4}$ l m r l, | r m r l | m r l, | ‖

263

However, accompany singing of the melody with beating the ♩ metrical unit, but in a very slow tempo.

II/59

In preparation practise the last two bars of the first and fourth lines of the melody in sequence:

1st line bars 3-4   4th line bars 3-4

II/77

To begin with sing the melody a few times in a very slow tempo.

II/96

This should be sung slowly to start with and accompanied by giving the ♩ unit beat; the tempo should then be made faster only gradually.

IV/75

Take the second and fourth motifs of the melody and practise them separately in a slow tempo, giving an accent on the first of every pair of eighths:

2nd motif   4th motif

As a result of these accents the intervals become separated out better and are grouped round certain tonal principal notes. This will later facilitate continuous, melodic singing of them.

IV/114

a) Sing this melodic sequence a few times:

b) In the eighth sequence in descending thirds, give a vigorous accent to the first note in the pairs of eighths:

No difficulty is presented by slow tempo singing of the motifs taken from these melodies (see page 262). Practise these individually and in groups. Singing of the complete melodies should only be attempted once the separate motifs are managed clearly and securely in the tempo considered correct.

New elements

$\frac{5}{4}$ TIME SIGNATURE = IV/108

The inner division of this compound bar is:

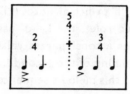

The first half of the asymmetrical combination, containing the main stress appears in the metrical role of the first half of the $\frac{4}{4}$ time signature, which is made up of $\frac{2}{4} + \frac{2}{4}$, whereas the $\frac{3}{4}$ part which holds the secondary stress is equal to the second half of the $\frac{6}{4}$ metre, made up of $\frac{3}{4} + \frac{3}{4}$. In keeping with these origins, beating time in $\frac{5}{4}$ evolves as follows:

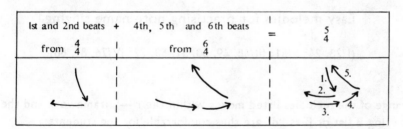

Sing the melody using solfa, then note names, a) in groups, b) individually, c) in answering form, d) alternating with inner, silent singing, and always with beating time.

THE m—r' MINOR SEVENTH INTERVAL UPWARDS = IV/115

The seventh m—r' will be a securely intonated interval in the melody if, in the given "l" pentatonic tonality, the students hear the l—r'—d' progression with certainty. The upper note of the m—r' minor seventh actually appears as a kind of upper changing note resolving onto "d".

For this reason, before singing the melody, practise the following pair of motifs:

$$\begin{array}{c}3\\4\end{array}\ \ \begin{array}{ccc}1 & d' & 1 & 1 \end{array}\ \ \Big|\ \begin{array}{ccc}r' & r' & d'\end{array}\ \ \ \ \Big|\Big|\ \begin{array}{ccc}1 & d' & m & m\end{array}\ \ \Big|\ \begin{array}{ccc}r' & r' & d'\end{array}\ \ \ \Big\|$$

THE l,—d' MINOR TENTH UPWARDS = I/59

The first two lines of the melody are connected by a minor tenth (10). Since in the first line of the melody the "l" principal notes ("l" — opening note; "l," — final note) are given a very exposed role, the l,—d' pattern is not heard or sung as an independent interval but as a tonal phrase related to the "l" principal note. If, even so, the "d" at the beginning of the second line is uncertain when it comes to singing the melody, practise this melodic sequence a few times in a slow tempo:

$$\begin{array}{c}2\\4\end{array}\ \ \begin{array}{cccc}1 & 1, & d & 1, \end{array}\ \ \Big|\ \begin{array}{cc}1, & & d' & 1\end{array}\ \ \Big|$$

Easy melodies for practising note name singing

(I/23, 24; II/51; III/48, 49, 50, 51, 53, 72; IV/76, 81, 88)

The range of the melodies listed moves within the r'—l, framework and the pitch levels using B flat or B as "d" are thus comfortable for the students:

r'— l,   r'— l,

In these two cases the notes as written are the same and the only difference is in their key signature:

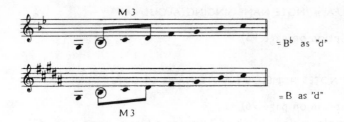

M 3

= B♭ as "d"

= B as "d"

M 3

Note name singing should first be practised in the system using B flat as "d", and singing using the note names where "d" is B should only be turned to once a certain orientation has been secured in B flat.

NOTE NAME SINGING PRACTICE FORMS

This work should only begin once the students have gained some familiarity with note name singing from hand-signs (see page 285).

SOLFA + NOTE NAME SINGING ALOUD

(Detailed description on page 95)
For example melody 1/23 of Pentatonic Music, with B flat as "d":

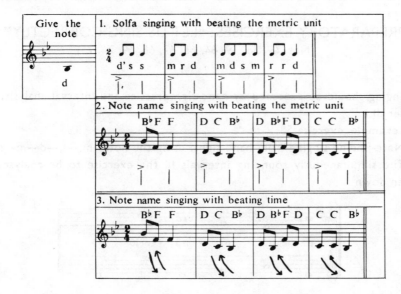

SILENT SOLFA + NOTE NAME SINGING ALOUD

(See description on page 95)

RANGE OF NOTES + MELODY NOTE NAME SINGING

(See description on page 96)

For example, melody III/48 of Pentatonic Music, using B as "d":

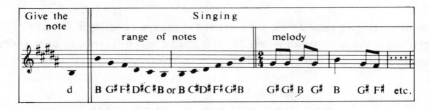

Give the note	Singing	
	range of notes	melody
d	B G♯ F♯ D♯ C♯ B or B C♯ D♯ F♯ G♯ B	G♯ G♯ B G♯ B G♯ F♯ etc.

SIGHT-SINGING TO NOTE NAMES

(See page 96)

Two-Part Material

PREPARATORY EXERCISES: "LET US SING CORRECTLY"
(Nos. 49, 58, 59, 64, 66, 67, 68, 69, 74, 75)

The singing should be preceded by hand-sign practice and interval analysis, as in Chapter III.

For example, exercise 58:

1. Note-finding singing from hand-signs, using the notes m,—l,—d—m—s.

2. The simultaneously sounding intervals in the exercise to be analysed and written down:

3. Two-part singing. (See 3., page 44)

TWO PART WORKS

Pentatonic range of notes

The two-part exercises listed here are notated in key signatures using one flat or four sharps. The reason for this is that in the pentatonic system with B flat as "d" the note E flat ("f") does not occur, and the note A sharp ("t") does not occur in the system with B as "d".

Since in this chapter there is no staff notation material among the unison melodies, it is necessary to practise note-finding singing from staff notation particularly thoroughly in connection with the two-part works, using both key signatures. With regard to the sight-singing material this sort of preparation should be carried out in the G and F clefs, using the range l,—m'.

a) with B flat as "d":

b) with B as "d":

BICINIA HUNGARICA II/67

1. It is a "l" pentatonic folksong theme with A A B C structure, and with an alto accompanying part.

2. Since an equally important role is played by the stretched (♩. ♪) and the snapped (♪♩.) rhythms in both the theme and its accompaniment, singing of

the separate parts should first be practised with a rhythm accompaniment composed of these rhythm patterns:

for the pattern ♩. ♪ the accompaniment ♪♩.
for the pattern ♪♩. the accompaniment ♩. ♪
for the pattern ♩ 𝄾 (or ♩) the accompaniment 𝄾 ♩

For example on this basis the alto part works out like this:

3. When the two parts are sung together only beating the metrical unit should be used as accompaniment.

BICINIA HUNGARICA IV/142

1. This is a "d" pentatonic theme, with A⁷ A,⁵ A,³ A structure, with a tonal fifth change in the third line:

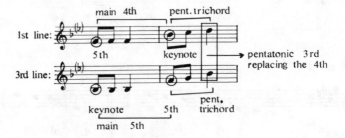

2. In the fourth line's fifth-changing melody "m" appears answering "d", that is the fifth is replaced by the pentatonic sixth:

3. On account of the alternating metre, practise with beating time.

1. A "d" pentatonic theme, with $A^7 A^5$, $A^3 A$, structure, with a tonal fifth change in the third line.

2. The alto entry in bar 2 can be prepared for by the following two-part exercise:

3. The soprano imitation beginning in bar 10 starts off with the awkward r—l fifth. Perfect intonation of the interval can be secured by practising this sequence:

4. Two-part singing should definitely be accompanied here by beating time.

BICINIA HUNGARICA IV/178

1. A "d" pentatonic theme, with the structure $A^5 A^5$, A A,

2. The inner division of the bars of this $\frac{5}{4}$ theme is 2+3 since the last three notes of the motifs form an organic melodic unit:

Practise the theme with beating time (see page 265).

3. The inner stress relationships of the accompanying part's $\frac{5}{4}$ bars change. Of the two-bar melodic units which follow each other the first bar is 3+2, and the second — because of agreement in the cadential phrases — is 2+3. For example:

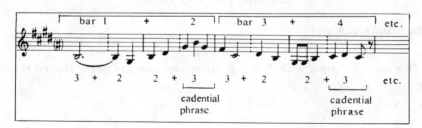

The quintuple bar made up of 3+2 agrees in its basic principle with the beating time required in the bar made up of 2+3 (see page 265).

It is therefore carried out as follows:

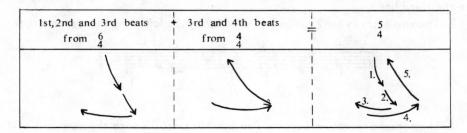

1st, 2nd and 3rd beats from $\frac{6}{4}$	3rd and 4th beats from $\frac{4}{4}$	$\frac{5}{4}$

The accompaniment material (alto bars 1—4 + soprano bars 5—8) should be practised with alternating the time beating in keeping with the music, with individual and then group singing:

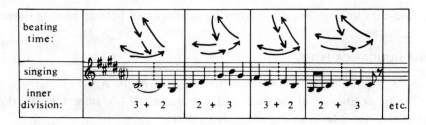

beating time:					
singing					
inner division:	3 + 2	2 + 3	3 + 2	2 + 3	etc.

4. When singing the exercise in two parts, the performance should be accompanied by giving the metrical unit beat only, if the different time beating required for the different parts causes any difficulty.

SUGGESTED FURTHER EXERCISES: Bicinia Hungarica IV/144, 145.

Diatonic range of notes

BICINIA HUNGARICA II/87

1. This aeolian theme, with A A B B, structure, uses the notes around the final note:

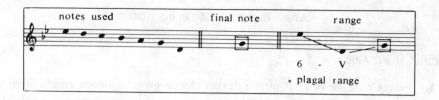

notes used   final note   range

6 - V
= plagal range

2. Sing it a few times with the ostinato $\frac{2}{4}$ ♫ ♩ so that the first ♪ of the synco-pated cadences will not tend to become shortened after the preceding ♫. ♪ˌ rhythm pattern.

66 TWO-PART EXERCISES/16

In the music of this exercise it is only the melodic sequence of bar 6 in the alto that needs preparation. Not so much in itself, but together with the preceding bar (5) it can cause intonation problems, for several reasons:

bar 5   –   6

5th↓   5th↑ 4th↓

a) The downward fifth of bar 5 is followed by an upward fifth and then a fourth moving back downwards.

b) The securely heard s—d fifth is followed by the rarer and less characteristic r—l fifth.

c) The melodic difficulty is aggravated further by the rhythmic division into shorter notes. Singing this motif sequence will provide some preparation:

At all costs it is necessary to concentrate in every case on perfect intonation of the top note "l".

Range including altered notes

1. The melodic movement of the dorian theme gives vigorous emphasis to the minor character of the tonality by the third having the most prominent role after the keynote among the exposed melody notes.

Notes used in the theme:		diatony							+ altered note
		r	m	f	s	l	t	d'	
Prominent notes and number of times they occur:	a) motif beginnings	1	1	2	1	2		1	
	b) final note	1							
	c) note arrived at by melodic leap	3	2		1				
	d) top note							1	

The main notes which occur most often are thus:

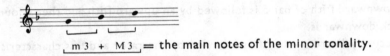

m 3 + M 3 = the main notes of the minor tonality.

For this reason it is better to sing the theme to comparative note names (see page *291*) instead of diatonic solfa names.

2. The notes used in the alto's accompanying material also supports the interpretation of G as "l" because apart from one melodic phrase it moves consistently in the system with two flats. On the basis of all this the complete two-part exercise should be sung throughout with the same "d" — using B flat as "d".

Range of notes changing key

1. This is a folksong-like theme structured A A^5 B + A,

A	A⁵	B	+	A.
alto: bars 1-4	soprano: bars 5-8	sop.: bars 9-10		sop.+alto: bars 11-14
G aeolian	D aeolian real upper fifth change	G aeolian rhythm contrast		G aeolian varied recapitulation
closed line	closed line		open +	closed line

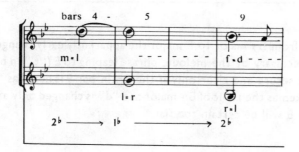

Dominant

Tonic → → Tonic

2. Suggested places for changing "d":

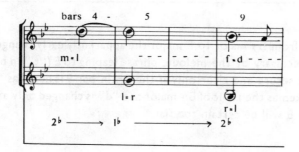

bars 4 -   5   9

m.l   - - - - - - -   f.d - - - -

l.r

r.l

2♭ ——→ 1♭ ——————→ 2♭

3. To prepare the entry of the soprano, practise this:

t, r f m   l,   l, m   l   l m· l,   l, l

66 TWO-PART EXERCISES/34

1. With the exception of the last note the alto part beginning in the second bar is a precise mirror inversion of the soprano. In spite of the identical melodic construction, however, the colour of the intervals differs. For example, bar 3 and its inversion:

m 2 dim.4   etc.

M 2   p 4 etc.

275

2. The colouring of the alto's B♭—E (f—t) augmented fourth into a perfect fourth brings about the change to B♭ major, in the eighth bar, which is then rein-forced by the soprano part.

Suggested places for changing "d":

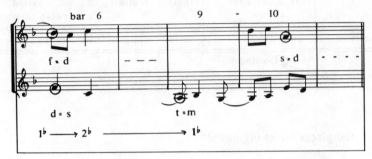

At the return from B♭ major to F major the apparently early change of "d" in the alto is made necessary by the melodic phrase leaping to E ("t") in bar 10. This "t" will indeed be secure and clear only if the B♭ in bar 9 is heard as "f" in F major. If this B♭ is taken as the tonic of B♭ major and "d" is changed only after it has been sung, the note E will be certain too flat.

FIFTEEN TWO-PART EXERCISES/13

1. The thematic material of this two-part exercise does not follow the customary four-line folksong structure but appears as a baroque fugal subject. Thus the four-bar theme appearing at the beginning of the work is the musical principal thought of the two-part exercise, which comes later sometimes in the alto part and sometimes in the soprano part — in new keys as well — in the form of a real or tonal answer.

The music material is thus fugal in structure.

2. The tonality of the theme — on the basis of the notes used and the final note — is a minor hexachord:

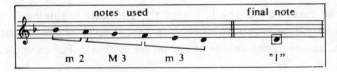

(A hexachord is six adjacent notes of the given tonal system — in this case the diatonic system. Minor hexachord is six diatonic adjacent notes the interval succession of which corresponds with the interval sequence in the first six notes in the minor. Cf. pentachord on page *207*.)

3. In the course of the exercise the theme is transformed — that is, it appears in a tonality of a different character — in a major hexachord instead of the minor. These transformed theme entries are to be found in bars 21, 24 and 26. For example, the notes used in the soprano theme in bars 21—25, together with the final note:

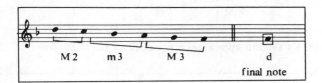

4. Outline of keys on the basis of the appearances of the theme:

	Theme 5 - 9	leading	Theme 13 - 17	trans-ition	Theme 21 - 25	Theme 26 - 30	trans-ition		Theme 40-44	
	A "l" hexach. (real answer)	back	D "l" hexach.		F "d" hexach. (transformed)	C "d" hexach.			G "l" hexach.	
Theme bars 1- 5					Theme 24 - 28			Theme 36 - 40		Theme 46 - 50
D "l" hexach.					C "d" hexach. (transf.)			Bb "d" hexach. (transf.)	leading back	D "l" hexach.
					condensation					

1b ——→ 0 ————————→ 1b —————————→ 0 ——→ 1b ————→ 2b ————————————→ 1b

Ton. —→ Dom. ————————→ Ton. ————→ Dom. →Ton. →Subdom. ————————→ Ton.

This presents a typical baroque outline of keys, touching the subdominant key before the end so that arrival of the tonic has the effect of the same sort of relative ascent as the modulation from the tonic level to the dominant at the beginning.

5. Suggested places for changing "d":

277

1. The musical material is fugal in structure.
2. The key of the theme is a "l" (minor) pentachord:

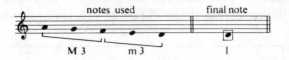

3. The theme's second appearance produces a tonal answer:

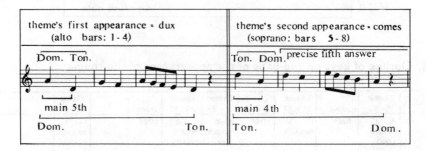

4. The minor pentachord key of the theme is coloured — that is, transformed — in the middle section (bars 17—24) to a major pentachord, first of all with F as the keynote, then C:

The final note in both cases is "d".

5. In the alto in bars 25—28 the theme appears in mirror inversion. The interval structure of the melodic patterns corresponds exactly with the original theme, difference occurring only in their colouring:

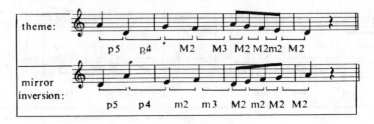

278

6. In its last appearance (bars 33—36) the theme comes divided between the two parts: the first note is sung by the soprano and the continuation is sung by the alto.

7. Outline of keys used, on the basis of the theme entries:

	Comes 5-8	trans-	Dux 17- 20			Dux 29- 32	
	A "l" pentach. (tonal answer)	ition	F "d" pentach. (trans- formed)			G "l" pentach.	
Dux bars 1- 4				Dux 21 - 24	Dux 25- 28		Dux 33 - 36
D "l" pentachord				C "d" pentach. (transf)	D "l" pentach. (mirror inversion)		D "l" pentachord

1♭ ⟶ 0 ⟶ 1♭ ⟶ 0 ⟶ 1♭ ⟶ 2♭ ⟶ 1♭

T ⟶ D ⟶ T ⟶ D ⟶ T ⟶ S ⟶ T

In this exercise, too, it is the already familiar baroque outline of keys that is to be found.

8. Suggested places for changing "d":

bar 6   14   21   25   28   32 - 33

l = r --- f = d ---- d = f --- f = d ---- l = m --- t = m --

d - f   ta - f   r - s   r - l   r = l   fi = t

1♭ → 0 ⟶ 1♭ ⟶ 0 ⟶ 1♭ ⟶ 2♭ ⟶ 1♭

SUGGESTED FURTHER EXERCISES: 66 Two-Part Exercises /35; Bicinia Hungarica I/55; 55 Two-Part Exercises/29.

279

Bitonality in the two-part material

1. In this exercise there is dual tonality: the first two motifs of the pentatonic theme appearing with the major third F—A are imitated from bar 4 by the alto in a canon at the lower fifth — that is, in the pentatonic system using the B♭—D major third. Although the theme's third motif is strongly varied in the last, cadential bars of the alto, the two different pentatonic systems remain consistently present throughout.

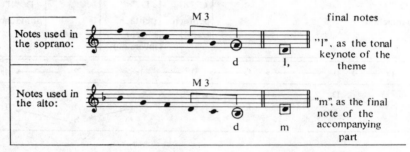

2. The alto entry can be prepared in the following way:
a) Sing the theme's first motif and its fifth imitation as if the six bars were fifth-changing melodic unit within the D "l" pentatonic key:

b) Practise bars 3—4 with a change of "d" in keeping with the pentatonic canon at the fifth:

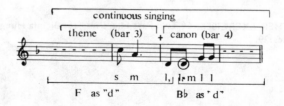

c) Once the students find the alto starting note with certainty in this way, begin the imitation — as appropriate to the new "d" — straight away with "m":

280

s m   m

F "d"   Bb "d"

BICINIA HUNGARICA II/79

1. After the alto entry two minor pentachord tonalities with a fifth between them are heard simultaneously:

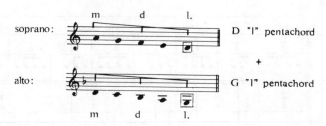

soprano: m   d   l.   D "l" pentachord

+

alto: m   d   l.   G "l" pentachord

Although the notes used in the two pentachords can be reconciled with the |♮ system, this would in the present case be extremely formal. For here, with the exception of the last bar, it is not a question of a melody + its accompaniment, but of the simultaneous sound of a pentachord theme and its canon at the fifth.

In the alto the cadential motif which appears in place of the fourth motif of the melody — which also moves away from the fifth canon structure used hitherto — would, however, be more properly sung in accordance with the D "l" tonality:

l = r

2. To prepare the alto entry practise the lollowing:

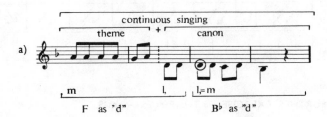

a)

continuous singing

theme + canon

m   l,   l,= m

F as "d"   Bb as "d"

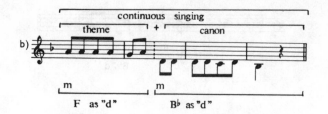

b)

continuous singing

theme + canon

m m

F as "d" B♭ as "d"

3. As a result of the canon at the fifth starting at an unstressed beat, the accents in the lower part do not coincide with those of the soprano:

	1st motif		2nd motif		3rd motif		4th motif	
soprano:	$\frac{2}{4}$	$\frac{2}{4}$	$\frac{2}{4}$	$\frac{2}{4}$	$\frac{2}{4}$	$\frac{2}{4}$	$\frac{2}{4}$	$\frac{2}{4}$
alto:	$\frac{2}{4}$	$\frac{1}{4}$	$\frac{2}{4}$	$\frac{2}{4}$	$\frac{2}{4}$	$\frac{2}{4}$	$\frac{2}{4}$	$\frac{3}{4}$

1st motif 2nd motif 3rd motif +

cadence

If the group is a good one, try two-part singing with different beating of time for the soprano and alto. In this the teacher should certainly give the metrical unit beats.

soprano:	$\frac{2}{4}$	$\frac{2}{4}$	$\frac{2}{4}$	$\frac{2}{4}$	$\frac{2}{4}$	$\frac{2}{4}$	$\frac{2}{4}$	$\frac{2}{4}$
alto:	$\frac{2}{4}$	$\frac{1}{4}$ $\frac{2}{4}$	$\frac{2}{4}$	$\frac{2}{4}$	$\frac{2}{4}$	$\frac{2}{4}$	$\frac{3}{4}$	
unit beat:								

SUGGESTED FURTHER EXERCISE: 66 Two-Part Exercises/9.

282

Three-Part Material

BICINIA HUNGARICA III/101.a

1. The already familiar dorian folksong theme (see Bicinia Hungarica III/101 on page 274) has a "l" based character which is made unmistakable here, too, by the major imitation beginning with the alto fifth B♭—F and by the chord progression in the music of the last five bars. And so the theme — that is, the soprano part — should be sung with B♭ as "d" in this exercise, too.

2. The melodic progression of the accompanying parts in the first bars is likewise associated with G as "l" and B♭ as "d" as main notes. But from bar 7 both the mezzo and the alto touch on D minor and F major and so the 'd" must be changed in both. Points at which "d" may be changed are:

3. Since the students already know the theme it is only necessary to join the mezzo and alto into the part singing. Stages recommended for this process follow:
   a) Sing the mezzo part (with the changes of "d" given above).
   b) Prepare the alto entry by practising this melodic sequence:

   c) Sing the mezzo and alto parts together (with the changes of "d" given above).
4. Following this try three-part performance.

TRICINIA/9

Apart from a few very short momentary modulations the music is in G minor or B♭ major throughout. It is therefore unnecessary to change "d".
   In the melodic phrases, coloured with alteration, the notes "fi", "si", "di" and "ta"

283

appear, evoking as it were the 11 degree set of notes of the Palestrina style (see page *235*).

The Renaissance style is likewise hinted at by the polyphonic cadence marking the ends of the two main formal sections:

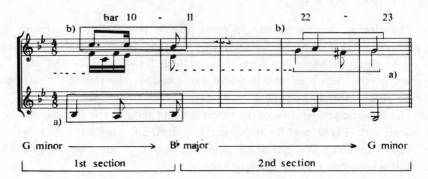

In each cadence there is suspension of the leading-note resolving onto the keynote — melodic element **a)** —, and there is also a melodic movement by a descending second onto the keynote — melodic element **b)** —, which details are fundamental stylistic features of Renaissance cadences. Of the two cadences, the second is the stronger because the lowest — the third — part complements the two-part melodic cadence with the 5—1 (later Dominant-Tonic) pattern.

The two section structure connected with the given tonal arrangement is at the same time a characteristic form type of the baroque style.

THEORETICAL INFORMATIONS AND
TECHNICAL EXERCISES
Range of Notes, Hand-Signs

Pentatony

SOLFA SINGING TO HAND-SIGNS

Practise the following interval progressions of pentatony:

4+6 (s,—d—l and r—s—m'; r'—l—d and l—m—s,).

6+4 (d—l—r' and s,—m—l; l—d—s, and m'—s—r),

5+6 (d—s—m' and l,—m—d'; m'—l—d and s—d—m,) and

6+5 (d—l—m' and m,—d—s; d'—m—l, and m'—s—d).

In practising these difficult patterns the important thing is not the singing of long hand-sign melodies but rather that the interval sequences to be practised should be given a place in short note series concentrating on the essential point. For example

a) d—s, —d—l—d' —m—l, or b) d' —r' —l—d—l—m—s, etc.

NOTE NAME SINGING TO HAND-SIGNS

The teacher provides a pentatonic hand-sign melody and the students sing it using the names of the pentatonic notes connected with B♭ or B as "d". For example, this sequence at the pitch where B is "d":

The teacher's hand-sign melody	d' l s l m s d' r l s d s l, r d etc.
The students's singing	B G♯ F♯ G♯ D♯ F♯ B C♯ G♯ F♯ B F♯ G♯ C♯ B
Actual pitch	

Diatony

SOLFA SINGING TO HAND-SIGNS

Practise the characteristic diatonic seventh (7), ninth (9) and tenth (10) intervals, ascending and descending. For example

    a) d—t,—d'—m—r—d'—t,—f—m   or   b) d—s—t,—l—s,—t—d'—m—f—m,— r—t,—d   or   c) d—m—f—t,—d--m'—f'—t—d etc.

NOTE NAME SINGING TO HAND-SIGNS

The teacher gives a diatonic hand-sign melody and the students sing it using the names of the notes in the system with 2 flats or that with 5 sharps. For example this series of notes using the key signature with 2 flats:

The teacher's hand-sign melody	d m f t, d l f r t d' t, f m r s t, d' etc.
The students' singing	B♭ D E♭ A B♭ G E♭ C A B♭ A E♭ D C F A B♭
Actual pitch	

Diatony + alteration

SOLFA SINGING TO HAND-SIGNS

Practise melodic phrases using "fi" and "ta" in which the altered notes come in a more difficult melodic environment:

    a) the melody reachers the altered note by a second, but then moves away from it by a larger interval, and

    b) the melody arrives at the altered note by a leap and then moves away by another leap (not step-wise, that is).

SOLFA SINGING FROM STAFF NOTATION

Extend the range of notes for note-finding singing from staff notation using the 2 flat or 5 sharp key signatures to include all the altered notes (fi, di, si, ri, li: ta, ma, lo, ra).

    a) In the G clef:

or:

b) In the F clef:

or:

287

The teacher sings melodic phrases, with altered notes, at the pitch using B♭ or B as "d" and the students answer this with note names. For example, the series of notes d—fi—s—ta,—l,—ri—m—di—r—lo—s—t,—d using B as "d":

The teacher's solfa singing:		d	fi	s	ta,	l,	ri	m	di	etc.
Actual pitch:										
Students' note name answer:		B	E♯	F♯	A	G♯	C♯	D♯	B♯	

Keys and Modes

The pentatonic modes using B♭ or B as "d"

(M) The students should sing (having been given the note "d") any pentatonic mode upwards or downwards to solfa and then straight away to the note names appropriate to the given "d".

For example, "s" pentatonic with B as "d" (ascending):

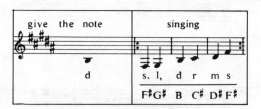

give the note	singing
d	s, l, d r m s
	F♯G♯ B C♯ D♯F♯

or "d" pentatonic with B♭ as "d" (descending):

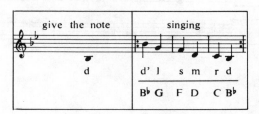

give the note	singing
d	d' l s m r d
	B♭ G F D C B♭

etc.

Major and minor keys with two flats or five sharps

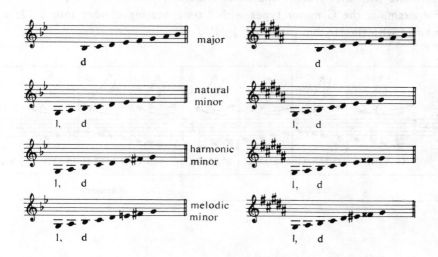

FORMS OF PRACTISING FOR THE MINOR

1. (M) Sing the natural, harmonic and melodic G minor — G♯ minor — in the direction ⟶, moving in even metrical units, and accompany this continuous singing with beating quintuple time (see page 272).

For example, the G♯ minor types with $\frac{5}{4}$ beating time divided into 2+3:

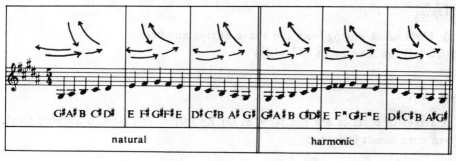

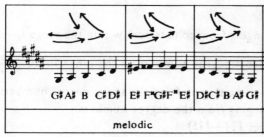

289

2. (M) Connect singing accompanied by beating time with a certain rhythm pattern and with that practise the three minors.

For example, the G minor types with $\frac{5}{4}$ time beating divided into 3+2, and combined with the rhythm pattern $\frac{5}{4}$ ♩ ♩ ♩. ♪ :

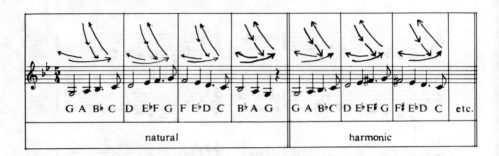

G A B♭ C	D E♭F G	F E♭D C	B♭ A G	G A B♭C	D E♭F♯ G	F♯ E♭D C	etc.

natural	harmonic

Note finding exercises in major and harmonic minor

IN B♭ MAJOR

   1. Note name singing from solfa letters in the range I,—m' (   ).

   2. Solfa + note name singing from degree numbers within the range VI—10

( ).

   3. Note name singing from the above degree numbers.
(Cf. 1, 3 and 4 on pages *122—123*)

IN B MAJOR

The stages of practice are the same as for B♭ major. The pitch is adapted to the given note names here, too.

IN G MINOR

   1. Note name singing from solfa letters within the range I,—m' (   ).

   2. Solfa singing from degree numbers, in the range 1—10 (   ).

   3. Solfa + note name singing from the above degree numbers.
   4. Note name singing from the degree numbers.
(Cf. 2—5 on pages *124—125*)

The practice stages are the same as for G minor. The pitch is adapted to the key signature with 5 sharps here, too.

Church modes (Modal keys)

NEW METHOD OF PRACTISING THE KEY SIGNATURES

The teacher names a note which is the keynote of each of the church modes. The students determine these modes and their key signatures.

Take for example the named note [musical notation] as keynote. The modal keys which have F as keynote are: F ionic = 1♭; F dorian = 3♭; F phrygian = 5♭; F lydian = 0; F mixolydian = 2♭; F aeolian = 4♭; F locrian = 6♭.

This kind of practice should be repeated until the interrelationships between the modes and the key signature systems become quite clear to everyone.

THE MAJOR OR MINOR CHARACTER OF THE CHURCH MODES

We can only speak of major or minor character in the case of those perfect fifth keys which, although they resemble either the major or the minor, do not correspond precisely to either. On this basis the locrian and the ionic and aeolian modes are excluded from the possibility of comparison (see page 200). The major or minor character of the other four modes is determined by their third in relation to the keynote: the minor third modes have a minor character and those with a major third are major in character.

This major or minor character is frequently accompanied by a melodic quality which makes us hear the given folksong or folksong-like theme — in keeping with its character — as having "d" or "l" as its keynote. In such cases we can make use of the so called comparative names in place of the diatonic solfa names based on the key signature.

COMPARATIVE NAMES OF THE MINOR-CHARACTER MODES

Comparison with the minor is most easily illustrated using A minor and the modes with A as keynote.

a) A dorian = 1♯

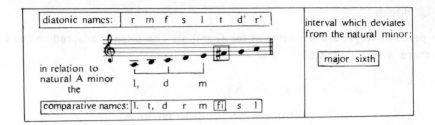

b) A phrygian = 1♭

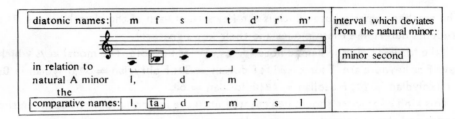

COMPARATIVE NAMES OF THE MAJOR-CHARACTER MODES

Comparison with the major is most easily illustrated using C major and the modes with C as keynote.

a) C lydian = 1♯

b) C mixolydian = 1♭

On the basis of the comparative names the lydian and dorian, and the mixolydian and phrygian modes come into close relationship:

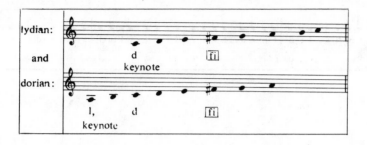

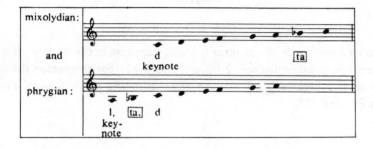

PRACTICE TO MAKE THE COMPARATIVE NAMES CONSCIOUS

1. (M) Moving in even quarters sing the sequence of the minor-character modes in any order to solfa and using the same starting note, with the following variations:
  a) Upwards to the diatonic names and downwards to the comparative names.
  b) Upwards to the comparative names and downwards to the diatonic names.
  c) Downwards to the diatonic names and upwards to the comparative names.
  d) Downwards to the comparative names and upwards to the diatonic names.
  For example, the phrygian — dorian sequence according to variation c):

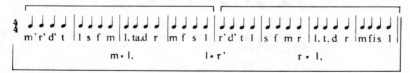

etc.

2. (M) Practise the modes which are major in character in a similar way.
For example, the lydian — mixolydian sequence according to variation b) in 1.:

etc.

Metre

The new time signature in the chapter is $\frac{5}{4}$ which appears in the Kodály material in both its forms (with inner division 2+3 and also 3+2). For this reason the ways of beating time also became fixed in connection with the given Kodály exercises (see pages 265 and 272).

Intervals

Practice of fourths and fifths

1. (M) Sing a fourth sequence in G harmonic minor, to solfa.
a) Upwards:

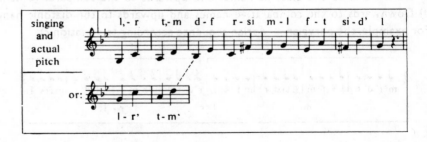

b) Downwards:

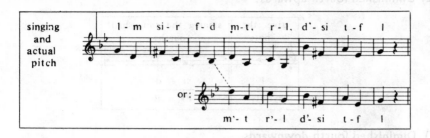

2. (M) Practise the sequences given in 1. with solfa + note name singing as well.
For example, upwards:

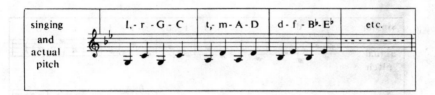

3. (M) Sing the above sequences (in 1. and 2.) in G♯ harmonic minor, too.

4. (M) To solfa and then to note names sing all the G harmonic minor's fourths of different kinds as they come in the key — after being given the tonic.

a) Perfect fourths upwards:

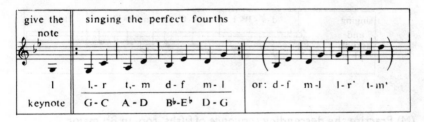

b) Perfect fourths downwards.
c) Augmented fourths upwards:

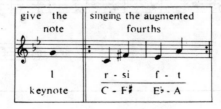

295

d) Augmented fourths downwards.

e) Diminished fourth upwards:

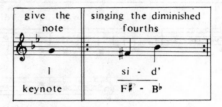

give the note	singing the diminished fourths
1	si - d'
keynote	F# - B♭

f) Diminished fourth downwards.

5. (M) In a similar way practise the fourth types in G# harmonic minor, too.

6. (M) Sing an ascending fifth sequence in B♭ major.

a) To solfa:

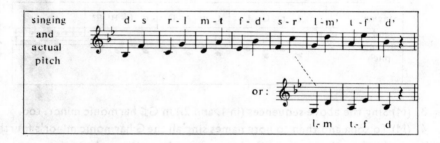

b) To solfa + note names:

7. (M) Practise the descending sequence of fifths, too, in B♭ major.

a) To solfa:

296

b) To solfa + note names:

8. (M) Sing the fifth sequences, as given in 6 and 7., in B major as well.

The intervals of the diatonic pentachords

1. (M) To solfa sing — at any pitch desired — any diatonic pentachord upwards and then starting from the basic note of the pentachord sing the intervals beginning with the largest and afterwards name them.

For example, the intervals of the ascending pentachord from "t":

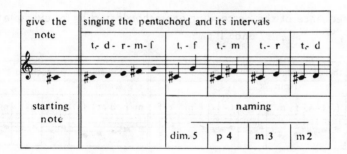

etc.

2. (M) Practise the intervals of the descending pentachords in a similar way. For example, the intervals of the pentachord descending from "l":

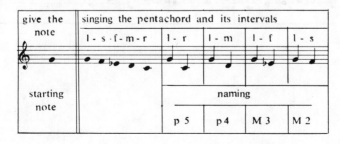

etc.

3. Sing the a) ascending and b) descending diatonic pentachords' intervals according to a predetermined order.

For example in the predetermined order 3, 2, 5, 4.

a), The sequence of the ascending pentachords starting for example from "s", "r", "l", "d", "t", "m" and "f":

give the note	"s" pentachord					"r" pentachord				
	s - l - t-d'- r'	s- t	s- l	s-r'	s- d'	r-m- f - s - l	r- f	r-m	r- l	r- s

	"l" pentachord					etc
	l,- t,- d - r- m	l,- d	l,- t,	l,- m	l,- r	

etc.

b) The sequence of the descending pentachords starting for example from "t", "m", "d", "f", "s", "r" and "l":

give the note	the descending pentachord from "t"					the descending pentachord from "m"				
	t - l - s - f - m	t - s	t - l	t - m	t - f	m- r- d - t,- l,	m-d	m-r	m-l,	m-t,

	the descending pentachord from "d"					etc.
	d'- t - l - s - f	d'- l	d'- t	d'- f	d'- s	

etc.

298

Practice of sixths
(List on page *131*)

1. (M) Sing a major third downwards and then from the same starting note its inversion, the minor sixth upwards, using any appropriate solfa names:

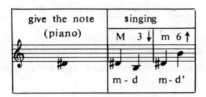

give the note	singing	
(piano)	M 3 ↓	m 6 ↑
	m - d	m - d'

Then sing this same pair of intervals using all the major and minor solfa possibilities and state which major or harmonic minor includes the pair of intervals sung to the different names from the given starting note D♯ ;

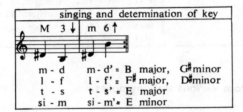

singing and determination of key	
M 3 ↓	m 6 ↑
m - d	m - d' = B major, G♯minor
l - f	l - f' = F♯ major, D♯minor
t - s	t - s' = E major
si - m	si - m'= E minor

Sing this sequence using different starting notes.

2. (M) Practise the upward major third and its inversion the downward minor sixth in the same way. For example, from A♭:

give the note	singing and determination of key	
(piano)	M 3↑	m 6↓
	d - m	d - m, = A♭ major, F minor
	f - l	f - l, = E♭ major C minor
	s - t	s - t, = D♭ major
	m - si	m - si, = this would have 8♭

Practise this, too, from several starting notes.

3. (M) Sing the sequence of minor third downwards — major sixth upwards as in 1. For example, from C:

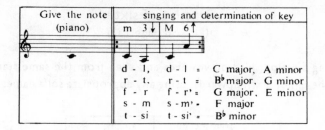

Give the note (piano)	singing and determination of key
	m 3↓ M 6↑
	d - l, d - l = C major, A minor
	r - t, r - t = B♭ major, G minor
	f - r f - r' = G major, E minor
	s - m s - m' = F major
	t - si t - si' = B♭ minor

Sing the same progression from different starting notes.

4. (M) Similarly practise the minor third upwards — major sixth downwards sequence. For example, from G:

Give the note (piano)	singing and determination of key
	m 3↑ M 6↓
	l - d' l - d = B♭ major, G minor
	t - r' t - r = A♭ major, F minor
	r - f r - f, = F major, D minor
	m - s m - s, = E♭ major
	si - t si - t, = A♭ minor

Sing the exercise from various starting notes.

Chords

Revision practice with triads

1. (M) In B♭ major and G harmonic minor — and in B major and G♯ harmonic minor — sing the triad series to solfa and then to note names (cf. 1—2, pages 210—211).

2. (M) Likewise in B♭ and B major, and G and G♯ minor, practise the sequence of the different types of triad as they occur within the given key, to solfa and note names (cf. page 213, 5 and 214, 6).

Inversions of the triad

In works of music the triads do not always appear with their root as the lowest note sounding: frequently the third or the fifth of the chord comes in the lowest part. In such cases the intervals between the notes of the chord change in order:

Lowest note of the chord	root	third	fifth
Interval order of the three notes	*(5 [3 [3)* fifth / third / root	*(6 [4 [3)* root / fifth / third	*(6 [3 [4)* third / root / fifth
Name of chord	root position triad	first inversion (sixth-chord)	second inversion (sixth-four chord)
Sign for the chord	$\binom{5}{3}$	6	6 4

The above interval structure of chord inversions is the same for all triad types: in the first inversion $\begin{smallmatrix}4\\3\end{smallmatrix}$ are built on each other and in the second inversion it is always $\begin{smallmatrix}3\\4\end{smallmatrix}$ which are placed on one another. The chord's original bass (the root of chord) comes in both cases as the upper note of the fourth interval.

This identical structure, however, becomes associated with different colours in the inversions of the different types of triad.

First inversion (6-) chords
in the major and harmonic minor keys

IN MAJOR

Degree	I6	II6	III6	IV6	V6	VI6	VII6
Type	major	minor	minor	major	major	minor	diminished
Intervals of first inversion	] p4]] m3]m6	]p4]]M3]M6	]p4]]M3]M6	]p4]]m3]m6	]p4]]m3]m6	]p4]]M3]M6	] aug.4]] m3]M6

301

Degree	I⁶	II⁶	III⁶#	IV⁶	V⁶	VI⁶	VII⁶#
Type	minor	dim.	aug.	minor	major	major	dim.
	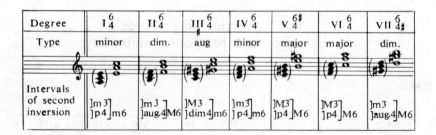						
Intervals of first inversion	]p4] M3]M6	]aug4] m3]M6	]dim4] M3]m6	]p4] M3]M6	]p4] m3]m6	]p4] m3]m6	]aug4] m3]M6

Second inversion (⁶₄-) chords
in the major and harmonic minor keys

IN MAJOR

Degree	I ⁶₄	II ⁶₄	III ⁶₄	IV ⁶₄	V ⁶₄	VI ⁶₄	VII ⁶₄
Type	major	minor	minor	major	major	minor	diminished
Intervals of second inversion	]M3]]p4]M6	]m3]]p4]m6	]m3]]p4]m6	]M3]]p4]M6	]M3]]p4]M6	]m3]]p4]m6	]m3]aug.4]M6

IN MINOR

Degree	I ⁶₄	II ⁶₄	III ⁶₄#	IV ⁶₄	V ⁶₄#	VI ⁶₄	VII ⁶₄#
Type	minor	dim.	aug	minor	major	major	dim.
Intervals of second inversion	]m3]]p4]m6	]m3]aug.4]M6	]M3]dim4]m6	]m3]]p4]m6	]M3]]p4]M6	]M3]]p4]M6	]m3]aug.4]M6

302

Singing exercises with first inversion (6-) chords

1. (M) Sing the series of first inversions in B♭ major to solfa and then to note names.

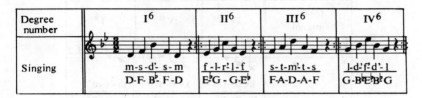

Degree number	I⁶	II⁶	III⁶	IV⁶
Singing	m-s-d'- s-m D-F- B♭- F-D	f-l-r'-l-f E♭-G - G-E♭	s-t-m'-t-s F-A-D-A-F	l-d'-f'-d'-l G-B♭-E♭-B♭-G

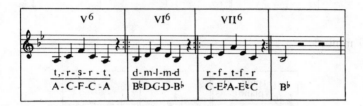

	V⁶	VI⁶	VII⁶	
	t,-r-s-r-t, A - C-F-C -A	d- m-l-m-d B♭-D-G-D-B♭	r-f- t-f- r C-E♭-A-E♭-C	B♭

2. (M) In a similar way practise the first inversions in G harmonic minor as well

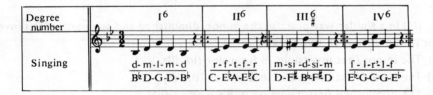

Degree number	I⁶	II⁶	III⁶	IV⁶
Singing	d-m-l-m-d B♭-D-G-D-B♭	r-f-t-f-r C- E♭-A-E♭-C	m-si-d'-si-m D-F♯-B♭-F♯-D	f- l-r'-l-f E♭-G-C-G-E♭

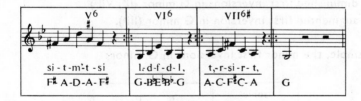

	V⁶	VI⁶	VII⁶♯	
	si - t -m'-t -si F♯ A-D-A-F♯	l,-d-f- d- l, G-B♭-E♭-B♭-G	t,-r-si-r- t, A-C-F♯-C- A	G

3. (M) After listening to the tonic — in the 2♭ keys — sing the sequence of major first inversions as they come in order, first to solfa and then to note names.

a) In B♭ major (adapting to the given pitch, it is best to begin with IV⁶ or V⁶):

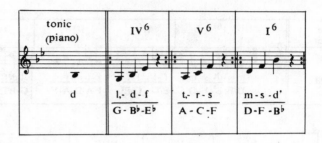

tonic (piano)	IV⁶	V⁶	I⁶
d	l,- d - f	t,- r - s	m - s - d'
	G - B♭-E♭	A - C - F	D - F - B♭

b) In G minor:

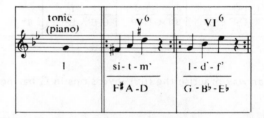

tonic (piano)	V⁶	VI⁶
l	si - t - m'	l - d' - f'
	F♯A - D	G - B♭ - E♭

4. (M) In a similar way practise the minor, diminished and augmented first inversions in the keys with two flats.

a) The minor first inversions in B♭ major (II⁶, III⁶, VI⁶).
b) The minor first inversions in G minor (I⁶, IV⁶).
c) The diminished first inversion in B♭ major (VII⁶).
d) The diminished first inversions in G minor (II⁶, VII⁶).
e) The augmented first inversion in G minor (III⁶).

For example, the minor first inversions in G minor:

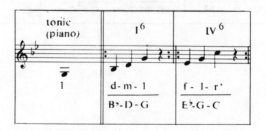

tonic (piano)	I⁶	IV⁶
l	d - m - l	f - l - r'
	B♭-D - G	E♭-G - C

etc.

304

5. (M) In a similar way practise the exercises given in 1—4 in the keys (major and harmonic minor) which have five sharps as well.

6. Sing a sequence of first inversion chords in a certain predetermined order, after listening to the keynote of B♭ major, G minor, B major or G♯ minor, to solfa and then to note names.

For example, the sequence II⁶—VII⁶—I⁶—III⁶—VI⁶—IV⁶—V⁶—I⁶ in **B major**:

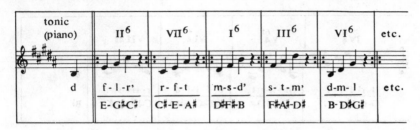

tonic (piano)	II⁶	VII⁶	I⁶	III⁶	VI⁶	etc.
d	f - l - r'	r - f - t	m - s - d'	s - t - m'	d - m - l	etc.
	E - G♯C♯	C♯-E-A♯	D♯F♯-B	F♯A♯-D♯	B- D♯G♯	

The teacher should make up similar sequences.

Singing exercises with second inversion (⁶₄-) chords

1. (M) Sing the series of second inversion chords in B♭ major to solfa and then to note names.

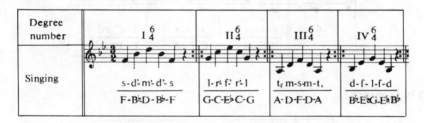

Degree number	I ⁶₄	II ⁶₄	III ⁶₄	IV ⁶₄
Singing	s-d⁻m⁻d⁻s	l-r⁻f⁻r-l	t₁ m-s-m-t₁	d-f-l-f-d
	F-B♭-D-B♭-F	G-C-E♭-C-G	A-D-F-D-A	B♭-E♭-G-E♭-B♭

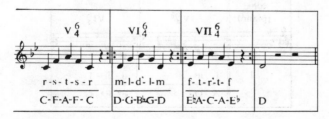

V ⁶₄	VI ⁶₄	VII ⁶₄	
r - s - t - s - r	m-l-d⁻-l-m	f - t - r⁻-t- f	
C - F-A-F - C	D-G-B♭G-D	E♭A-C-A-E♭	D

2. (M) Practise the series of second inversions in G minor, too.

305

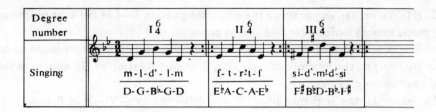

Degree number	I_4^6	II_4^6	III_4^6
Singing	m-l-d'-l-m	f-t-r²-t-f	si-d'-m¹d²-si
	D-G-B♭-G-D	E♭-A-C-A-E♭	F#-B♭-D-B♭-F#

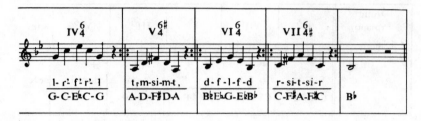

IV_4^6	$V_4^{6\#}$	VI_4^6	$VII_4^{6\#}$	
l- r²- f²-r²- l	t,-m-si-m-t,	d- f- l-f-d	r- si-t-si-r	
G-C-E♮-C-G	A-D-F#-D-A	B♭-E♭-G-E♭-B♭	C-F#-A-F#-C	B♭

3. (M) After listening to the tonic in the two-flat keys, sing the major second inversions as they come in order in the keys, first to solfa and then to note names.

a) In B♭ major:

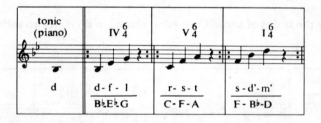

tonic (piano)	IV_4^6	V_4^6	I_4^6
d	d- f- l	r- s- t	s - d'- m'
	B♭-E♭-G	C- F- A	F - B♭-D

b) In G minor:

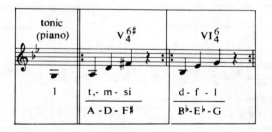

tonic (piano)	$V_4^{6\#}$	VI_4^6
l	t,- m- si	d- f - l
	A -D- F#	B♭-E♭- G

306

4. (M) In a similar way practise the second inversions of the minor, diminished and augmented chords, in the keys with two flats. (Cf. page *304*, 4.)

For example, the diminished $^6_4$ chords in G minor:

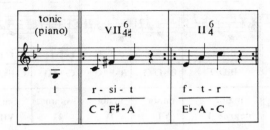

etc.

5. (M) Similarly, practise the exercises in 1—4 in the major and harmonic minor with five sharps as well.

6. After listening to the keynote of B♭ major, G minor, B major or G♯ minor, sing a sequence of $^6_4$ chords in a certain predetermined order, first to solfa and then to note names. For example, the sequence V$^6_4$—I$^6_4$—IV$^6_4$—II$^6_4$—VI$^6_4$—VII$^6_4$—V$^6_4$—VI$^6_4$ —III$^6_4$ in G sharp minor:

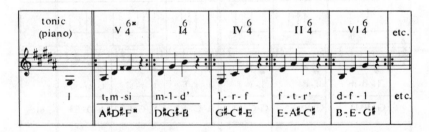

The teacher should make up similar sequences.

General revision exercises with triads

1. (M) a) Sing from each note of B♭ major or B major a root position triad, a first inversion and a second inversion, to solfa and to note names, so that the given note of the scale always comes as the lowest note of the chords. Then

b) name the type of the individual chords and the degree number within the given key.

The exercise in B♭ major, for example:

Structure of the chord:	root	6	6 4	root	6	6 4
	[3 ↑ [3 ↑	[4 ↑ [3 ↑	[3 ↑ [4 ↑	[3 ↑ [3 ↑	[4 ↑ [3 ↑	[3 ↑ [4 ↑
Singing +	d-m-s	d-m-l	d-f-l	r-f-l	r-f-t	r-s-t
	B♭-D-F	B♭-D-G	B♭-E♭-G	C-E♭-G	C-E♭-A	C-F-A
naming	major degree I	minor VI	major IV	minor II	dim. VII	major V

etc.

2. (M) Practise the exercise in 1, in G and G♯ harmonic minor, too.
For example, in G minor:

root	6	6 4	root	6	6 4	etc.
[3 ↑ [3	[4 ↑ [3	[3 ↑ [4	[3 ↑ [3	[4 ↑ [3	[3 ↑ [4	
l₋ d-m	l₋-d-f	l₋- r- f	t₋- r- f	t₋- r- si	t₋- m- si	etc.
G-B♭-D	G-B♭-E♭	G-C-E♭	A-C-E♭	A-C-F♯	A-D-F♯	etc.
minor degree I	major VI	minor IV	dim. II	dim. VII	major V	

Chord analysis

In the quotations **207—220** only root position triads and first inversion chords appear. Those from **221** to **226** include second inversion chords as well. The analysis and the singing exercises in connection with the analysed chords should be carried out according to the stages described in details in Chapter III (see pages *214—216*).

207. LULLY: ALCESTE. III.

The minor extract ends on the major first degree. A typical stylistic feature of the Renaissance and the baroque. The major third of the final tonic chord in a minor key is known as the Picardy third.

208. CORELLI: CONCERTO GROSSO IN D MAJOR, OP. 6., NO. 4.

This quotation stops on the dominant — thus it remains open.

209. MOZART: PIANO SONATA IN A MAJOR. IV. (K. 331)

210. MOZART: THE MARRIAGE OF FIGARO. I.

211. LULLY: ALCESTE. III.

212. HANDEL: MESSIAH. III.

213. HANDEL: PIANO SUITE IN G MINOR. PASSACAGLIA.

214. MOZART: THE MAGIC FLUTE. I.

215. HANDEL: SAMSON. I.

216. J. S. BACH: FREU' DICH SEHR, O MEINE SEELE. CHORALE.

217. J. S. BACH: ALLEIN GOTT IN DER HÖH' SEI EHR'. CHORALE.

218. J. S. BACH: WO SOLL ICH FLIEHEN HIN. CHORALE.

219. J. S. BACH: JESU, JESU, DU BIST MEIN. CHORALE.

220. J. S. BACH: DU GROSSER SCHMERZENSMANN. CHORALE.

221. LULLY: ALCESTE. III.

222. MOZART: THE MAGIC FLUTE. II

223. MOZART: IL SERAGLIO. III.

224. MOZART: IL SERAGLIO. OVERTURE.

225. MOZART: IL SERAGLIO. III.

226. MOZART: THE MAGIC FLUTE. II.

SIGHT-SINGING

Unison Extracts from the Musical Literature

MATERIAL USING STAFF NOTATION

Pentatonic range

227. LISZT: VIA CRUCIS.

228. BARTÓK: BLUEBEARD'S CASTLE. (or.: 3♭)

229. FAURÉ: REQUIEM, OP. 48. (or.: 1♭)

230. LISZT: DIE SELIGKEITEN. (or.: 7♯)

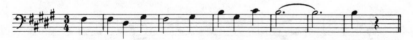

231. DEBUSSY: L'ENFANT PRODIGUE. (or.: 6♯)

232. LISZT: SPOSALIZIO.

233. BARTÓK: BLUEBEARD'S CASTLE. (or.: 0)

234. DEBUSSY: IBÉRIA. (or.: 5♭)

235. DELIBES: LAKMÉ. I. (or.: 1♭)

236. DEBUSSY: TROIS CHANSONS DE FRANCE. (or.: 0)

237. LISZT: DIE HEILIGE CÄCILIA. LEGENDE. (or.: 5♭)

238. VAUGHAN WILLIAMS: THREE POEMS BY WALT WHITMAN. (or.: 0)

239. LISZT: SEPTEM SACRAMENTA. (or.: 0)

240. KODÁLY: PEACOCK VARIATIONS.

241. BRITTEN: PETER GRIMES I.

(or.: 6♭)

a)

(or.: 4♯)

b)

242. DVOŘÁK: SONATINA IN G MAJOR, OP. 100. II. (or.: 1♯)

243. PUCCINI: TURANDOT. II. (or.: 1♯)

317

244. BORODIN: PRINCE IGOR. II. (or.: 2♯)

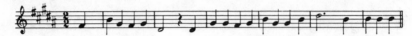

245. BARTÓK: DANCE SUITE. III. (or.: 3♯)

246. GAY—BRITTEN: THE BEGGAR'S OPERA. II. (or.: 0)

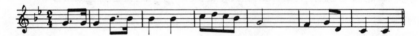

247. PUCCINI: TURANDOT. II. (or.: 0)

248. KODÁLY: DUO, OP. 7. III. (or.: 0)

249. GAY—BRITTEN: THE BEGGAR'S OPERA. I. (or.: 3♭)

a)

b)

250. STRAVINSKY: THE WEDDING.

(or.: 7♭)

a)

(or.: 6♯)

b)

251. DVOŘÁK: SONATINA IN G MAJOR, OP. 100. IV. (or.: 1♯)

252. DEBUSSY: BRUYÈRES. PRELUDES, II. (or.: 3♭)

Diatonic range

253. J. S. BACH: CANTATA, NO. 212.

254. HANDEL: JUDAS MACCABAEUS. I. (or.: 0)

255. MOZART: COSÌ FAN TUTTE. II. (or.: 0)

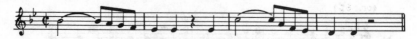

256. HANDEL: CONCERTO GROSSO IN G MAJOR. FUGUE. (or.: 1♯)

257. J. S. BACH: CANTATA, NO. 110. (or.: 2♯)

258. MOZART: COSÌ FAN TUTTE. I. (or.: 0)

320

259. MOZART: THE MAGIC FLUTE. I.

Range including altered notes

260. LULLY: ISIS. II.

261. H. PURCELL: HAIL! BRIGHT CECILIA. ODE. (or.: 0)

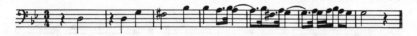

262. LULLY: BELLÉROPHON. II.

263. H. PURCELL: HAIL! BRIGHT CECILIA. ODE. (or.: 0)

264. J. S. BACH: CANTATA, NO. 102. (or.: 5♭)

265. HANDEL. JUDAS MACCABAEUS. II. (or.: 0)

266. H. PURCELL: THY GENIUS LO! (or.: 3♭)

267. HANDEL: MESSIAH. II. (or.: 0)

268. LULLY: PHAÉTON. III. (or.: 1♯)

269. J. S. BACH CANTATA, NO. 110. (or.: 3♯)

270. BEETHOVEN: PIANO SONATA IN E MAJOR, OP. 109. II. (or.: 1♯)

271. LULLY: PSYCHE. V. (or.: 2♯)

Modulating melodies

272. J. S. BACH: CANTATA, NO. 202. (or.: 2♯)

This melody modulates from B♭ major to D minor. The altered note E in **bar 5** becomes a diatonic note in the system with one flat. Suggested place for changing "d";

bar 5 - 6

fi = t

323

273. LULLY: BELLÉROPHON. II. (or.: 3♭)

The five-bar period is heard twice in the extract, first in G minor and then in D minor. Change of "d":

274. CARISSIMI: SVENTURA, CUOR MIO.

The last G (bar 11) of the G minor cadence in bars 10—11, at the same time as it represents an ending, also starts off the material to be heard in the new key:

275. J. S. BACH: CANTATA, NO. 4. (or.: 1♯)

After the G minor melodic unit of bars 1—4, the musical material of bars 5—10 is heard in D minor, and then from bar 11 the melody returns to G minor. The changes of "d":

| G minor 1 | | s-d | D minor | 1 | | 1-m | G minor |

EXTRACTS IN SOLFA LETTERS

The following extracts should be sung only to note names, using the key signatures with two flats or five sharps, accompanying with beating time.

276. J. S. BACH: WERDE MUNTER, MEIN GEMÜTE. CHORALE.

277. J. S. BACH: WACHET AUF, RUFT UNS DIE STIMME. CHORALE. (or.: 3♭)

278. LULLY: ALCESTE. IV. (or.: 0)

279. J. S. BACH: STRAF' MICH NICHT IN DEINEM ZORN. CHORALE. (or.: 3♭)

280. CARISSIMI: SVENTURA, CUOR MIO.

281. MONTEVERDI: L'INCORONAZIONE DI POPPEA. I. (or.: 1♯)

282. RAMEAU: DARDANUS. III. (or.: 2♯)

283. J. S. BACH: EIN' FESTE BURG IST UNSER GOTT. CHORALE. (or.: 2#)

d' | d'd's l t | d't l s d' | t l s l | f m r d ‖ d | s l s fis | s d s |

l t d' t | d't l s l | l s l s f | m d' t l | s l s f m | r d ‖

284. J. S. BACH: ALLE MENSCHEN MÜSSEN STERBEN. CHORALE. (or.: 2#)

s d' s l | s f m m | s s f m | r d d ‖ r r m fis | s fis s |

l t d' d' | t l l | m m l s | s fis s | l s f m | r d d ‖

285. J. S. BACH: ES IST GENUG, SO NIMM, HERR. CHORALE. (or.: 3#)

d r m fi fi s r r f | m r m fis s fis s d | r m fi |

fis r r f m r m fis | s fis r r r m r f m m r |

r r r m r f m m r s m r d s m r d ‖

286. J. S. BACH: O GOTT, DU FROMMER GOTT. CHORALE. (or.: 4#)

s m r d s s l l r r s f m r d s l l s f m r |

m fis l t l s s s s d' ta l l l l r'd' t s |

l s l t d' s s f m r r d ‖

327

Material in Several Parts

287. LASSUS: MOTET. (or.: 0)

In this motet only three of the four altered notes in the eleven-note range of the Palestrina style occur — "ta", "fi" and "di". The note "si" — that is, the aeolian leading note — is not included.

The whole motet, in keeping with the key signature, should be sung with B♮ as "d". (Cf. Lassus, "Expandi manus mea", on page 234.)

288. LASSUS: MOTET. (or.: 1♭)

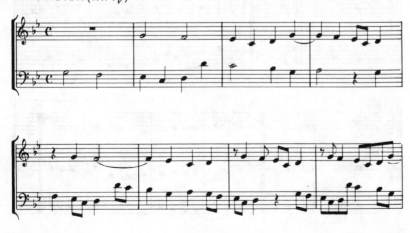

289. MARENZIO: OCCHI DOLCI. MADRIGAL. (or.: 0)

In this choral work all eleven of the notes in the Palestrina style range appear (the diatonic notes + the altered notes "fi" , "di" , "si" and "ta"). It should be sung according to the key signature — with B♭ as "d" and without any change of "d".

290. PALESTRINA: ESURIENTES. MOTET. (or.: 0)

291. J. S. BACH: WER WEISS, WIE NAHE MIR. CHORALE.

The third line of the chorale modulates into the relative major. The closing tonic chord of the last G minor cadence has a Picardy third.

292. H. PURCELL: THE NAVIS.

The musical material of bars 5—10 and 16—24 appears in F major. In the

bass progression of bars 7 and 18 the E♮ is the altered note "ta" leading to chord IV⁶ in F major, preparing the subdominant chord which begins the cadence. Suggested place for changing "d":

293. SEVERINO CORNETI: CHE T'AGGIO FATTO. MADRIGAL. (or.:0)

294. J. S. BACH: HERZLIEBSTER JESU, WAS HAST DU. CHORALE.

DEVELOPMENT OF MUSICAL MEMORY

Memorizing and Transposing a Unison Melody

From the sight-singing material in staff notation it is mainly the extracts with altered notes that should be used for memorizing. The way of checking the memorized melody is the same as for Chapter III (see page 243).

After a certain time **transposition singing** of the melodies must be made an organic part of the working process. Depending on the range of the melody, transposition can be practised in the keys using C, C♯, C♭, F, F♯, B♭ and B as "d", in the way already familiar (see page 243).

Memorizing Two—Part Material

As in Chapter III it is only with the help of the inner ear that the students will learn the selected extracts (see page 244). If the memorizing work requires a lot of time, the given "d" can be sounded several times, so that the notation and its absolute pitch should become fixed in accordance with reality in the inner musical imagination of the students.

THE TWO-PART QUOTATIONS

295. J. S. BACH: ENGLISH SUITE IN A MINOR. GIGUE. (or.: 0)

296. LASSUS: MOTET. (or.: 1♭)

297. J. S. BACH: MENUETT IN G MINOR.

298. LA RUE: MOTET.

299. CARISSIMI: BEGLI OCCHI, PIETÁ. (or.: 2♯)

300. LASSUS: MOTET. (or.: 1♭)

301. BEETHOVEN: STRING QUARTET IN C MAJOR, OP. 59, NO. 3. IV. (or.: 1♯)

302. ROTENBUCHER: MOTET.

303. J. S. BACH: ENGLISH SUITE IN A MINOR (or.: 0)

304. H. PURCELL: SONATA III. (or.: 0)

305. LE JEUNE: MADRIGAL.

306. HANDEL: FUGUE IN G MINOR.

EAR TRAINING

Recognition of Intervals

Intervals in the diatonic pentachords

The intervals of the ascending and descending diatonic pentachords display five different interval sequences in relation to the starting note:

	The interval sequence starting with the smallest	Direction and starting note of the pentachord
a)	maj. 2 maj. 3 perf. 4 perf. 5	ascending from "d" and "s"
		descending from "l" and "m"
b)	maj. 2 min. 3 perf. 4 perf. 5	ascending from "r" and "l"
		descending from "r" and "s"
c)	min. 2 min. 3 perf. 4 perf. 5	ascending from "m"
		descending from "d"
d)	maj. 2 maj. 3 aug. 4 perf. 5	ascending from "f"
		descending from "t"
e)	min. 2 min. 3 perf. 4 dim. 5	ascending from "t"
		descending from "f"

As with the pentatonic note-groups these interval sequences should be worked into the ear training exercises in a similar way: the teacher selects one of the sequences and plays its intervals in any order from the same lowest or highest note, while the students write down the intervals as they sound.

For example the series in c) in the order 4, 3, 5, 2, with A as the top note:

1. Recognition.

342

2. Individual checking, filling in omissions.

3. Group checking, with naming the intervals: perf. 4, etc.

4. Singing (first of all from the unchanging note and then from the note which changes from interval to interval).

a) To interval names.

b) To solfa names.

(Cf. 1—4, page 158).

The interval pairs of the triad inversions

In the inversions of the triads it is always a third and fourth or a fourth and third that are to be found (see page 301). In the course of this ear training only those interval pairs should be used which from the point of view of structure and colour— even without the tonal framework — can be clearly distinguished from each other. These are the following:

a) $\dfrac{\text{p 4}}{\text{m 3}}$ = major⁶   b) $\dfrac{\text{p 4}}{\text{M 3}}$ = minor⁶   c) $\dfrac{\text{aug. 4}}{\text{m 3}}$ = dim.⁶

d) $\dfrac{\text{M 3}}{\text{p 4}}$ = major⁶₄   e) $\dfrac{\text{m 3}}{\text{p 4}}$ = minor⁶₄   f) $\dfrac{\text{m 3}}{\text{aug. 4}}$ = dim.⁶

These six types of interval pairs should be practised from the recognition point of view as the pairs of thirds were in Chapter III (see page 250).

For example, the sequence a)—f)—d)—c)—e)—b):

1. Recognition.

Teacher (piano)						
Students: (writing)	↑ p4 / ↓ m3	↑m3 / ↓aug 4	↑ M3 / ↓ p4	↑aug.4 / ↓ m3	↑ m3 / ↓ p4	↑ p4 / ↓ M3

2. Individual checking and filling in of omissions.

3. Group checking, with naming of the interval pairs: $\dfrac{\uparrow\text{perf.4}}{\downarrow\text{maj.3}}$ etc.

4. Solfa singing starting from the central note (with all appropriate names occurring in major and harmonic minor keys):

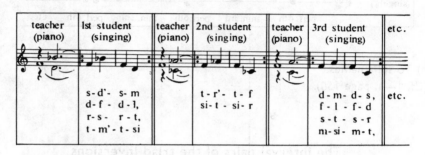

teacher (piano)	1st student (singing)	teacher (piano)	2nd student (singing)	teacher (piano)	3rd student (singing)	etc.
	s - d'- s- m / d- f - d -1, / r- s- r - t, / t - m'- t - si		t - r'- t - f / si- t - si- r		d - m- d- s, / f - l - f- d / s- t - s -r / m-si- m- t,	etc.

(Cf. 1—4, page 251.)

Interval recognition from "Let Us Sing Correctly"

In this chapter use exercises 34, 38, 39, 41, 42, 43, 44, 45 and 46 for ear training purposes, in accordance with the detailed stages described earlier (see page 248). Since their range presents the possibility to do so, exercises 34, 38 and 39 should be played preferably in the two flat or five sharp systems so that singing of them to note names will be related to the key signature area already practised in this chapter.

Chord Recognition
Root position triads

TYPE RECOGNITION

The teacher plays the four kinds of triad in various orders, but with the lowest note of every chord — in this case the root — remaining the same.

This ear training exercise should otherwise be carried out in a way similar to interval recognition.

For example, the sequence minor—augmented—major—diminished—major:

1. Recognition.

2. Individual checking and filling in of omissions while the chords are played again.
3. Group checking with naming: minor, etc.
4. Solfa singing using all the appropriate names for the given type within the major and harmonic minor keys:

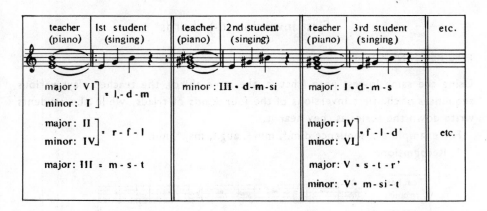

(See the triad types on page 209.)

TRIADS PLACED WITHIN TONALITY

After giving the tonic note of some major or harmonic minor key, the teacher plays the various chords of the given tonality and the students, with the help of singing to solfa, establish the degree number within the key of each chord.

For example the sequence V—VI—IV—II—V—III—VII—I in the minor (tonic = "I"):

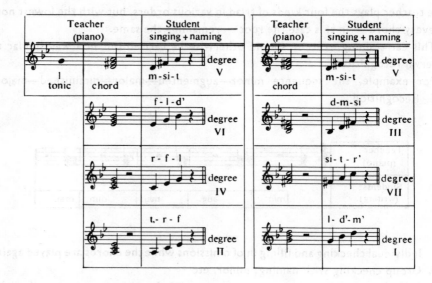

The teacher should make up similar sequences.

First inversion (6-) chords

TYPE RECOGNITION

Using the same lowest note (that is, the same third), the teacher plays various sequences of the first inversions of the four kinds of triads, while the students write down the series as they hear it.

For example the sequence dim.⁶, min.⁶, aug.⁶, maj.⁶, min.⁶:

1. Recognition.

2. Individual checking, and filling in of omissions.

346

3. Group checking, with naming of the chords: dim.⁶, etc.

4. Solfa singing of the given chord using all its possible names which occur in the major or harmonic minor keys:

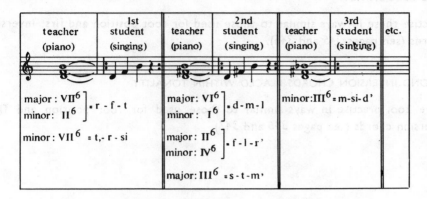

teacher (piano)	1st student (singing)	teacher (piano)	2nd student (singing)	teacher (piano)	3rd student (singing)	etc.

major : VII⁶ ⎫
minor : II⁶ ⎭ = r - f - t

minor : VII⁶ = t,- r - si

major: VI⁶ ⎫
minor : I⁶ ⎭ = d - m - l

major : II⁶ ⎫
minor : IV⁶ ⎭ = f - l - r'

major: III⁶ = s - t - m'

minor:III⁶ = m - si - d'

FIRST INVERSION CHORDS PLACED WITHIN TONALITY

After giving the tonic note of any major or harmonic minor key, the teacher plays various first inversions from the given tonality while the students, with the aid of solfa singing, establish the degree number of the various chords within the key.

For example, the sequence II⁶—V⁶—I⁶—IV⁶—III⁶—VII⁶—VI⁶ in the minor (tonic = "I"):

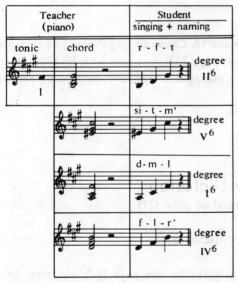

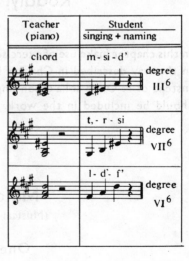

The teacher should make up similar sequences.

347

Second inversion ($^6_4$-) chords

TYPE RECOGNITION

Practise these in ways similar to those used for root position and first inversion chords (see pages 345 and 346).

SECOND INVERSION CHORDS PLACED WITHIN TONALITY

Here, too, practise in ways similar to those used for root position and first inversion chords (see pages 346 and 347).

Rhythm Dictation
(Musical material on page 417.)

The stages used in practising are the same as hitherto (see page 79).

Kodály: 24 Little Canons

In this chapter make use of exercises 6,9 and 16. Canon singing should be performed in the way described in Chapter III (see page 252), but now with B♭ or B as "d" instead of F. Once solfa canon singing is managed successfully, note name practice should be included in the work.

Melody Dictation
(Musical material on page 421).

One-part dictation

The preparatory stages are the same as hitherto (see page 162) but now B♭ is used as "d" in keeping with the given musical material.

Melody dictation should be carried out similarly to the way described in Chapter III (see page 252).

Two-part extracts
(Musical material on page 424.)

At this stage it is necessary to start memorizing by ear simple two-part extracts containing no more than one motif — as follows:

1. The teacher performs the selected extract on the piano and repeats it as necessary until volunteers are able to sing it from memory, singing the parts one after the other to solfa and beating time as accompaniment.

2. Once everyone knows the music of the different parts, checking in two parts follows:

a) Singing either part to solfa + showing the other part to hand-signs.

b) Singing either part to solfa with the hand-sign accompaniment of the same melody + showing the other part to hand-signs at the same time.

c) Simultaneous performance of both parts to hand-signs, without singing.

d) As in a) with note name singing.

e) As in b) with note name singing.

f) Singing one part to solfa + playing the other part on the piano.

g) As in f) but with note name singing.

h) Writing down the complete material in staff notation.

3. Group checking.

a) One or several students sing individual parts one after the other to note names reading them from their exercise books.

b) Volunteers perform the whole of the music from memory on the piano.

If in one part of the selected extract there is an altered note which has no hand-sign, then those stages of the checking in two parts which become unrealistic as regards their practical realization will naturally be omitted.

Bach Chorale Extracts
(Musical material on page 427.)

The learning and practising process is the same here as in Chapter III (see page 253).

PLANNING SUGGESTION

(See the diagram at the end of the book.)

CHAPTER V.

MUSICAL ANALYSIS OF AMERICAN FOLKSONGS

307. RAIN, RAIN,

(150 A. F. S.,* page 10)

Rain, rain, go a-way, Come again some other day.

The range of the melody is the maj. 2 / min. 3 pentatonic trichord, the lowest note of which is also the last note of the folksong:

final note

Being familiar with the pentatonic trichords we can hear the melody as ending on either "l" or "m":

r - d - l,
l - s - m

The basic idea of the music is the one-bar motif using a descending minor third, which does not, however, come as an opening element in the second half of the melody — here it appears as the closing phrase of a new two-bar unit:

bar 1	bar 2	bar 3	bar 4
		B	
a	a,		a,

* 150 A.F.S. = "150 American Folk Song" collected by Katalin Komlós, selected and edited by Peter Erdei at the Kodály Musical Training Institute. Wellesley

Bars 3 and 4 merge indivisibly into one because bar 3, from the melodic and rhythmic angles alike, requires a continuation: a) The upward fourth moves round the main note F and in this way opens up the melody; b) the continuous eighth movement virtually runs into the material of the final bar.

The various musical motifs of the folksong together unfold the whole form:

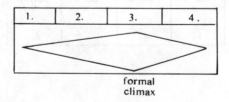

motivic construction	a	a,	B b (a₊) + a,	
closing notes — bar final note			4	
closing notes — motif final note	①	①	——————→	①
rhythmic movement	1st element	2nd element	3rd element	4th element (recapitulation)
kind of rhythm cadence (see rhythm cadences on page 172)	with unstressed ending — weak	relatively stressed ending — strong	the most unstressed ending — weak	— strong
the role of the various rhythmic elements in the form	neutral starting element	braking therefore closing element	a carrying over element	closing element

Taking the melody as a whole it is the third formal unit (in the present case the third bar) which brings something new, a contrast, as a result of which it is also here that the form's inner dynamism reaches its climax:

1.	2.	3.	4.

formal
climax

356

308. HOT CROSS BUNS

(150 A. F. S., page 9)

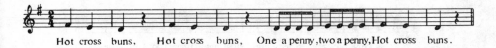

Hot cross buns, Hot cross buns, One a penny, two a penny, Hot cross buns.

The notes used are the thichord m—r—d , with "d" as final note:
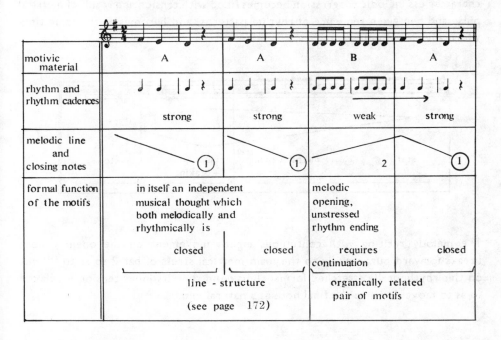 The material is structured A A B A , where the A motifs
form self-contained melodic and formal units. In the clearly divided four-line
melody it is again the third form element which produces the contrast: a) instead
of the melodic line descending by seconds the new material rises; b) the quarter
stepping is replaced by busy eighth movement; and c) in contrast with the independent and closed A lines, the B motif wins its justification only together
with the following bars.

The form-creative role of melody and rhythm appears in organic unity:

motivic material	A	A	B	A
rhythm and rhythm cadences	strong	strong	weak	strong
melodic line and closing notes	①	①	2	①
formal function of the motifs	in itself an independent musical thought which both melodically and rhythmically is	closed	melodic opening, unstressed rhythm ending	closed
	closed	closed	requires continuation	closed
	line - structure (see page 172)		organically related pair of motifs	

357

309. HICKETY

(150 A. F. S., page 13)

Hickety, hickety   horny cup   How many fingers do I hold up?

The notes used form the $\xrightarrow[\text{maj.2}]{\text{min.3}}$ pentatonic trichord. As in the preceding melodies, the final note is the same as the lowest note of the range used, and so its melodic line has a falling tendency.

Here, too, the melody may be interpreted in two ways tonally: it can be taken as ending on "s" or on "r". The exposed melodic main note, however, absolutely suggests interpreting it as ending on "s".

In the musical material only one motif and its repetition are heard. The motif's melodic line is extremely simple: after recitation on the highest of the notes used, there is a descent by degrees to the lowest note which is also the last note. This characterless melodic progression becomes filled with tension as a result of metrical pulse and the given sequence of rhythm patterns, and becomes at the same time a formally closed unit:

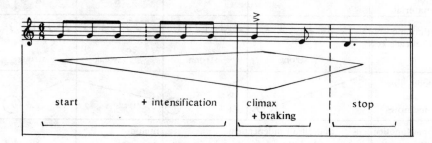

The melody reciting with continuous eighth movement on the opening note breaks forward purposefully to the main metrical stress of bar 2 so as to fill out on this rhythmically stretched formal climax and then its inner tension is relaxed so as to move down to the final note as a natural end.

358

310. HUNT THE SLIPPER

(150 A. F. S., page 9)

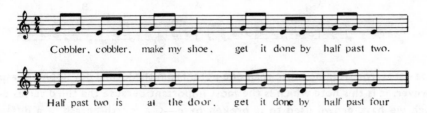

Cobbler, cobbler, make my shoe, get it done by half past two.

Half past two is at the door, get it done by half past four

As in the preceding song the notes used make up the $\xrightarrow[\text{maj.2}]{\text{min.3}}$ pentaton trichord but in this case it is the highest note which becomes the final note. Because of this melodic movement it is the d—l,—s, interpretation that we are most likely to feel natural:

final
note

d   l,   s,   d

As far as its motivic material is concerned the folksong is very closely related to the song beginning **Rain, Rain.** In both a minor third descending from the stressed beat of the bar to the unstressed is the essence of what happens melodically, but whereas in the above song each third-phrase appears as an independent form

element:

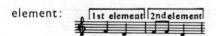

1st element   2nd element

here the arrangement of the rhythm patterns groups pairs of third-phrases into one motivic unit:

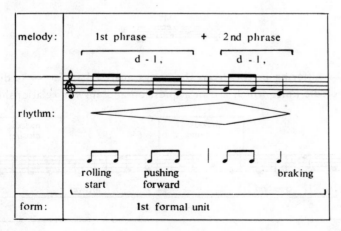

melody:	1st phrase	+	2nd phrase
	d - l,		d - l,
rhythm:			
	rolling start	pushing forward	braking
form:	1st formal unit		

In the melody the seven-syllable rhythm pattern occurs four times, associated with the A A A, B motivic material:

A, deviates from A in no more than one note. From the formal development aspect however, it is this note which is the most important because the third series d—l, which we have grown used to is broken by d—s, a fourth-phrase of a different character. This "s" motif ending is a very significant detail in the song from several points of view:

a) The music material, hitherto differentiated by rhythm alone, is now enriched by a new melodic detail. b) After the equal A motifs this melodic opening appears with the need for closing, making the third formal unit dynamic, and at the same time the whole form. c) It reinforces the definite melody closing function of the "d" ending in the last motif because the natural melodic objective of this "s" is to arrive at "d".

311. BYE, BYE BABY

(150 A. F. S., page 11)

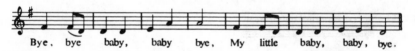

Bye, bye baby, baby bye, My little baby, baby, bye.

Its range is a pentatonic tetrachord with "d" as the keynote — and so major in character:

The music — differing in this from the songs analysed so far — is divided into only two melodic units which are in a question and answer relationship:

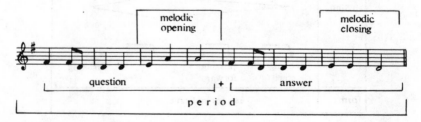

The two halves of the melody are built from identical material and they differ from one another only in their last phrase:

Since the song does not evolve its form from folskong-like lines but presents the typically art music period framework, it is better for the way of indicating the form also to be adapted to art music formal analysis practice:

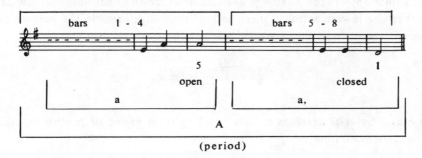

(period)

The melody's basic rhythmic movement is quarter stepping the even pulse of which is interrupted only in two places — formally very important places — in the first and last bars of each half of the melody:

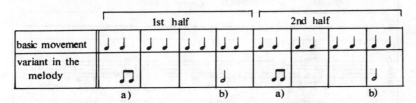

The element marked a) ♫ provides the opening half of the melody, leaning down towards the keynote, with appropriate forward-pushing force, while the element marked b) ♩ first of all increases the intensity of the melodic opening and prepares the new start in the second half of the melody, and in the second place it reinforces the final coming to rest of the melody.

312. POOR LITTLE KITTY PUSS

(150 A.F.S., page 13)

The range of notes used here is the m—r—d—l, pentatonic tetrachord, with "d" as final note. In the folksongs analysed thus far the final note was the same as either the lowest or the highest note of the range used. In the present case, however, the melody moves around the final note:

The music material develops strictly speaking from varied or precise repetition of the same motif (line):

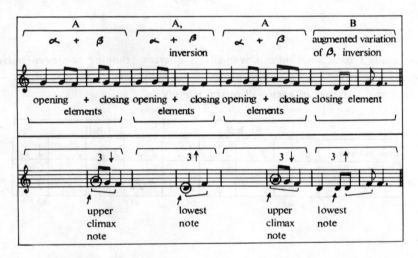

The development and evolution of the element marked "β" are therefore closely related to the inner life of the form:

a) As a motif-ending element, it is heard as a descending third phrase filled out with a passing note. b) As an element which ends a larger formal section (half-melody) it moves from the lowest note back to the keynote. c) As an element which ends the whole melody it likewise bends back upwards from the lowest note but here — as if to emphasise the importance of the closing motif's formal function — the original phrase of two beats broadens into a motif taking four beats. Working in the knowledge of these finer inner relationships in the melody perhaps the more correct formal outline would be A A, A B[a.]

313. DRAW A BUCKET OF WATER

(150 A. F. S., page 14)

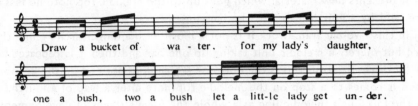

Draw a bucket of wa-ter, for my lady's daughter,

one a bush, two a bush let a litt-le lady get un-der.

The notes used here are  in which the pentatonic major

third appears as its inversion, the minor sixth. Thus the melody is in the pentatonic tetrachord with "m" as the keynote.

In this melody there are really only two kinds of motivic material to be found:

In the "A" material here — as opposed to the preceding song — the start of the song is varied and the identical element is preserved by the cadential pattern:

If we write these motifs using the rhythm pattern $\frac{2}{4}$ ♩♪♪♩ | ♩ ♩ | familiar from the other songs, we are faced with a clear representation of the melodic development of the "α" element:

Motif "A" starts the melody off with a sudden upward fourth from a static keynote, thus giving it impetus.

Motif "A," — coming in the centre of the form — keeps the music on the same melodic plain.

Motif "A,," — as the material which ends the melody — comes by a descending line to the low final note which has not yet been heard in the course of the motif.

It is into this formal framework that the "B" material of the third motif is fitted becoming again the most exposed form element in the melody:

a) It presents new material which goes up to the melodic top note no less than twice, and by a fourth leap into the bargain.

b) In this two-bar framework it is not a motif with a longer arching line that is heard but merely a melodic unit taking up one bar and then it is repeated.

c) Of the four motifs this is the only one which does not end on the keynote — indeed it comes to a stop on the melodic top note after a leap of a fourth.

In the folksong's melodic line as a whole the form's stages of development are outlined with virtually artistic perfection:

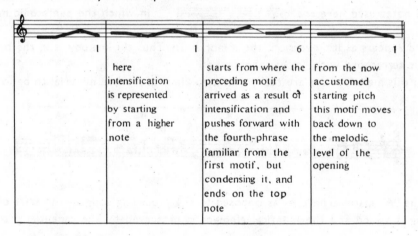

1	1	6	1
	here intensification is represented by starting from a higher note	starts from where the preceding motif arrived as a result of intensification and pushes forward with the fourth-phrase familiar from the first motif, but condensing it, and ends on the top note	from the now accustomed starting pitch this motif moves back down to the melodic level of the opening

It is not here that the folksong's second motif appears for the first time. We met this same melodic movement in the folksong beginning **Rain, Rain,** bars 3 and 4:

Rain, Rain   (bars 3 - 4)   Draw a Bucket of Water   (A.)

What happens melodically is identical and the only difference is in the rhythm which adapts to the text. In one respect, however, there is an essential difference between the two: whereas in the **Rain, Rain** motif — through the effect

364

of the melodic environment — two different tonal interpretations are possible, the latter song's "A," motif — likewise on account of the given environment — fits within a definite tonal framework and is thus tonally unambiguous:

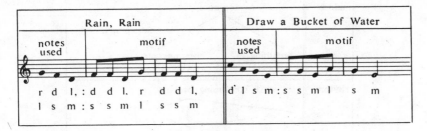

Rain, Rain		Draw a Bucket of Water	
notes used	motif	notes used	motif

r d l,:d d l, r   d d l,   d' l s m:s s s m l   s   m
l s m:s s m l   s s m

This motif incidentally recurs in many American folksongs and so it can be considered as something of a motif-type.

314. BLUEBIRD

(150 A. F. S., page 17)

Here comes a   bluebird   through the   window.   Hey,

diddle- dum a   day   day   day.

Here the range of notes embraces the complete pentatony, with "d" as the final

note: 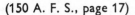 Its key is thus "d" pentatonic.

In the first half of the melody comes an independent and closed motif, with a

precise repetition: The closed unity of this motif is

secured by the melodic and rhythmic elements together:

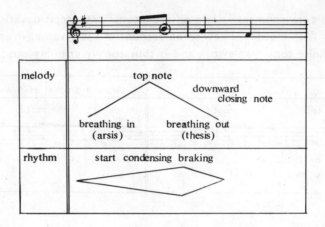

melody	top note downward closing note breathing in breathing out (arsis) (thesis)
rhythm	start condensing braking

As a continuation of this motif pair, self-contained in this way, the B+C material brings the close of the song as a whole. Its melodic motif is the phrase which descends to the keynote, and its reinforcement; and the rhythmic motif is the expansion of the previous rhythmic arrangement, making it more comprehensive:

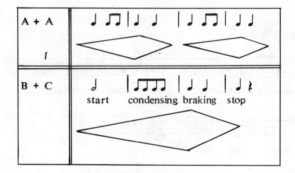

The form details of the song, conspicuous even externally, may be displayed clearly in the following table:

notes used final note	key	range	bar numbers music material last notes of motifs	characteristic rhythm pattern or rhythm sequence
l s m r d	"d" pentatonic	6 - 1	2 2 2 + 2 4 A A B + C 3' 3' (2) 1	♩ ♫ | ♩ ♩ ――――― ♩ | ♫♫ | ♩ ♩ | ♩ ♪

366

The first line of the folksong's secord stanza expands to seven syllables and it is for this reason that the "A" motif appears with its rhythm broken up into shorter values:

If we compare with this the last motif of the song beginning **Draw a Bucket of Water,** we discover another motif-type which can be found in several American folksongs:

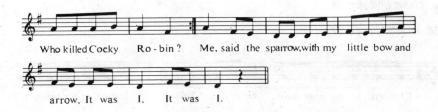

315. COCKY ROBIN

(150 A. F. S., page 18)

Like the preceding song this, too, is a "d" pentatonic melody. Its formal construction is asymmetrical, divided as it is into 4-bar and 6-bar units:

The 4-bar first half of the melody divides clearly into the already familiar motif pairs A—A. The 6-bar second half appears to be a sequence of three motifs:

367

But if we look more closely at the text and the melody the expansion from four to six bars looks much more like the result of augmentation:

Even without these augmentations the text and melody form a complete half-melody.

Thus the form of the whole folksong is:

316. DANCE JOSEY

(150 A. F. S., page 27)

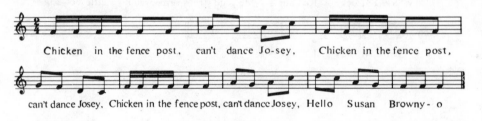

The notes used here in the "d" pentatonic melody cover the range of a ninth around the final note "d":

(= plagal range, see page 273)

Its motivic structure is A A, A B:

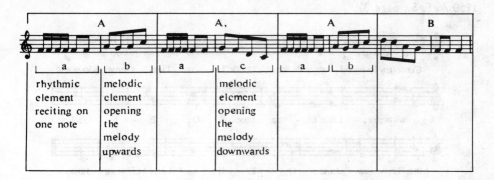

It is characteristic of the "A" material that the first bar, appearing with the rhythm pattern ♫♫♪, recites on the keynote, whereas the second bar with the eighth movement ♪♪♪♪ leads to the opening of the melody.

Motif "B" is a contrast in character. Its first bar leads back the melody towards the keynote after the open ending of motif "A", while its second bar really stays on the keynote, and with this brings the whole form to an end. In spite of this the B motif draws its musical material from A:

The melodic elements, identical in origin, have exchanged their formal roles: a) element "c" opens, and element "c⁵" prepares the close; b) element "a" starts off the motif, but "a," by drawing together the original ♫♫♪ rhythm values (♪♪♪♪ = ♪ ♩) finally brakes the music.

The melodic outline and the cadences of the folksong are also interesting:

The "A" and "A," motifs are identical in function: each starts from the exposed keynote and moves to the fifth. But since this fifth, as a melodic target, always comes in a different register and as the result of melodic progression in contrasting directions, the music does not become monotonous in spite of the repetition: it reaches the last B motif by constant wave motion.

369

317. LIZA JANE

(150 A. F. S., page 3)

Come my love and go with me, Little'Li - za Jane, Come my love and
go with me, Little'Li - za Jane. O, E - li - za!
Little'Li - za Jane, O, E - li - za! Little 'Li - za Jane.

This song presents a characteristic form type: in its four lines the A and A, of the first half are in a question and answer relationship, just as the B and B, of the second half of the melody. Thus in the four lines the opening and closing process appears twice:

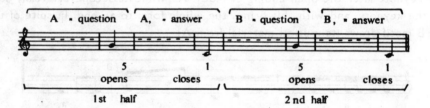

The A A, B B, indication, however, suffices only to define the formal framework divided symmetrically into two parts. If we wish to show the inner organisation of the music's smaller melodic units we require more detailed formal points of reference:

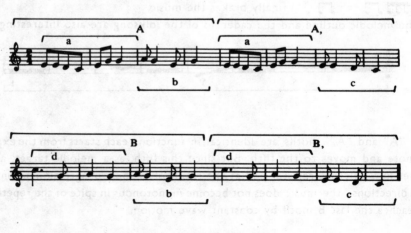

Each of the four melodic elements — "a" "b" "c" and "d" — fulfils a definite formal function:

"a" is the starting element in the lines in the first half,

"d" is the starting element in the lines in the second half,

"b" is the question-like opening element in the first and third lines,

"c" is the answer-like closing element in the second and fourth lines.

Thus the first melodic element in the lines forms organic units of the two pairs of lines directly related to each other while the second melodic element in the lines secures the melodic and formal rhyming of the even and odd lines:

	The folksong's			
	1st element		2nd element	
1st line	a	(starts)	b	(opens)
2nd line	a	(starts)	c	(closes)
3rd line	d	(starts)	b	(opens)
4th line	d	(starts)	c	(closes)

A particularly interesting point in this folksong is that the way the unchanged melodic elements being differently fitted together produces the development of the form as a whole.

318. ROCKY MOUNTAIN

(150 A. F. S., page 18)

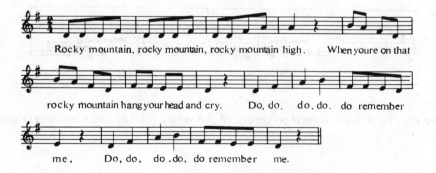

Rocky mountain, rocky mountain, rocky mountain high. When youre on that rocky mountain hang your head and cry. Do, do, do, do, do remember me. Do, do, do, do, do remember me.

371

This melody is A B C C, in structure, once more using double opening and closing. If we examine the melodic and rhythmic content of the lines which appear to contain contrasting music material, here, too, we find the organic elements which hold the sequence of the lines together, securing the folksong's individual appearance and its organic unity.

These details are as follows.

The "B" line draws on "A" for, on the one hand, the rhythm pattern which moves in continuous eighth and only brakes itself at the end(♫♫|♫♫|♫♫|♩ ♪), and on the other hand for the 1+1+2 bars inner division of the 4-bar formal unit:

Line "C" is connected even more organically to "B". a) Its first 2-bar melodic unit is none other than the augmented crab inversion of the "ɣ" element in "B" (augmented rhythmically in proportion):

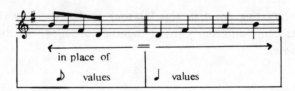

b) Its second 2-bar melodic unit is a variant of the "d" material in line B, which opens out like a question:

And thus here is the formal structure of the whole melody, with its interrelationships:

372

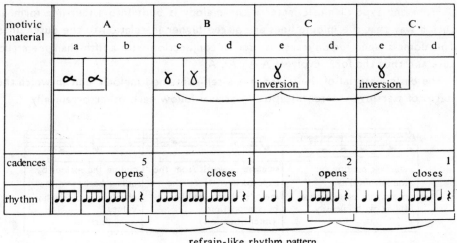

motivic material	A		B		C		C,	
	a	b	c	d	e	d,	e	d

refrain-like rhythm pattern

319. THE RIDDLE SONG.

(150 A. F. S., page 45)

I gave my love a cherry that has no stone, I gave my love a chicken that has no bone, I gave my love a ring that has no end, I gave my love a baby, there's no cryen.

All the songs so far analysed which contained all the notes of pentatony have been "d" pentatonic melodies. This folksong moves away from the "d" pentatonic frame-work with its novel melodic movement, and comes in a different tonality:

final note -s

And so its key is "s" pentatonic.

From one type of music material the melody is built into a four-line form, in such a way that the middle lines are placed higher in relation to the outer lines. This dome-shaped melodic arch is used in conjunction with a fifth-changing structure and thus the form evolves: A A⁵, A⁵, A,,.

The basic material of the folksong is a self-contained melodic unit in which the stages of starting — intensification — arrival follow each other organically:

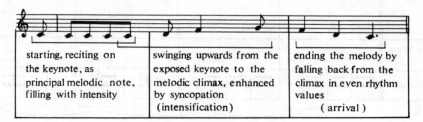

| starting, reciting on the keynote, as principal melodic note, filling with intensity | swinging upwards from the exposed keynote to the melodic climax, enhanced by syncopation (intensification) | ending the melody by falling back from the climax in even rhythm values (arrival) |

The smaller or greater variation which presents itself in the remaining lines is likewise produced by the formal development's inner regularity mentioned above:

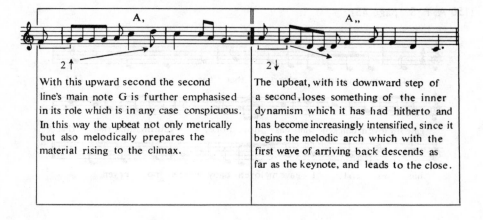

2↑	2↓
With this upward second the second line's main note G is further emphasised in its role which is in any case conspicuous. In this way the upbeat not only metrically but also melodically prepares the material rising to the climax.	The upbeat, with its downward step of a second, loses something of the inner dynamism which it has had hitherto and has become increasingly intensified, since it begins the melodic arch which with the first wave of arriving back descends as far as the keynote, and leads to the close.

On this basis the folksong strictly speaking lives a double life:

A			A,5			A,5	A,,		
starts	intens-ifies	arrives	starts more dynam-ically	intens-ifies	arrives		starts the first wave of arriving back	intens-ifies	finally arrives
starts			intensifies			remains on the intens-ification level	a r r i v e s		

The tension arrangement in the form as analysed above in the individual folksong lines and in the complete folksong produces that inner undulation which enchants the melody into a living organism as it were.

320. MY GOOD OLD MAN

(150 A. F. S., page 3)

Where are you going my good old man? Where are you going my sugar, my lamb? Best old man in the world.

The key of the melody is "l" pentatonic:

The formal structure is A A⁵, B which appears extraordinary, particularly after the preceding song. It is not so much as a result of the three-line melodic structure as because of the fact that the song has no completing "A" or "A," line to secure symmetry. We feel the melody to be more or less unfinished, all the more so because the last line, B, does not contain as many metric groups as the preceding lines:

375

	independent rhythm patterns producing metric groups	+ last note
A	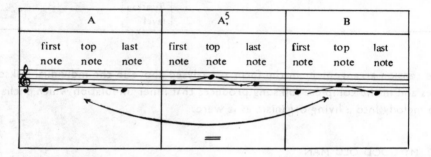	♩
A⁵		♩
B		♩

In spite of all this the symmetry principle — which is one of the fundamental formal regularities particularly in three-section musical forms — is also present in this song, in the melodic sweep of the folksong's lines:

A			A⁵			B		
first note	top note	last note	first note	top note	last note	first note	top note	last note

In this outline of the melody it also becomes clear that the A⁵ line presents a tonal fifth change, for the A line covers the range from the keynote to the fifth, whereas the A⁵ line goes from the fifth only to the keynote (that is, to its octave).

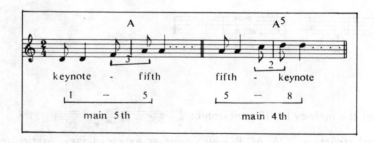

SUPPLEMENT

MUSIC MATERIAL FOR EAR TRAINING EXERCISES

This supplement containes the music quotations which serve as material for rhythm and melody dictation. This material, divided as it is into chapters, is connected with the appropriate chapters of the book and is built in organically to the study material they contain. (See the "Planning Suggestion" tables in the book.) The book's various chapters provide detailed information concerning the pedagogical stages involved in the individual ear training forms and the ways of using the quotations.

CHAPTER I

(See ''Melody Memorizing by Ear'' ''Rhythm Dictation'' and ''Planning Suggestion'',
on pages *75, 79* and *81.*)

Melody Memorizing by Ear (=Melody Dictation)

Unaccompanied unison pentatonic melodies

The extracts which follow are taken from Kodály's ''333 Elementary Exercises''.
(Their original numbers are to be found in the numbers on the right.) From this
material the teacher should select those parts which he considers most useful for
the given group of students.

EASY $\frac{2}{4}$ MELODIC SECTIONS

MAJOR SECOND RANGE

(These melodic phrases can be sung by students using any of the pentatonic major
2nd names: d—r   r—m   or   s—l)

(These phrases can be sung in two ways within pentatony by the students:
d—l,—s, or s—m—r)

326.  **327.**

328.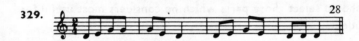

329.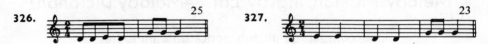

MAJOR SECOND
MINOR THIRD RANGE

(The phrases can be sung both with r—d—l, and with l—s—m names.)

330.  **331.**

332.

333.  **334.**

335.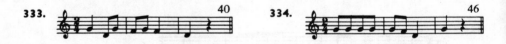

(Because of the major third this set of notes can be interpreted in only one way within the pentatony: as a m—r—d trichord.)

MAJOR SECOND
MINOR THIRD
MAJOR SECOND RANGE

(This can be taken once more in two different ways: as a r—d—l,—s, tetrachord or as l—s—m—r)

381

MAJOR SECOND
MAJOR SECOND
MINOR THIRD RANGE

(Can be sung in only one way: as a m—r—d—l, tetrachord.)

MINOR THIRD
MAJOR SECOND
MAJOR SECOND RANGE

(= s—m—r—d tetrachord)

383

(m—r—d—l,—s,)

364.

365.

366.

367.

368.

369.

370.

Pentatonic melodies with accompaniment

390. BARTÓK: FOR CHILDREN III.

(Concerning the $\frac{3}{8}$ time signature, see p. 64)

391. BARTÓK: BLUEBEARD'S CASTLE.

392. MUSSORGSKY: BORIS GODUNOV II.

393. BARTÓK: BLUEBEARD'S CASTLE. (or.: from D)

394. KODÁLY: ODE TO FRANZ LISZT.

395. BARTÓK: 44 DUOS.

Rhythm Dictation

In all cases it is the upper part — that is, the melody — of the extract the rhythm of which the students have to record. If in a given extract there is a sung melody together with its accompaniment (e. g. Nos. 396, 404, etc.) it is naturally the rhythm of the vocal material which the students should pay attention to and write down.

396. FRESCOBALDI: SE L'AURA SPIRA.

397. HANDEL: SAMSON II.

398. J. S. BACH: ST. MATTHEW PASSION I.

(Before playing it, the teacher can mention the time signature of the extract.)

399. HANDEL: SAMSON II.

400. HANDEL: RODELINDA III.

401. J. HAYDN: PIANO SONATA IN C MAJOR II.

402. MOZART: IL SERAGLIO II.

403. CARISSIMI: VITTORIA, VITTORIA.

404. FRESCOBALDI: SE L'AURA SPIRA.

405. HANDEL: SAMSON I.

406. F. VITALI: PASTORELLA.

407. MOZART: THE MAGIC FLUTE I.

408. MOZART: PIANO SONATA IN B FLAT MAJOR III. (K. 570)

409. MOZART: PIANO SONATA IN D MAJOR II. (K. 284)

410. BEETHOVEN: PIANO SONATA IN G MAJOR, OP. 79. III.

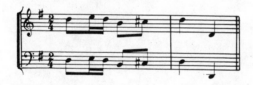

411. MOZART: IL SERAGLIO II.

412. HANDEL: RODELINDA III.

413. MOZART: THE MAGIC FLUTE II.

CHAPTER II

(See "Ear Training" and "Planning Suggestion" on pages *158 — 166*).

Rhythm Dictation

414. MOZART: PIANO SONATA IN D MAJOR III. (K. 311)

415. MOZART: PIANO SONATA IN F MAJOR III. (K. 332)

416. CALESTANI: ACCORTA LUSINGHIERA.

417. J. HAYDN: PIANO SONATA IN E MINOR III.

418. BEETHOVEN: 6 VARIATIONS IN G MAJOR.

419. MOZART: RONDO IN F MAJOR (K. 15hh)

420. J. S. BACH: CELLO SOLO SUITE IN G MAJOR. GIGUE.

421. HANDEL: RODELINDA. OVERTURE.

422. HANDEL: SAMSON I.

423. MOZART: PIANO SONATA IN D MAJOR I. (K. 576)

424. BEETHOVEN: 12 VARIATIONS IN C MAJOR.

425. J. S. BACH: CELLO SOLO SUITE IN G MAJOR. GIGUE.

426. J. HAYDN: PIANO SONATA IN G MAJOR III.

427. MOZART: PIANO SONATA IN D MAJOR I. (K. 576)

428. J. S. BACH: CELLO SOLO SUITE IN G MAJOR. GIGUE.

429. MOZART: PIANO SONATA IN G MAJOR III. (K. 283)

430. MOZART: PRESTO IN B FLAT MAJOR (K. 15ᴵᴵ)

Melody Dictation

PENTATONIC MELODIES

431. PUCCINI: TURANDOT II. (or.: 3♭)

432. PUCCINI: TURANDOT I. (or.: 3♭)

433. KODÁLY: PEACOCK VARIATIONS. (or.: 1♭)

(The upper part is to be written down.)

434. PUCCINI: TURANDOT I. (or.: 4♯)

435. BARTÓK: 44 DUOS. (or.: 1♭)

436. BRITTEN: PETER GRIMES II. (or.: 1♭)

DIATONIC MELODIES

437. HANDEL: SAUL I.

438. MOZART: CONTRADANCE. (K. 15e) (or.: 1♯)

(The upper part is to be written down.)

439. STRADELLA: SE NEL BEN.

440. HANDEL: MESSIAH III. (or.: 2♯)

441. MOZART: IL SERAGLIO II.

442. MOZART: PIANO SONATA IN C MAJOR III. (K. 279)

(The melody of the bass is to be written down.)

399

443. HANDEL: SAMSON I. (or.: 1♭)

444. MOZART: COSÌ FAN TUTTE I.

445. HANDEL: SAUL I.

446. MOZART: THE MAGIC FLUTE II.

447. HANDEL: JUDAS MACCABAEUS II. (or.: 2♯)

Bach Chorale Extracts

448. WIE SCHÖN LEUCHTET DER MORGENSTERN. (or.: 2♯)

449. O HERRE GOTT, DEIN GÖTTLICH WORT. (or.: 1♯)

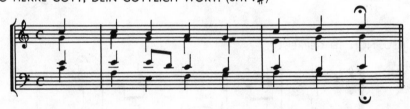

450. ALLE MENSCHEN MÜSSEN STERBEN. (or.: 2♯)

451. ES IST GEWISSLICH AN DER ZEIT. (or.: 2♭)

452. GOTTES SOHN IST KOMMEN. (or.: 2♯)

453. WER NUR DEN LIEBEN GOTT LÄSST WALTEN. (or.: 2♯)

454. JESU, NUN SEI GEPREISET.

455. JESUS, MEINE ZUVERSICHT.

456. HEUT' TRIUMPHIERET GOTTES SOHN.

457. WAS MEIN GOTT WILL, DAS. (or.: 2♯)

458. HERR CHRIST, DER EIN'GE GOT'S SOHN.

CHAPTER III

(See "Ear Training" and "Planning Suggestion" on pages 248—255.)

Rhythm Dictation

459. HANDEL: SAMSON I.

460. MOZART: PIANO SONATA IN F MAJOR I. (K. 547.a)

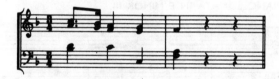

461. MOZART: PIANO SONATA IN C MAJOR III. (K. 309)

462. VIVALDI: SINFONIA FOR STRINGS IN C MAJOR.

463. BEETHOVEN: STRING QUARTET IN F MAJOR, OP. 18, № 1. I.

464. HANDEL: SAMSON I.

465. J. HAYDN: PIANO SONATA IN C SHARP MINOR III.

466. J. HAYDN: PIANO SONATA IN E MINOR III.

467. MOZART: PIANO SONATA IN D MAJOR (K. 311)

468. HANDEL: SAMSON III.

469. BEETHOVEN: PIANO SONATA IN G MAJOR, OP. 31, № 1. I.

470. MOZART: PIANO SONATA IN F MAJOR III.

471. HANDEL: SAMSON II.

472. BEETHOVEN: STRING QUARTET IN E MINOR, OP. 59, № 2. III.

407

473. MOZART: RONDO IN F MAJOR (K . 494)

474. MOZART: IL SERAGLIO III.

475. MOZART: PIANO SONATA IN F MAJOR I. (K. 533)

Melody Dictation

PENTATONIC MELODIES

476. MUSSORGSKY: BORIS GODUNOV IV. (or.: 3♯)

477. BARTÓK: BLUEBEARD'S CASTLE. (or.: 0)

(The melody of the upper part is to be written down.)

478. BARTÓK: SECOND SUITE IV. (or.: 3♭)

479. BARTÓK: MICROCOSM III. (or.: 1♯)

(The upper part is to be written down.)

480. BARTÓK: SECOND SUITE IV. (or.: 2♭)

481. BARTÓK: HUNGARIAN PICTURES. (or.: 1♯)

MAJOR AND MINOR MELODIES

482. HANDEL: MESSIAH I.

483. HANDEL: SAMSON I. (or.: 3♯)

484. MOZART: COSÌ FAN TUTTE I. (or.: 2♯)

485. MOZART: CONTRADANCE (K. 587) (or.: 0)

486. HANDEL: JUDAS MACCABAEUS I. (or.: 3♯)

487. MOZART: GERMAN DANCE (K. 600/2.)

488. J. S. BACH: CELLO SUITE IN D MINOR. GIGUE.

489. MOZART: CONTRADANCE (K. 123)

490. J. S. BACH: CELLO SUITE IN D MINOR. GIGUE.

491. HANDEL: JUDAS MACCABAEUS II. (or.: 3♯)

492. MOZART: GERMAN DANCE. (K. 600/2.)

493. HANDEL: ISRAEL II.

Bach Chorale Extracts

494. O HAUPT VOLL BLUT UND WUNDEN. (or.: 2♯)

495. JESU, MEINE FREUDE.

496. ACH GOTT, VOM HIMMEL SIEH' DAREIN. (or.: 0)

497. WO GOTT ZUM HAUS NICHT GIBT.

498. VATER UNSER IM HIMMELREICH. (or.: 3♭)

499. ICH DANK' DIR SCHON DURCH DEINEN SOHN.

500. HERZLICH LIEB HAB' ICH DICH, O HERR. (or.: 2♯)

501. DAS WALT' GOTT VATER UND GOTT SOHN.

502. DURCH ADAMS FALL IST GANZ VERDERBT. (or.: 3♭)

503. HERR CHRIST, DER EIN'GE GOTT'S SOHN.

504. O WIE SELIG SEID IHR DOCH, IHR FROMMEN.

415

505. DES HEIL'GEN GEISTES REICHE GNAD'.

506. NIMM VON UNS, HERR, DU TREUER GOTT.

CHAPTER IV

(See "Ear Training" and "Planning Suggestion" on pages *342—351*).

Rhythm Dictation

507. MOZART: PIANO SONATA IN C MAJOR III. (K. 309)

508. MOZART: IL SERAGLIO II.

509. J. HAYDN: PIANO SONATA IN D MAJOR III.

510. J. HAYDN: PIANO SONATA IN G MAJOR III.

511. HANDEL: ALCINA I.

512. MOZART: MENÜET IN G MAJOR. (K. 1)

513. MOZART: "SONATA FACILE" IN C MAJOR III. (K. 545)

514. MOZART: PIANO SONATA IN F MAJOR I. (K. 547.a)

515. MOZART: "SONATA FACILE" IN C MAJOR III. (K. 545)

516. MOZART: PIANO SONATA IN F MAJOR III. (K. 332)

517. MOZART: PIANO SONATA IN F MAJOR I. (K. 547.a)

518. MOZART: PIANO SONATA IN F MAJOR III. (K. 332)

519. HANDEL: RODELINDA I.

419

520. HANDEL: SAMSON I.

521. HANDEL: SAMSON II.

522. MOZART: PIANO SONATA IN B FLAT MAJOR II. (K. 281)

523. J. S. BACH: THREE-PART INVENTION IN A MINOR

524. BEETHOVEN: PIANO SONATA IN C MINOR, OP. 13. III.

Melody Dictation

One-part dictation

PENTATONIC MELODIES

525. RAVEL: L'ENFANT ET LES SORTILÈGES.

526. PUCCINI: TURANDOT I. (or.: 3♭)

527. CHOPIN: MAZURKA IN C SHARP MINOR, OP. 50, NO. 2.

528. MOZART: IL SERAGLIO II. (or.: 2♯)

529. HANDEL: JUDAS MACCABAEUS I.

530. MOZART: THE MAGIC FLUTE I. (or.: 2♯)

(The melody of the bass is to be written down.)

531. MOZART: CONTRADANCE. (K. 123)

532. J. S. BACH: MENUET.

533. MOZART: IL SERAGLIO I.

534. J. S. BACH: MENUET.

(The upper part is to be written down)

535. MOZART: THE MAGIC FLUTE II.

536. J. S. BACH: MENUET. (or.: 4♭)

537. MOZART: CONTRADANCE. (K.: 462/5.)

Two-part extracts

538. MOZART: CONTRADANCE. (K. 123)

539. HANDEL: FUGUE IN G MAJOR. (or.: 2♯)

540. MOZART: ANDANTE. (K. 15mm)

541. BYRD: MASS IN FOUR PARTS. AGNUS DEI.

542. MOZART: RONDO. (K. 15hh)

543. H. PURCELL: SONATA VIII. (or.: 2♯)

544. J. S. BACH: ENGLISH SUITE IN E MINOR. PASSEPIED I. (or.: 1♯)

545. MOZART: PIANO SONATA IN C MAJOR I. (K. 309) (or.: 1♯)

546. H. PURCELL: SONATA VI. (or.: 1♯)

547. J. HAYDN: STRING QUARTET IN E FLAT MAJOR I. (or.: 3♭)

548. MOZART: PIANO SONATA IN B FLAT MAJOR III. (K. 333)

Bach Chorale Extracts

549. WACH' AUF, MEIN HERZ.

550. SINGEN WIR AUS HERZENS GRUND.

551. HERR CHRIST, DER EIN'GE GOTT'S SOHN.

552. WACH' AUF, MEIN HERZ.

553. IN DICH HAB' ICH GEHOFFET, HERR.

554. HERZLIEBSTER JESU, WAS HAST DU.

555. WER WEISS, WIE NAHE MIR.

556. WO SOLL ICH FLIEHEN HIN.

557. ACH GOTT, VOM HIMMEL SIEH' DAREIN.

429

558. JESU, DER DU MEINE SEELE.

559. WIR CHRISTENLEUT'.

ZOLTÁN KODÁLY

PEDAGOGICAL INSTITUTE OF MUSIC

Printed by Petőfi Printing House, Kecskemét, Hungary

ZOLTÁN KODÁLY
PEDAGOGICAL INSTITUTE OF MUSIC

Printed by Petőfi Printing House, Kecskemét, Hungary